Education and development:
strategies and decisions in Central America

International Institute for Educational Planning

Education and development: strategies and decisions in Central America

Sylvain Lourié

Trentham Books

British Library Cataloguing in Publication Data

Lourié, Sylvain
Education and Development: Strategies and Decisions
in Central America
1. Education. Central America
I. Title
370′.9728

ISBN 0 94808 14 0

Cover design: Venus God — detail from the Dresden Codex.

English language edition co-published by the United
Nations Educational, Scientific and Cultural
Organisation, 7, place de Fontenoy, 75700 Paris and
by Trentham Books Limited, 151 Etruria Road,
Stoke-on-Trent ST1 5NS, England.

Unesco ISBN 92-803-1114X
Trentham Books ISBN 0 948080 14 1
© Unesco 1989

Preface to the English Edition

This book was written in the wake of a five-year intensive contact with education in Central America. Its intention was to assess the limits of economic analysis as a possible instrument for measuring the extremely complex social phenomenon which education represents. Today, almost ten years after that experience and some three years after the French edition was published, it was felt that it might be useful for English-speaking readers to share the lessons gleaned by the author during his close involvement with decisions and strategies affecting the educational scene of several countries. His skewed view, from the angle of an 'educational planner', enabled him to enter his complex educational zone with the analytical tools of the economist but forced him — during his stay — to shift to the more evasive instruments of sociology and political science.

The book attempts to reflect the non-economic dimensions of most of the decisions reached and to suggest that whilst economic analysis may well be a necessary condition to assess those quantitative dimensions which call for readily identifiable measures (employment, financial resources, students' enrolments and flows', etc.), it is in no way a sufficient condition.

The Central American scene, in the late 70's, was characterized in the field of education by a surging demand for school places at all levels. Costa Rica and Panama were the exceptions as both moved towards total enrolment at the primary level and a rather impressive expansion of secondary and higher education. Neither of these countries had at the same time much recourse to non-formal education structures or programmes.

In all six cases, however, and in particular the two cases which are being analyzed in detail in the book (Guatemala and Costa Rica), it cannot be said that the dimensions affecting the response to the demand were intrinsically of an economic nature. An attempt has been made therefore to understand the main difference between the fabric of two rather different societal organizations such as Guatemala and Costa Rica. Paradoxically, it is in a highly complex and intimately woven network of a democratic type such as Costa Rica, that decisions are difficult to come by, because of opposing forces, in particular that of different lobbies. In Guatemala, on the other hand, once

5

simple rules of the game designed to respect the main power structures were followed, artifacts of innovations were allowed to occur.

The book seeks to understand these various forces which enabled decisions either to affect slowly a sophisticated social establishment or to make an impact on such structures and establishments as were tolerated by the prevalent authorities.

The view taken to analyze these forces was that of an outside 'planner' or 'expert' who attempted to act as an informer and mediator, exceptionally as a catalyst. This vantage position, that may prove unrewarding because of its marginal impact on reality, enabled these pages to be written as a reflection on the nature of the social and political and cultural forces which in fact forced, in a relatively short span of time, what came to be decisions affecting educational policy.

Since the book was written and, on occasion, simultaneously as it was being written, other authors (McGinn and Schiefelbein at Harvard, Benveniste at the University of California at Berkeley, Farrell at the University of Ontario, etc.) contributed very rich analyses on comparable phenomena affecting other countries, some in Latin America. This convergence of preoccupations is in itself an indication of the need to go beyond the linear and causal processes which so often suggest that one can move from the 'diagnosis' of the educational situation to the foundation of decisions. Fortunately, or unfortunately for the experts, decisions are never linear. Points of decisions are theoretical notions, just as T.S. Elliot reminded us that every decision brings in its wake others that will 'reverse it'.

After the book had been written, the author was fortunate enough to benefit from the wisdom of decision-makers from the whole world who came for training or research to the International Institute for Educational Planning (IIEP), which the author was responsible for between 1982 and 1988. Thus was he able to enrich the lore of intuition and sensitivity which had been accumulated not only in Central America but over some twenty years of experience both in the field and through international agencies. From this varied experience, and the confrontation with what at times appears to be a no-win battle against illiteracy, a refinement and a confirmation of the theoretical model proposed in the latter part of this book gradually appeared. In a publication of the Institute entitled 'Educational planning in the context of current development problems' (Paris, 1984), some first thoughts were couched concerning a systematic approach to classify the nature of the forces which affect decision-makers in the complex field of education.

The contributions of these educationists, making up consecutive groups of trainees who attended six annual programmes in Paris and of participants in various intensive training courses in all regions on issues dealing with education and public finance or education and employment, confirmed the essential importance of the two directions whence forces impact on the decision-maker.

Schematically speaking, (since no decisions are clear cut and can be analyzed 'in vitro' without constant modifications, including from the examiner himself) we find that 'upstream' forces, which affect the decision-maker prior to his taking any decisions, are marked by exogenous forces lying outside, say, a Ministry of Education or from its actors. These considerations, known as 'political' in nature, may be socio-cultural as well as financial. Yet they are the ones that define the area, limited in nature, in which the decision-maker can actually operate with a modicum of freedom. An example of one such external force is that of the International Monetary Fund's demands on heavily indebted countries to 'adjust' public finances through limitation — inter alia — of their social policies, in particular of public outlay for education.

The second set of forces which affect any decisions in the field of education are those which take place 'downstream' from the decision-maker after the theoretical 'point of decision' has been passed and when the hour of implementation has struck. These 'downstream' forces spring essentially from the establishment itself, and are influenced by its inertia or self-defence mechanisms which limit its innovative capabilities. This does not mean that no external factors affect such implementation processes. A simplistic example will suffice: micro-planning based on school-mapping exercises can easily be negated by parochial decisions of local representatives preferring that a school be built in a politically advantageous location rather than in another which is considered technically 'justified'.

Fundamentally, *actors* whether outside the school system or within it will determine the magnitude and orientation of these forces. They will be the vectors who will influence the decision-maker. Yet, these vectors themselves will be qualified by the *structures* within which they operate, the *functions* which they have taken on to themselves and the *products* which these actors are supposed to put on 'the market' (plans, programmes, projects, ordinances, decrees, etc.). Thus, we find that any analysis 'upstream' or 'downstream' from the decision-maker may be facilitated by checking out the identity of the actors, their functions, their structures and finally the products for which they are responsible.

This grid might be seen as a complement to the 'action systems' based on Crozier's work which are discussed in depth in the last part of this book.

If one were to study the Central American scene from an education point of view some ten years after this was looked at through the following pages, one would find an overall deterioration. In general, non-formal education, which should spring from a democratic and participatory fabric of society, has not expanded. The Sectorial Unit on Educational Planning of the Ministry of Education of Guatemala has not become the driving force for speeding resource optimization techniques and management criteria. Costa Rica, so remarkably exceptional in its political commitment to education, has had to reduce its outlay for education dramatically and in proportions which cannot be exclusively explained in terms of the demographic slump. It is therefore no 'accident' if education has taken the backseat in that part of the world where ideally speaking one might be tempted to say that it represented the key to economic and social organization and strength. It is suggested that the grid proposed concerning the nature, role, limitation and functionality of actors may serve to explain considerably more the present situation than raw statistics dealing with central government expenditures, school enrolments and qualifications of teachers.

An attempt to analyze the shortcomings of some of the popular instruments of the 60's and 70's applied to education (manpower approach, rate of return, social demand, etc.) will be made on the occasion of an IIEP international workshop aimed at defining educational strategic planning for the nineties and which will be held this year. Its results should be published in 1989. This workshop organized on the occasion of the XXVth Anniversary of the International Institute for Educational Planning will attempt to understand the notion of 'strategic planning' as applied to education and conceived as a process of high flexibility, not linear or causal in nature, and meant to permit a constant shift of the centre of gravity of decisions between objectives, resources and obstacles.

Generally speaking, the 80's showed up the extraordinary vulnerability of education when confronted with non-educational factors. Whilst the objective demand for truly universal and 'quality' primary or 'basic' education is strongly felt, the unemployment crisis, adjustment policy, international terms of trade, rapid — and often dangerous — modifications of socio-cultural values, (moving either towards radically traditionalist positions or in the direction of international scientific, technological and cultural standardization) all affect the body politic of education more than qualitative, systematic and 'logical' inventories of the dysfunctions of its conventional components. It is hoped that the 1989 IIEP publication might bring to light some further arguments in favour of a more general analytical instrument, flexible in nature and readily adaptable to the concept of strategic thinking as opposed to the 'numbers game' approach of educational planning so attractive to economists and quantitative analysts the last 70 years.

Today, the key message which justified the attempt to put down in a few pages the author's experience in Central America, but which should be broadened to other parts of the world, appears to be still applicable. It spells out an obvious need to identify, know and understand the real forces which affect any social policy and in particular education. This imperative demand for a broad, complex and constantly enriched information base seems to be the key to any forward thinking in the analysis of decision-making in the field of education. The broader the base, the more discreet will the decision-maker's position become as he moves in the extremely limited space of non-previously committed decisions and within which he can theoretically leave his mark. Such an information base must no longer be limited to raw statistics but must embrace the entire range from exceptional surveys, preferably of a participatory nature, to regular systematic surveys encompassing both household, enterprises and individuals and finally to the census itself which, as the previous surveys become consolidated, will attempt to include previously covered key questions. Issues such as the role of teachers' unions, students' associations, parents' associations, certainly need to be taken into consideration. The role and commitment of the community and of the 'users' cannot be ignored and it is precisely with reference to the latter that new sampling and survey techniques based on socio-cultural trends will want to be improved upon. For several decades now, the private commercial sectors have relied on such surveys to determine the nature of marketed products. Yet no such action has been systematically taken for education which remains one of the most expensive products in terms of public resources. Such analysis would shed new light on the very concept of the 'social demand'. The relationship between aspirations of educational attainment and its economic value might be examined from the angle of cultural values and behaviour patterns which affect the notion of work, income, wages, leisure, etc. These dimensions need to be handled simultaneously and so on a macro scale if education as a social, cultural and functional process is to be addressed.

Further studies on the complex issue of collective and individual decisions in the field of education are imperative. It is hoped that others will study educational situations both at the institutional, programme or collective level. Such studies may reveal the real nature of more global phenomena which education, used as a proxy, may bring out. Thus we will understand better the 'upstream' intrinsic constraints, both national and international, and the intrinsic constraints which affect the 'downstream' side of the decision-maker. We might finally come up with a more diversified and subtle theory than 'rate of return' analyses to explain individual and collective choices.

Can anyone say that decisions in the field of education today are independent of adjustment policies, of international fashions or values, of technological innovations affecting the use of computers, telematics or global communications? At the domestic end of it, can anyone suggest that attitudes towards mass media, the family, the elders, immigration and emigration, new minorities, etc. do not have a heavy impact, not only on the content, but on the future significance of education?

Answers to these and many other such issues call for a more reliable awareness of education's own laws of supply or demand, which are ceaselessly waxing and waning. This, in turn, is only accessible to those who will take time out to watch, listen to and respect all its actors. In the long run this may lead to the detection of those social forces that will both take education out of a bureaucratic corset and mobilize the means to carry out directly the responsibilities, and reap the rewards, inherent in the unfettered role of education as an instrument of social justice and cultural development.

Paris, July 1988

Contents

Introduction

The economics of education is a discipline which can look back on over a quarter of a century's experience. Its thinkers and researchers have shown a truly creative quality in selecting from the 'sciences' of education identifiable elements whose development could be followed and therefore analyzed. In this way, for example, certain quantifiable values have been recognized, such as the number of pupils produced by an educational system, and it has then been possible to study the *cost* of their production by the system and their *value,* once they have left the school system, as agents for producing goods and services in the national economy.

The quantification of a phenomenon such as education, which by virtue of the intellectual, spiritual, metaphysical — and even symbolic — nature of its purpose rejects *a priori* any subordination to a purely materialist school of thought, has inevitably given rise to polemics and misunderstanding. The former, which call themselves theoretical, are in fact purely interprofessional, setting economists and educationists at loggerheads; the misunderstandings, labelled 'strategic', are essentially tactical and political, and give rise to quarrels between ministers and officials on one side and advisers or 'experts' on the other.

Over the years a number of educationists have come to accept a certain amount of quantification in order to improve budgetary planning, while more and more economists have become aware of the difficulty of reducing the elements of the learning process to a set of measurable parameters. If there are still 'diehards' in both camps, this may be because in their fervent devotion to the service of their own profession they see — or think they see — the manifold failings of the opposing camp or, conversely, the unending possibilities of their own discipline, ignoring the petty squabbles of a world which understands neither the learning process nor the subtleties of econometric models. In other words, polemics are no longer in fashion, and we daily see proof, if not of perfect complementarity, at least of the unavoidable co-existence between researchers, whether they be educationists or economists, on the one hand, and decision-makers on the other.[1]

What is in fact the state of the relations between national officials and these popularizers of educational economics, the 'experts'[2] in educational planning, strategy or policy? These latter are situated at the point of articulation between the daily activity of the decision-maker and the technical rigour which validates their professional contribution. This rôle of intermediary between thought and action becomes even more complex if it is accompanied by full appreciation of the fact that there is no such thing as 'neutral' education.[3] This is obvious in the case of an adviser or 'expert' from an international organization whose terms of reference may be unambiguous from a conceptual point of view but have little practical significance since the nature and extent of their mission are determined by the Member States themselves. It cannot prescribe operational standards without interfering in the domain of national sovereignty.

While it would be an exaggeration to speak of real misunderstanding between the two groups concerned, their relationships still cannot be described as really complementary. The activity or the policy of the educational decision-maker — nearly always the Minister concerned — is characterized by immediate necessities and by unforeseen (or unforeseeable) circumstances. The frame of reference in which his routine activity takes place is composed of 'officials', the teachers and, very often, representatives of the young and not so young taking part in the 'learning process'.

On his side, the expert — national or foreign — will be hoping to impose his own ideas, or those which he believes to be — or which are — those of the organization which influences him or employs him. But these ideas will all be aimed at a hoped-for improvement of the system — in the *abstract*. At best, they will be proposals which can be carried out in a medium or long term; at worst, they will be utopian dreams. In either case the decision-maker (with rare exceptions) will see them only as a 'means' of meeting the demands of everyday affairs, and not as 'final answers' that should influence the way in which these same affairs are run. But the expert, often only partly aware of the nature of the demands that press upon the decision-maker, will not always be able to demonstrate convincingly that what is important in his eyes may *also* be important for that decision-maker. To do so would call for measures to be taken *hic et nunc,* so that the machine of which the Minister

1. Unesco International Colloquium, *Research and practice in education: how to strengthen links between research and practice in order to improve general education.* Bucharest, C.E.P.E.S., 10-15 November 1980.
2. See the excellent publication by Guy Benveniste, *The politics of expertise,* (Berkeley, Cal., The Glendessary Press, 1972) which defines the rôles of the 'Pandit' (the 'wise man') and the 'Prince' (the decision-maker).
3. Paulo Freire, 'Neutral education does not exist', in *Education on the move,* Paris, Unesco, 1975.

is in charge can be steered, regardless of obstacles, towards an objective which will not be reached within a time-span directly controlled by the same decision-maker. In the normal course of events he will no longer be in charge when the seeds which the expert would like to see planted are really for harvesting.

While this kind of difference can exist between every decision-maker and adviser, whatever the field of their common activity, it is practically inevitable in the educational field, where even more than in other sectors every significant change comes up against the inertia of custom and of institutions, and must make its effects felt through a long period of conventional educational cycles which do not allow the results to be seen or measured until six, nine or even twelve years later.[4]

It would seem, then, that the first obstacle to a common language is the problem of time, viewed very differently by the decision-maker and by the adviser. But there is another problem too: the way in which each of them regards the educational phenomenon.

Almost all studies, plans or reports by national specialists or international experts in educational strategy, educational planning or educational financing are based on a simplified version of the methods of the medical profession, using the term 'diagnosis' for the opening phase or first part of their work. By its content and its form this diagnosis enables the adviser to stay — or become — faithful to the discipline of the 'economics of education'. All the data he gathers are in essence quantitative, and inevitably confuse the individual fields of education and economics. The economic analysis will deal essentially with two aspects: the costs and financing of the system or sub-system being studied, and the links between the 'products' of the system (pupils, students, participants, etc., whether graduates or non-graduates) and the structure of the labour market expressed in terms of jobs, income or wages corresponding to the classifications or diplomas or duration of studies in the educational system or subsystem in question (in relation to the criteria of 'return' of the system itself). In this way the mechanics of the 'internal' and 'external' efficiency[5] of the system are compared with criteria outside the system, such as employment or the 'rate of return' of the education received.

As for the educational analysis, this is usually concerned with the 'stocks' (the number of pupils or students — and students — by levels, types and years of study, pupil/teacher ratios, etc.) and the 'flows' (transition rates from one year to the next, numbers of repeaters, drop-outs, graduates, etc.,

4. In this respect the agricultural sector presents similar characteristics in that the impact of a proposed change must also overcome resistances and inertia over a long period.
5. This second 'efficiency' will frequently be touched upon only superficially, since the data provided by decennial censuses, household or factory surveys and other studies are not presented in a manner compatible with the educational indicators either in terminology or in periodicity. In most cases all that can be done is to reproduce statistical tables that employ terms relating to the labour market but not touching on the 'stocks' and 'flows' of the educational system.

classes by level and type of studies), and also with the indicators describing the nature and size of the infra-structure (number of schools, area per school, per classroom, special rooms, laboratories, etc.) and of the equipment (furniture, laboratory and workshop equipment, etc.). These various data will be either aggregated at the national level or broken down (by regions, provinces, counties, urban centres and rural areas, etc.).

To judge by the universality of this procedure, and the standardization of its content, it is easy to conclude that such a diagnosis, with a pronounced economic slant, corresponds in fact to a preference expressed not only by governments but also by the international or regional organizations and banks that both require and produce them.

From the decision-maker's point of view this type of diagnosis has the advantage of quoting official figures, of providing data in a relatively simple form, and above all of being an instrument containing no value judgements. He can therefore make use of it as he wishes in dealing with parliament or with the media, in order to ask for — or justify — a budgetary increase, a new teacher-recruitment policy, or the opening of new schools. There is no appeal against the data, and their use depends on the discretion, the experience and the imagination of the user, who can take advantage of the adaptability of the information to make it fit in with his proposed policy.

From the point of view of the international organizations, a diagnosis is an official common denominator, enabling data to be compared internationally and tendencies in each country to be studied, and, above all, not offering occasion for any accusations of criticizing a national educational system.

For the 'expert', the diagnosis is a means of inserting himself into the power game by providing the decision-maker — without antagonizing him — with apparently 'objective' data and a common frame of reference to open the dialogue about the conclusions which the decision-maker will wish to draw from them or the consequences which the expert intends to propose.

By means of the diagnosis, and with the time available to him (the expert can devote his time exclusively to drawing up proposals, unlike the decision-maker, who is constantly called upon to find solutions to the 'urgent' problems that arise daily) the expert can make an analysis of the 'dysfunctioning' of the system. He will base this analysis on three criteria:

— an ideal model: for example, 100 per cent internal efficiency for primary education;
— an explicit model, usually corresponding to a government policy: for example, providing primary-education cover in rural areas equal to that available in urban zones;
— an implicit model, perhaps inspired by universal standards approved by a government in the international arena but not followed through by any national decision: for example, democratization of primary education.

It is the weighing of such criteria, and the choice between them, that demonstrate the 'interior vision', the subjectivity — perhaps even the ideology

— of the expert, who will use the data in the diagnosis in proposing 'his' policy.

On his side the decision-maker, as we have seen, would like to make use of the data from the diagnosis in shaping his own policy, but owing to lack of time, and of practice in the professional techniques involved, he will not usually have been able to carry his analysis of the dysfunctions as far as the point reached by the expert. Instinctively, he will substitute for this analysis his own political understanding.

It is at this point that the dialogue breaks down, because it is based upon entirely different premises. The decision-maker, in a subjectivity[6] of his own, checks over the various factual elements which will enable him to draw up a political project. Some of these elements have been provided by the diagnosis, which he can use as he thinks fit.

All the same, the really essential elements come from his appreciation of all the factors which play their part in justifying the decision that he wants to take and that will bring the advantages that he can foresee — or thinks he can. But these factors are not to be found in the diagnosis, since they are neither measurable nor 'objective'.

They form part of his real — or presumed — knowledge of such factors as the past history of his country; the importance attached (or not) by the national culture to certain forms of teaching, instruction, education or apprenticeship; to the relationships existing between himself and his staff, between his own Ministry, on the one hand, and other government departments, the Head of State, the interested pressure groups, the private associations, and so on, on the other.

The expert, having only the diagnosis and the dysfunctions he has identified from the numerical data, will probably not be listened to, even if he obtains a hearing at all. One of two things will happen: either he will let himself be influenced (perhaps with a certain measure of self-interest) by the local considerations that will be stressed by the decision-maker (in that case, the international criteria will provide an excuse for a policy which does not reflect them, and only the decision-maker's choice will see the light of day, uninfluenced by the expert); or alternatively the expert will insist upon the importance of some international criterion which may well have no place in the national tradition or system of values. His contribution may be listened to with interest, but it will not be respected in the decision finally taken since it offers no intelligible solution to a problem which forms part of the panorama of national reality as perceived by the decision-maker.

As suggested earlier, this is a case of a dialogue which is both out of proportion and out of step. Each of the partners is placed differently in the 'landscape' of power. The one plays his part visibly, in the public eye, and if he

---

6.In Part III, Chapter 1, section 3, we shall consider the concept of 'criteria of satisfaction' for the decision-maker (as identified by Herbert Simon), which clarify this notion of 'subjectivity'.

fails he places his whole political future at risk. His intention, his activity, his reactions must be rapid, since they are measured by the yardstick of elections or of the personal decision of the man who appointed him. The other plays a rôle far less in the public eye. He tends to work below the surface, not on it, but the risks he runs are limited since he will be judged more by his competence than by his instinct; and even if his analysis has been taken into account he will be only marginally affected by the failure of decisions which he will have influenced only slightly. He has time for reflection, and by transposition he sees the chessboard of educational policy in a temporal framework which takes in not merely one or more five-year plans but even some 'prospective plans' as well.

Nevertheless, we saw that the opening phase of the relationship seemed to augur success for this dialogue. Indeed, over the diagnosis, the starting-point of the process, there was a promising consensus of opinion. The decision-maker, his collaborator, and the international bodies all agree that it is an indispensable instrument. Only in the following stage, that of the analysis of dysfunctions, do we see the first signs of the gulf that will yawn wider and wider until the final decision is taken.

And yet it is precisely the many different reasons that the principal actors have for wanting, or for insisting on, the diagnosis that lie at the root of the halting dialogue and the possibility of disagreement.

The so-called objectivity of the diagnosis may hide the fact that it is incapable of revealing the true dimensions of the origins — or even the consequences — of a decision. This 'objectivity' of the instrument is limited to the visible part of the education 'iceberg'. The part below the surface is not entirely unknown to the decision-maker, and therefore it is by a deliberate choice that he prefers to use, apparently with reason, the part that everyone can see. The international bodies, for their part, acting on behalf of the concert of nations, cannot make use for their analyses and inter-country comparisons of data which these same nations do not provide in the standard presentation. The expert, acting on behalf of a country or of an international body, becomes the hostage of this self-criticism. This explains why this economic instrument, with its limited objective, has gradually become a useful tool for everybody, economist or not.

But the discipline of educational economics, which the expert represents 'in the field' — surely it serves some purpose in the narrow field of manoeuvre which is open to him?

In other words: in the absence of other techniques for the rapid identification of a particular educational 'landscape', the educational economists have perfected an instrument — the diagnosis — which in fact contains all the information which they themselves require for their studies and research.

The diagnosis, or a more detailed form of it, is in fact both the necessary and the effective means of analysing the education sector's contribution to the GNP[7] and its share of the State budget,[8] the real nature of the redistribution that results from the public financing of education,[9] the extent of the private financing of education,[10] the cost per graduate by type of training,[11] and the relationship between education and manpower.[12] By including certain supplementary information on incomes by educational attain-

7. Theodore W. Schultz, *The economic value of education,* New York and London, Columbia University Press, 1964; *Investment in human capital: the rôle of education and of research,* New York, The Free Press: London, Collier-Macmillan, 1971. Edward F. Denison, 'Measuring the contribution of education (and the residual) to economic growth', in *The residual factor and economic growth,* Paris, OECD, 1964; *Why growth rates differ,* Washington, Brookings Institute, 1967; *Accounting for the US economy growth,* Washington, Brookings Institute, 1976.
8. Friedrich Edding, *Methods of analysing educational outlay,* Paris, Unesco, 1966.
9. Jean-Pierre Jallade, *The financing of education: an examination of basic issues,* Washington D.C., World Bank, International Development Association, July 1973, (World Bank staff working paper No.157); *Public expenditures on education and income distribution in Colombia,* Baltimore, Johns Hopkins Press, 1974, (World Bank occasional papers No.18) *Basic education and income inequality in Brazil: the long-term view,* Washington D.C., World Bank 1977, (World Bank staff working paper No.268).
10. C.M. Izquierdo, 'Financiamiento de la educación privada in America Latina', in *Financiamiento de la educaciòn in America Latina,* Mexico, Fondo de Cultura Economica, Banco Interamericano de Desarrollo, 1978.
11. Jacques Hallak, *A qui profite l'école?* Paris, P.U.F., 1974.
12. This question has been dealt with by many authors; in particular: H. Parnes, 'Scope and methods of human resource and educational planning' in *Manpower forecasting in educational plannning,* Paris, OECD, 1967.
The work of F.H. Harbison marked a further stage: for example, Frederick Harbison and Charles A. Myers, *Manpower and education: country studies in economic development,* New York, McGraw Hill, 1965; *Educational planning and human resource development,* Paris, Unesco: IIEP, 1967 (Fundamentals of Educational Planning, No.3); *A human resource approach to the development of African nations,* Princeton N.J., Princeton University, Woodrow Wilson School of Public International Affairs, 1971; *Education sector planning for development of nation-wide learning systems,* Washington D.C., Overseas Liaison Committee, American Council of Education, 1973; *Human resources as the wealth of nations,* New York, Oxford University Press, 1973.
See also M. Debeauvais, *La quantification de variables sociales: quelques aspects concernant la planification de l'éducation et de la main-d'oeuvre,* Paris, Colloquium on Universities and National Development, Islamabad, November 1976.
The systematic and causal studies of J. Tinbergen also marked an important advance during a period of economic growth for demonstrating the relation between education and economic growth through increased productivity; see J. Tinbergen and H. Correa, *Quantitative adaptation of education to accelerated growth,* Division of Balanced International Growth, Reprint Series No.19, Rotterdam, 1962; J. Tinbergen and H.C. Bos, *Econometric models of education: some applications,* Paris, OECD, 1965; J. Tinbergen, 'Actual versus optimal income distribution in a three-level education model', in *Scritti in honore di Guglielmo Tagliacarne,* Rome, 1974.
A more critical, though less linear and causal, approach was adopted by M. Carnoy in *Schooling, income, the distribution of income and unemployment: a critical appraisal,* Paris, OECD Development Centre, 1973; *Education and employment: a critical appraisal,* Paris, Unesco: IIEP, 1977 (Fundamentals of educational planning, No.26);

tainment levels, the diagnosis enables the rate of return to be calculated for each level and type of education.[13]

Have these analyses and investigations — which have undoubtedly increased our knowledge of the theoretical relations between economy and education — not helped to attach even more importance to the diagnosis, the source of the 'raw material' of these investigations? Furthermore, the wider use of the diagnosis has perhaps strengthened the conviction of those who recommended it, that the economic dimension of education, as the only measurable one, was the only one deserving the attention of the decision-makers. And there is also the fact that diagnosis has been firmly adopted by financing bodies, who like to apply cost-benefit analysis to the projects submitted to them (whatever sector they come from) and for whom economic analysis is the only instrument that guides their choice.

To facilitate further consideration, let us liken the 'expert' to a specialist who regards his rôle as that of applying to the realm of education the strict discipline of the techniques and principles of economics. This expert, thus taken prisoner by his own discipline, is scarcely tempted to examine the submerged part of the iceberg. At the same time, however, his professional discipline and his habit of identifying certain causal relationships may in fact support and assist the decision-maker to understand fully, or understand better, this vague, shadowy area in which he is guided more by his instincts than by his knowledge.

But if the expert is to submit his diagnosis to criteria different from those he is accustomed to, it may perhaps be necessary to go back to the beginning. . .

A re-appraisal of the purposes of education, and an understanding both of what is at stake in major educational decisions and of how those decisions are arrived at, will oblige the expert to remain constantly aware of the dimensions of education, on the one hand, and to re-examine the contribution that an expert in educational economics might make towards a more satisfactory analysis of the inter-relationship between this sector and the society which provide its material and which, in return, sees in it the guarantee of its own future, on the other hand.

'Segmented labour markets', in *Education, work and employment,* Vol.II, Paris, Unesco: IIEP, 1980.

13. M. Blaug, *Economics of education: selected readings,* Harmondsworth, Penguin Books, 1968/69 (2 vols.); *An introduction to the economics of education,* London, Allen Lane The Penguin Press, 1970; *Education and the employment problem in developing countries,* Geneva, ILO, 1973.
G. Psacharopoulos, *The rate of return on investment in education at the regional level: estimates for the State of Hawaii,* Honolulu, University of Hawaii Economic Research Centre, 1969; 'Returns to education: an international comparison', in *Education and income: a background study for World Development Report 1980,* Washington D.C., The World Bank, 1980, (World Bank staff working paper No.402).

The rôle of the expert-economist in such an attempt is perhaps open to question, but should not he be the first to accord to his own science the relative importance that it deserves? This implies both assurance and modesty. Assurance, because economics has been able to introduce into the social sciences a method of rigorous analysis of certain aspects of human and community behaviour. Modesty, because these aspects are limited, and the laws of economics are always subject to human volition and human irrationality'.[14] This is all the more true when economics abandons the financial, fiscal or budgetary arena, in which its ability to foresee the future is still a long way from equalling its power of analysis, and introduces into another self-styled social 'science', such as education, analytical tools which, as we have tried to suggest above — grasp only a fraction of the phenomenon.[15]

We cannot end this discussion without one futher remark. Whilst it is true that sociology chooses for study units as homogeneous as possible — and therefore, by definition, of small magnitude — economics, for its part, cannot operate without universal laws. But should not the object of the economic analysis (in this case, an educational system) itself define the *limits* of its application, rather than allow the instrument (the economic analysis) to become an end in itself by determining the scope of its attention?

Education, the nature of which appears differently to each observer, is *also* the object of sociological analysis. The dimensions that permit of such analysis are not the same as those which delimit the economist's field of study. The economist regards education as an abstract function of production since it is — necessarily — universal. The sociologist will try to identify the forces at work in a given educational system or subsystem at a given moment. Nevertheless, it is in fact *this* particular system (which exists in relative independence as compared for example with monetary systems, interdependent by definition, which the economist can — and must — study at the international level) which has to play an economic rôle. This rôle will vary from one country to another, depending on the social stratification, incomes policy, trade union liberty, the rôle of women, the laws governing the employment of minors, dependence on international trends, and so on. The usefulness of the economic instrument will therefore depend upon its capacity to adapt itself to the particular features of the object of study — education in a given country at a precise moment. Indirectly, the economic function of such and such a type or level of education or training will be sufficiently fulfilled if the instrument is adapted to it.[16] We are tempted to sum up in this way the question

14. Edgar Morin, *Le paradigme perdu: la nature humaine,* Paris, Editions du Seuil, 1973.
15. See the numerous publications of Francois Perroux, in particular: *A New concept of development: basic tenets,* Paris, Unesco, London, Croom Helm, 1983. His approach as an economist is impressively described in 'Peregrinations of an economist and the choice of his route', in *Banco Nazionale de Lavoro Quarterly Review,* No.133, June 1980.
16. In this rapid summary we have not dealt with the *indirect* relationships between

which can serve as a practical test of the relevance of economics in educational matters: to what extent will the studies, analyses and reflections that describe the education/economics relationship enable a decision-maker to make an essentially different choice from the one he would have made independently of them?

The answer to this question must be sought in an empirical approach consisting in a return to the origins of a concrete educational fact (not merely an intention, such as a law still awaiting the decrees that will bring it into force) and in noting how and when, in the decision-making process, considerations arising from economic science as applied to education have played a part. Such an undertaking is not possible, since it would require an intimate and complete knowledge of all the factors, both foreseeable and accidental, that have operated between the first conception of an activity, synthesis of an idea and a volition, and its effective realization. To start with, it would require a capacity to assess attitudes and positions relatively, in the same way as many philosophers have attempted to demonstrate the subjectivity of 'the' truth, and which Pirandello succeeded in illustrating in his work. Next, it should follow the techniques of certain social scientists, who have studied administrative organizations by isolating the 'actors' and endeavouring to work out the details of their 'game' within the 'system'.[17] These techniques would need to adapt themselves to the 'interstructuration' of public bureaucracies and of interest groups.[18] Finally — and above all — it would require the capacity to evaluate the impact of an economic instrument on an educational *outcome*, and not only on the men and the structures that govern them.

Although it is not within our power to consider undertaking such a definitive work, we feel bound to add some supplementary brush-strokes to the picture which is being built up by many well-known contributors[19] and which

economics and education. This would demand an in-depth study of the effects of *all* types of education upon the finding of employment, on the prospects of promotion, or, in general, occupational mobility. See Blaug, Vaizey, Schultz, Andersen, Carnoy and others.

17. M. Crozier and E. Friedberg, *Actors and systems: the politics of collective action,* Chicago, Ill. University Press, 1980. This work provides a conceptual outline and an analytical technique which the present author has used to describe the field of play and the actors in the 'game' of education in Central America, and which he acknowledges with gratitude.

18. P. Gremion, *Le pouvoir périphérique,* Paris, Editions du Seuil, 1976.

19. J.G. March and H.A. Simon, *Organizations,* New York, Wiley, 1958. This is the masterly work on the decision-making process which has influenced a whole generation of researchers in North America and Western Europe.
See also H.A. Simon, *Sciences of the artificial,* Cambridge, Ma., MIT Press, 1969. For an understanding of the science of bureaucracies we prefer the works of M. Crozier, *The Bureaucratic phenomenon,* London, Tavistock Publications, 1964; *The Stalled society,* New York, Viking Press, 1973; and the work in collaboration with E. Friedberg

one day will possess the contours, the colours, the light and shade which will render it more nearly true to life. The educational economist will then be more faithful to the nature — and the limits — of his rôle in a context which he will not himself have defined, though his science will have made an effective contribution to the understanding of its complexity.

In order to assess the limitations of economic analysis on the one hand, and to discover the nature of the non-economic considerations which affect the decision-maker, these 'supplementary brush-strokes' will take the form of describing why and how certain decisions were taken by the educational authorities in some Central-American countries. This description will include the shadows cast by an inevitable subjectivity and by the use of its analytical tool — the diagnosis.

But before presenting the 'happenings' chosen as the subjects of analysis (Part II), it will be useful to set them in the context of the dimensions of education in the countries where the case studies took place (Part I). This overall concept should open up a wider panorama than that which would result from a quantitative diagnosis (Part III). After that the question can be asked: of what nature are the elements that should form part of an eventual analytical instrument that will be more complete and, in consequence, more useful and effective?

The two cases analyzed in depth, together with most of the items of information used in the following pages and the events described therein, date from at least ten years ago. This seemed necessary to the author, in order to give to the presentation the detachment that only the passing of time can provide. What follows is a description that is in the main historical, and not an up-to-date presentation of the contemporary educational systems in Central America or in other Latin-American countries referred to. The reader should appreciate that the principal aim of this work is to discover exactly where, in the complex education phenomenon, the invidious position of the 'planners' is to be found: the planners, who find themselves at the point of articulation between the teacher in the classroom, dealing with pupils whose destiny he hopes to influence and enrich, and the decision-maker who, aware of all the facts and phenomena of the day, hopes to direct them along the path corresponding to the vision of society which he shares with his colleagues in power.

Particular care has been taken to avoid even the slightest reference to any information which is not freely available to the general public. No allusion will be found in the following pages to any matters not to be found in official publications or press reports. Admittedly, every observer tends to give

---

mentioned above (page 13, note 2). In addition, a work dealing more directly with North American society has been consulted: G. Benveniste, *Bureaucracy,* San Francisco, Boyd and Frager Publishing Co., 1983 (2nd edn.).

his own interpretation of events which he has witnessed and which he is trying to describe, and subjectivity of this nature is bound to be present. At the same time, these pages should bear witness to my earnest intention not to abuse the confidence and friendship of those with whom these events were shared. Thus there are no value judgements and no opinions based upon friendship or provoked by sensitivity.

An undertaking of this nature is always a thankless task, since it cannot lay claim to any scientific veracity whatsoever that is open to proof. Nevertheless, it is not a purely personal view of affairs, since it has been received with approval and understanding by many of the 'actors' in the Latin-American educational world, who have by their comments enriched the analyses that are part of the text.

This introduction would be incomplete without an expression of profound gratitude to the Director-General of Unesco, who, by generously granting study-leave to the author, enabled him to analyse the documents and studies in his possession so as to reproduce their content in the pages that follow. This same study-leave also allowed the author to exchange views with, and obtain the opinions of, various colleagues in the Faculty of Economic Sciences at Aix-Marseille II, in particular the Deans, Jean-Louis Reiffers, Maurice Parodi and Joseph Brunet-Jailly. This combination of the generosity and understanding of an international organization and the critical and constructive spirit of the academic world symbolize, more than anything else could, the exceptionally favourable and encouraging conditions from which the author benefited. At the same time, it should be made clear that this study is entirely the author's responsibility, and in no way engages the responsibility of either Unesco or the University of Aix-Marseille II.

PART ONE

The Rules Of The Game

CHAPTER I

Education and development: statement of a hypothesis

The word 'education' covers realities that are distinct, not to say different. For some, education is a *process,* which can last throughout life but whose 'crowded hours' take place in the institutional setting of the school and last 6, 9 or 12 years, or even for 16 to 20 years, depending on the duration of higher education. The process includes or combines learning, instruction, teaching, training. For others, the word is given a more static meaning; limited in duration, education does not include any non-institutional, nonformal aspects. It is the sum of what is acquired during the institutional period. For others again, education is a collection of means: buildings, administration, personnel, etc. Finally, still others see education as one of the 'principal social institutions'.

For our part, we shall use a very simple application of sequential systems analysis, whose three stages — entry-process-exit — are useful for setting out the boundaries but do not claim to be a definition.

At the *entry* stage the 'elements' are, obviously, the 'educatees' and the human and material means provided to meet their needs.

The *process,* as defined by Simeon Tanguiane,[1] Assistant Director-general of Unesco and Head of the Education Sector of that organization, will take the form of 'a conscious activity, deliberate and organized, aiming at the transmission and mastery of a coherent system of knowledge, know-how and methods (general and professional) and at the development of thought, reflection, aptitudes, all the aspects of the personality'. This is where there takes place one of the first stages of the mysterious symbiosis ('black box') between the individual and the exterior world. Its progress will form the framework of this study.

The *exit* consists in the fulfilment of two purposes: an 'ultimate' purpose, subjective in nature, aimed at reaching a certain intellectual, spiritual or

1. S. Tanguiane, in 'Education and the problem of its democratization', *Prospects,* Vol.VII No.1, 1977, p.14-31 sets out the notions of 'process', 'results of the process' and 'social institutions'.

cultural level; and a more immediate one, concerned with meeting the demands of the world of work.

From the factors relevant to this study we have chosen three:

— the *values* which education transmits and can modify, but which represent an aspiration and a choice;

— the *function* of education — social rôle or economic aspirations.

Here there is interplay between individual aspirations and the conditions in which they may — or may not — be realized, depending either on a social consensus, on a political volition, on a cultural image, on the employment market, or on some combination of these various factors;

— the *structures,* the human, financial and material resources which make education a mainly public social institution.

The educational phenomenon, therefore, will be viewed differently according to the eye of the beholder: the three distinct factors, each of which in its own way can lend itself to analysis, spring from very different disciplines — or attitudes:

a) For the philosopher, the educationist, it is the system of values which takes pride of place: [2] a means of spiritual expression, a symbol, an enrichment, individual development and fulfilment, adhesion to the culture. Education, independently of its social, financial or institutional cost, is the sacred process by which mankind progresses, raises himself, and aspires towards universal unity.

b) For the sociologist and political scientist, education is an instrument developed by man in order to help create or strengthen collective structures such as the State, the political régime, the social structure, the means of production, etc. This functionalist approach[3] is basically concerned with an organism exercising one — or several — specific functions.

c) For the statesman, the trade unionist, the parents, the students, the teachers, *education* is a *machine*: a ministry and schools (whether or not directly under

2. Plato, *Laws,* Book II; *Republic,* Books III and IV. Montaigne, *Essays,* Book I, Ch.26. Alain, *Propos,* especially the one dated 1.7.1910 on 'L'enseignement monarchique'. E. Faure *et al., Learning to be,* Paris, Unesco, 1972. J. Piaget, *The Man and his ideas,* New York, E. Dutton, 1973.

3. Max Weber, especially *Protestant ethic and the spirit of capitalism,* New York McMillan, 1977. E. Durkheim, *Education and sociology,* New York, Free Press/McMillan, 1956. P. Bourdieu and J.C. Passeron, *Reproduction in education, society and culture,* London: Beverley Hills, Sage, 1977.

In countries with centralized planning, which set targets both for production and for educational organization, the supply and demand of employment are determined at the national level and maintained throughout the time-span laid down by the State. Thus, in practice, economic and educational goals are intimately linked, since both are subject to adjustments on orders from the planning authorities. (See V.A. Jamin and S.L. Kostanian, *Education and economic development,* Paris, Unesco, 1971, prepared for the International Commission on the Development of Education). The scale on which the educational and economic systems operate is identical within an essentially national framework.

State control). It is at one and the same time the instrument and the property of power.

The parable of the elephant and the blind men recounts that each of the latter envisaged a different animal, depending on the part of the beast that he discovered by his sense of touch. Similarly, education is what the philosopher, the sociologist or the official believes it to be, each of them deeply concerned with the rôle that he considers essential, sometimes to the extent of neglecting or belittling the rôles that others attribute to the phenomenon.

To overcome the limitations of the partial view of education described in the Introduction, of which the quantitative diagnosis was only one example, it must be accepted that education is, at least, simultaneously a system of values, a function and a machine.

A quick survey of the relationships between each of these aspects and some of the structures of Central-American educational systems should help us to see the field of application of the suggested hypothesis.

CHAPTER II

Education: a system of values or a social function?

When a philosopher develops a concept to the point of realizing the action which is tended to sanction it, it ceases to be what it was in the mind, the imagination or the vision of its author at the moment of its first expression. In the realm of education, identified by Plato with Virtue, as in all human endeavour, it has always been so: between the thought and the action distortion and contradiction flourish.

To the same extent that the phenomenon of 'learning' (not solely to acquire a trade, but to acquire knowledge in its widest sense) has become a communal activity, this aim, characteristic of mankind at all times and in all places, has been channelled, organized, structured, and — perhaps — devitalized.

Undoubtedly, if education is part of the system of values of the society which has engendered it, it cannot escape the fate that awaits every human undertaking: to be 'taken in hand' by those who are in control of society. Admittedly, in the 19th and early 20th centuries, especially in Europe and America, there were deep-seated movements to make education a means (a function?) which would lead to the rise of 'the working classes well above the level of the bourgeois and aristocratic classes', as Marx put it, and to the 'enlightenment of the masses from below and from within', in the words of Alain.

Similarly, José Marti, one of the most remarkable humanists of Latin America, reminded us that 'to be educated is the only way to be free', starting from the conviction that 'man grows only when he learns something'.[1]

Marx was the first to put forward the theory that 'all production and reproduction is production and reproduction not only of goods and services but also, at the same time, production and reproduction of the producers themselves and of social relationships'.[2] For him, economic science makes

1. José Marti, *Paginas escogidas,* Vol.2, Havana, Editorial de Ciencias Sociales, 1971.
2. K. Marx and F. Engels, *German ideology,* C.J. Arthur ed., New York, International Pubs Co., 1970.

the mistake of concentrating on the production of *things,* whereas it is the production of social relationships — corollary of the first — that is of prime importance in the process of production and reproduction. In Marx's view man, by producing and reproducing, reproduces himself at the same time, by virtue of reproducing the conditions of his existence.

The concept of reproduction in education was the subject of a work by P. Bourdieu and J.C. Passeron[3] who in 1970 tried a new approach which, in many respects, has since become unfashionable. Nevertheless, it reflected an important stage in the reflections arising from considerations not unrelated to the original Marxian thesis.

For these two authors, 'by reproducing the cultural arbitrariness that it inculcates' education contributes to 'to the reproduction of the relations of force that underlie its power'. They define this function as the 'function of social reproduction of the cultural reproduction'.

They explain this as follows: '. . . by the fact that it corresponds to the material and symbolical interests of groups or classes differently situated in the hierarchy of forces, this teaching work always tends to reproduce the structure of the division of cultural capital among these groups or classes, contributing at the same time to the reproduction of the social structure: in fact, the laws of the market which shape the economic or symbolical value — i.e., the value as cultural capital — of the cultural arbitrariness reproduced by the different kinds of teaching work and hence by their products (educated individuals) constitute one of the mechanisms, more or less determinant according to the type of social formation, defined as reproduction of the structure of the hierarchy of forces among the classes.[4]

P. Bourdieu and J.C. Passeron accord a fundamental rôle to primary education in this process of reproduction. They start from the hypothesis that the 'teaching work' is an irreversible process producing, in the time needed for inculcation, an irreversible disposition,[5] and they put forward the thesis that 'the primary teaching work (first education) which is accomplished in teaching work without antecedents (primary teaching work) produces a primary habitus, characteristic of a group or of a class, which is at the root of the subsequent constitution of all habitus'.[6] Let us leave the authors to develop this thesis in their commentary: 'The success of all school education, and more precisely of all secondary teaching work, depends basically on the primary education which has preceded it, (and above all) when the school rejects this priority in its ideology and in its practice, by making the history taught in school a history without prehistory; it is known that through the total of working knowledge connected with the daily conduct of life, and

3. P. Bourdieu and J.C. Passeron, op.cit.
4. *Ibid.*
5. They qualify this as unable to be checked or changed except by another 'irreversible process', producing in its turn a new irreversible disposition. *Ibid.*
6. *Ibid.*

especially through the acquisition of the mother tongue or the handling of the terms and relationships of kinship, it is the more or less complex and more or less symbolically elaborate dispositions, according to the groups or classes, which predispose unequally to the symbolic mastery of the operations implied by a mathematical demonstration just as well as by the deciphering of a work of art'.

In a study completed in 1972[7] Yves Barel attempted to use the concept of reproduction as a model for proposing a new theory and methodology for social planning. On the basis of results obtained in biology and epistemology he has tried to identify a 'dual and contradictory process' which on the one hand tends to reproduce the existing structure and hierarchy and on the other endangers this reproduction because 'the other adjustment of the structure involves the invention of new rules correcting the 'errors' which could not be foreseen in advance, and necessitates exchanges with the environment and the granting of 'significance' (on the integrating plan) to these exchanges. Thus, the function and the functioning can no longer be conceived as the simple and unilateral notion of conservation of existing structures and hierarchies'. The logical flaw underlying the concept of reproduction as 'survival' — or cyclic return on invariance — consists, the author claims on the basis of Piaget's work, in considering as finished structures and hierarchies which are not.[8]

The rôle of education in this methodological analysis arises from the overlapping of elements of the principal socio-cultural systems identified by the author in his investigations. Thus, he enumerates 41 processes of reproduction[9] which overlap each other. Since education acts upon 12 of these processes, its relative importance appears to be as an instrument of reproduction in so far as its multiplier effect or, conversely, sound-box effect is among the most powerful in the register of the socio-cultural system as defined by Barel.

Admittedly, neither Bourdieu and Passeron in 1982, nor Barel, claim that education is *only* reproduction ('without invariance'). It cannot be denied

7. Y. Barel, *La reproduction sociale: systèmes vivants, invariance et changement,* Paris, Anthropos, 1973.
8. Op.cit.
9. 1. General reproduction; 2. Social reproduction; 3. Natural reproduction; 4. Material reproduction; 5. Cultural reproduction; 6. Biological reproduction; 7. Natural cycles; 8. Economic reproduction; 9. Human reproduction; 10. Reproduction of works; 11. Reproduction of writing; 12. Reproduction of structures of organization; 13. Symbolic reproduction; 14. Vegetable reproduction; 15. Animal reproduction; 16. Reproduction of the human species; 17. Demographic reproduction; 18. Cultural reproduction of individuals; 19. Reproduction of health; 20. Reproduction of a work of art; 21. Reproduction of macro-objects; 22. Nations; 23. Classes; 24. Family; 25. Education; 26. Socio-cultural milieux; 27. Institutions; 28. Structure of power; 29. Language; 30. Sciences; 31. Techniques; 32. Ideologies; 33. Philosophy; 34. Religions; 35. Arts; 36. Morale; 37. Law; 38. Mental logic; 39. Social psychology; 40. Urban reproduction; 41. 'Humanization' of nature.

that in transmitting knowledge as well as values, the school cannot avoid the risk that these acquisitions from which the pupils 'benefit' will in due course provide ammunition for their own destruction. But it is none the less true that 'society' — as defined by Durkheim — sees its own reflection in the values which are transmitted by 'its' school.

In the Central-American context, then, what is the real nature of this education which, as Marti said, aims at liberation, but for which we have just foreseen a more coercive rôle? In the pages that follow we shall try to find a possible answer to the question. We shall then see more clearly, perhaps, whether education in Central America is essentially part of a system of values — for man — or whether it is (equally, or even more) an instrument which by-passes man in order better to serve 'society'.

This approach, presaged by the title of this chapter, will lead us to deal with primary education, education for production, and the less easily grasped forms of out-of-school education. This third aspect of the nature of education in Central America should help us to find an answer to our question — a question to which the other two aspects offer only partial solutions. But what about higher education? We have deliberately refrained from dealing with this other than by indirect references (since this work makes no claim to cover all the forms and types of education). As in a *tachist* painting, the light and shade have been suggested, but only in order to give some 'relief' to the map of education in Central America.

It may be objected that the University is the summit of the educational system, and that to leave it out is to reduce the presentation of the educational landscape to valleys and modest hills. In reply, it can only be said that too long an exposure to the light might perhaps prevent us from seeing the currents, often deep and sometimes hidden, which bring life to the lower areas of the relief.

But a more important reason lies in the extraordinarily complex nature of the various forms of higher education in Central America, sometimes crushed by the autonomy of a university cut off from the world of production, sometimes thrust to the front of the stage by a political affiliation finding (or not finding) a means of expression. This analysis of the heights, which would need to be carried to great lengths, does not therefore enter into the scope of this work.

Section 1. **Primary education**

The three characteristics which in practically all national constitutions describe primary education refer to it as being compulsory, universal and free. The avowed principle is to impose by law on all children aged from 7 to 12 years an education of 5, 6 or 7 years (depending on the country) on a basis of complete equality so that, as a result of standardized instruction, *all* citizens shall have the possibility of having the same intellectual grounding at the same age to enable them to set about the subsequent organization of their lives.

The facts which, in many Central-American countries, do not conform to these generous intentions are nevertheless worthy of analysis: to the obligation to send all children to school is opposed access limited to favoured minorities; to universality is opposed selectivity; and to gratuity is opposed loss of earnings and exorbitant costs for impoverished families. [10]

i) *Obligation:* whereas in 1970 Panama and Costa Rica had more than 80 per cent of the age-group (7-14 years) in school, El Salvador, Honduras and Nicaragua suffered from nearly 40 per cent absenteeism, and in Guatemala less than 50 per cent of the age-group were enrolled. But this information alone is insufficient for assessing the Central-American child's chances of taking part in a 'compulsory' and 'minimum' education: the rural child is even less fortunate. Enrolment of rural children in Panama and Costa Rica is about 80 per cent, in Honduras it is equal to that of urban children; in Guatemala and El Salvador rural children have only half the chances of schooling offered to urban children; and in Nicaragua, in 1979, they had barely a third.

The situation that emerges is clear: the school system does not take in all the children entitled to schooling. Evidently, therefore, access to primary schooling is far from being available to all children and, in addition, the urban child is considerably more favoured than the rural child of the same age. Access to schooling is directly linked with the child's place of residence — in other words, to his social class. Even the urban children, in peripheral or marginal areas, go to overcrowded schools, in which they make practically no progress from one year to the next.

ii) *Universality:* out of 1,500 children reaching the age for the first year of primary schooling, 1,000 have affective access to schools. Furthermore, in 1971, of these 1,000 only 280 reached the final year of their schooling. The proportion is exactly halved for rural children, even though the situations vary (30 in Nicaragua, 36 in Guatemala, 104 in Honduras, 184 in El Salvador, 334 in Panama and 387 in Costa Rica). This gap between the numbers who start and the numbers who finish is due to the drop-outs and repeaters. These latter result from the application of promotion criteria which are part of the system (ability of the child to demonstrate a certain level of knowledge recognized by the teacher). It is the same with the drop-outs, due partly to the attitude of certain heads of family who, confronted with the successive failures of their children, 'recuperate' them for work at home. Added to this, in very many cases the system does not provide rural schools of more than 2 or 3 years' schooling. So we find that in addition to the negative factor

10. The statistical data relating to the six Central-American countries used in this section have been published by the Proyecto Regional PNUD/UNESCO RLA/72/100 Red de Sistemas Educativos para el Desarrollo en Centroamerica y Panama, in the form of six monographs entitled: *Datos e indicadores para el area educación y desarrollo rural.* Guatemala, Unesco, 1987. (series I, vols. I to VI), for which all the data were taken from official publications of the governments concerned.

represented by the siting of a school in a rural area already mentioned, the retention of the child depends upon the application of promotion criteria based on substituting for the word 'universal' the word 'centralizing'. This is clear from the criteria for passing from one year to the next laid down by the Central Administration, reflecting academic principles which over the years have established themselves as dogmas, favouring mechanical memorization, abstraction and the deductive method.

To all this must be added, in a country such as Guatemala, the rejection of the native languages, which are not used by the educational system, thus obliging the 6-year-old child to come to grips simultaneously with the demands of deductive causality and those of its expression in a language which, to him, is foreign.

Even more significant is the real purpose of primary schooling: it is the means of access to secondary education. Given that the latter is concentrated in the towns (in Guatemala less than 1 per cent of the pupils at this level are in rural secondary schools), it follows that the curricula, the timetables, the contents of the textbooks, and — above all — the teacher/pupil relationship, are completely alien to the rural setting. In other words, the rural world, and that of the marginal urban areas, do not identify themselves with the examples, the illustrations, the elements of information or with the value judgements that primary schooling attempts to inculcate.

Even more serious is the lack of any kind of information or teaching that would enable the few pupils who can complete their primary schooling, but who have practically no chance of continuing their studies beyond that level, to face up more easily to the life that awaits them either in their original surroundings or in an urban centre in which, hypothetically, employment might be found. There is no question of the school's helping them either to achieve social integration, or to obtain for themselves better prospects in productive life.

iii) *Gratuity:* with the exception of Panama and Costa Rica, where the average *per capita* income in 1978 was some 4,000 francs, in the rest of Central America it varied between 1,200 and 2,000 francs. In 1976 the wage of a day-labourer during the coffee or cotton harvests ranged from 2 to 8 francs per day. Minors, in Guatemala and El Salvador, earn half the amount paid to their elders. But if the child wants to go to school, buying a shirt, a pair of shorts, an exercise-book and a pencil will take all he has earned. The cost of feeding the child who is going to school will also take a large share of the budget of an average family with five children, three of whom are old enough to work. If we add together the loss of earnings and the cost of the clothing and food needed by the child, the 'free' elementary school represents a charge amounting to not less than 20 per cent per child of the monetary budget of a rural family in Guatemala.

From this rapid survey of a situation which may appear completely foreign to inhabitants of Europe, North America or Japan, let us keep in mind the aspect which is, perhaps, not entirely foreign to the reality in industrialized countries. As compared with the actual situation in Central-American countries regarding compulsory, universal and free education the industrialized countries admittedly experience no problems concerning the first of these three conditions — but what of the others?

To sum up, bearing in mind our original intention of re-assessing the methods of quantitative analysis, it would appear that on the evidence of these figures alone the educational systems are 'inefficient'. The drop-out rates of over 90 per cent between the first and sixth years of rural primary schooling (60 to 70 per cent even in Panama and Costa Rica) are sufficient evidence of a 'bad' return. This information from the diagnosis is accurate, numerically speaking; sociologically, however, it is false. Any 'return' must be judged in relation to the proposed objective. Had the objective of the system been to produce, from 100 new entrants, 100 or even 90 primary-school graduates six — or even seven — years later, its content and its methods would have reflected the reality of the world which surrounds the population to be reached: children for the most part rural, or 'marginal' in the towns. But since neither the methods of teaching nor the curricula reflect this reality, the objective must be different. It consists in selecting the few individuals whom it can shape in the urban mould as defined by criteria of academic origin. In such conditions a system which selects only 10 out of 100 children in the rural setting is faithful to its mission, which consists precisely in choosing those judged most capable of preserving the values, the customs and the attitudes of those who have produced the system with the 'natural' aim, as Hobbes would say, of maintaining themselves in power. Thus society reproduces itself by means of a *highly* efficient system.

But it is this same system of primary education which economic studies have shown to be the most 'profitable'[11] in the sense that the cost/benefit ratio (benefit expressed in terms of the income expected by a graduate of this level) is more favourable than for second- and third-level education, where the higher costs do not 'bring back' proportional *rates* of return.

It is probable that if primary education were to be provided on a lavish scale, with the prospect of really offering to 100 per cent of the age-group schooling equivalent to six consecutive years of classes in which the curricula and methods were inspired by the needs, problems and real interests of the pupils, the rate of 'return' would be lower, since such an education would obviously cost more — but it would then be 'universal' and 'free' without the 'compulsion' to benefit from it being a snare and delusion.

Section 2. 'Short' courses and economic production

This same function of 'social reproduction' which we have just observed has also constructed two very different roads in secondary education:

11. See M. Blaug and G. Psacharopolous, op.cit.

a) the 'royal road', called 'general', with its specialized sections (humanities, mathematics, natural sciences, etc.) leading to the university — and to the selection of the ruling élite;
b) the 'sidings' of technical education.

Admittedly, over the last few decades, a technical education has been developed to respond more precisely to economic and social demands. This viewpoint seemed to open up a vision of hope, and of the birth of a system turning its back on the 'royal road'. Unfortunately, technical education is the alternative in a binary system ('yes' or 'no' to the élitist and ruling social rôle). The selection criteria for pre-university education, based on values called intellectual (deduction or abstraction and memorization are the two essentials), reject into the 'no' category all those whose instinct, motivation and natural disposition are based on different criteria (induction, empiricism, concrete or graphic representation, visual memory, etc.). To individuals of this type who wish to progress in the educational system, the 'technical' offers an alternative. In Costa Rica, for example, until 1965 a graduate from technical education (four years of secondary) wishing to go on to university had to 're-take' three years of general studies (the second cycle of secondary) and apply for admission as a product of so-called 'academic' education.

At the same time, those who stay in technical education have an attitude towards their possible employment which is in exact contradiction to that of 'society' and, more especially, to that of their possible employers.

In the stratification of the Central-American labour market the products of this education (called 'vocational') are much closer to the 'white-collar' workers than to the 'dirty-handed', as typified by the labourers, the non-qualified workers, the specialized workers and the foremen — these last nearly always 'risen from the ranks' of the other categories. It follows that the graduates from technical education — even if they feel 'inferior' as compared with students from general or academic education — identify themselves more with these latter than with the mass of agricultural workers and labourers, usually illiterate or with only incomplete primary education. In other words, a technical-education graduate's studies will have inclined him to seek employment connected with the tertiary sector. The great majority of technical-education students enrolled in commerical sections (in 1976: Cost Rica 70 per cent, Guatemala 72 per cent, El Salvador 83 per cent), like those of the agricultural and industrial sections, do their utmost on graduating to find employment in either public or private administrative posts.

A final count in an indictment of technical education which has already been anticipated[12] is that this type of education has often inherited the heaviness and would-be academic style of conventional schooling, but never-

---

12. See P. Foster, 'The vocational school fallacy in development planning', in A. Andersen and M.J. Bowman (eds.), *Education and economic development,* Chicago, Aldine Publishing Co., 1965, and M. Blaug in *Economics of education,* op.cit.

theless still does not generally manage to train satisfactory technical personnel. The courses, usually under the aegis of the Ministry of Education, are still widely separated from the world of work. The majority of the teachers, for example, have as their only professional experience the training they received a generation ago, at best in a technical teacher-training college. The potential employers have very little influence on the nature of the teaching provided in these courses. They are in no hurry to offer employment to the graduates, who, as we have seen, do not have the same idea of their professional function as the employers who, for their part, regard them as technicians capable of assisting — but not directing — the foremen.

This is precisely the level at which economic production must depend upon the capacity of the training system to provide the specialized manpower needed, either to ensure a return on the capital invested (in a free economy) or to enable the declared goals of society to be met (in a centrally-planned economy). But in the free economies the inexactitude of manpower forecasts, the inertia of the educational system in responding to what could well be 'signals' from the labour market, and the motivation of the students in 'the technical', render completely hypothetical the economic function of education, as applied at the level of what would seem to be the most 'functional' form of it. It is in this context that we must question the value of projections of manpower needs based on the 'objective' data provided by forecasts of product growth by economic sector of activity.

An analysis of the origins of this approach[13] would perhaps show that it was begun, and subsequently perfected,[14] in economic circumstances of growth in free-economy countries. All analysis was based implicitly on the causality of this growth, which was believed to be due — in addition to the capital and the 'quantity' of manpower — to a continual improvement in the relationship between these two factors leading to productivity. And this latter was explained both by technical progress and by the 'residual factor', namely the qualification (in other words, the education) of the manpower.

Thus, a forecast of growth in the aggregate of a sector assumed a corresponding increase (by reason of a 'technical coefficient', as it was called by Tinbergen, varying by country and sector) in its manpower by levels of qualification, these latter corresponding to those of the educational systems.

If such models could illustrate *a posteriori,* in industrialized countries during a period of growth (assumed in the 1960s to be continuous), a certain relationship, for example, between graduates from agricultural schools and the growth of the agricultural sector, there were many economists and planners who, by extrapolation, estimated that this theory could be used equally well for forecasting, especially for the emerging economies of the developing countries.

13. H. Parnes, op.cit.
14. J. Tinbergen, op.cit.

The audience that welcomed these intentions was large, well-wishing, and respectable. For example, in the 1970s the director of an international financing institution visiting an East African country, and noting on the one hand the importance of the agricultural sector in the national economy and on the other hand the absence of schools of agriculture, drew the — logical — conclusion that a greater number of such schools would provide the country with the necessary technicians to increase the productivity of this key sector. Unfortunately the provision, at great expense, of such institutions, and in due course the production of graduates, did not have the desired effect.

In the event, the very great majority of the agricultural technicians trained (in establishments financed from the exterior, with standards of comfort and modernity very different from the realities of the local peasant environment) had experienced a change in their professional aspirations during the course of their studies. If some of them still envisaged returning to the fields, the great majority could only hope to find employment in the Ministry of Agriculture, with agricultural machinery manufacturers or in agricultural banks. Admittedly, their training will not have been worthless to them, but it in no way corresponded to what the country's agriculture clearly needed. But agriculture, estimated by branch but in aggregates, could give the illusion of being able to use x technicians for each v of value added for the product concerned. Unfortunately, only 20 per cent of the production units were of sufficient size to produce at least one v. Since a single technician cannot split himself into parts and give full-time service to several units, and since each unit functions as a family cell with no need for assistance from even a fraction of a technician, the result was 80 per cent non-absorption of the technicians trained for the aggregate of the population foreseen for the agricultural production sector.

This example is not exceptional and shows that the insurmountable difficulty in economics is the need to define a law having universal application once certain relationships, which are considered unchangeable, have been established. Furthermore, the planning of education or of particular levels of the educational system has no means of basing its projections on the effective use that the labour markets intends to make of its products.

In the first place, as the example just cited suggests, the overall behaviour of the labour market does not correspond to that of its most modern portion. Secondly, the fluctuations of the labour market are subject to changes in the general situation which are difficult to predict for the medium or long term, as demonstrated by the world economic crisis of recent years which replaced the period of continuous growth. Thirdly, the partitioning and rigidity of conventional educational systems prevent at one and the same time the 'signals' of the labour market from getting through to the fortified enclosure of the system, and the system from reacting sufficiently quickly in order to adapt itself to short-term needs, which are the only trustworthy demands of the labour market. Finally, the complexity of the division of labour gives

41

rise to a strong link between professional function and scholastic level. Every post filled often represents a specific 'route', made up of schooling, training, employment, promotion and transfer, or a combination of parts of these various components.

At a meeting called by OECD in 1971 there took place, in this Organization which ten years earlier (in a Mediterranean Regional Project) had recommended its use, the formal 'burial' of the technique called 'manpower forecasting' in the practice of educational planning in industrialized market-economy countries. The search can therefore be abandoned for a single economic function of education which such a forecasting instrument could provide in countries which do not have a single system known as 'centralized' planning.

Besides an appreciation of the economic climate, and of the application of deliberate measures (such as a wages or even an incomes policy, a social policy, etc.), a knowledge of the actual behaviour of the labour market and of the motivation — or aspirations — of the present and future manpower is considerably more determinative than a correlation of factors which it may be tempting to interpret as a particular causality.

The problem remains: cannot economics provide an instrument for analysing and forecasting which would establish a link between the labour market and the educational process? The experience of Honduras, ignoring the macro-economic projections of manpower needs, seems to confirm the usefulness of a link between new forms of training and specific in-depth socio-economic surveys, both among potential employers and among those who cannot aspire to the 'royal road' but who, as a result of specialized studies, count on receiving a given level of remuneration.

The authorities, envisaging the creation of 'short courses' in agriculture at the secondary and higher levels of education, had in mind a flexible system meeting the needs of the agricultural sector (plantations and agro-industrial, both national and foreign). It only remained to decide upon the modalities of the training and ascertain the real nature of the demand. The survey by the Honduran government as part of the National Project 'Pilot survey of the demand for short courses in the Honduran labour market' was speedily put in hand (in under one year, 1977-78). It was able to show that while the short courses (post-primary or post-secondary) should not be envisaged without considerable precautions — in view of the preconceptions both on the supply side (future students and their families) and the demand side (employers), they would nevertheless be likely to benefit the children of families in the lower socio-professional categories. The demand for technicians able effectively to meet the qualitative demands of the market was high, and the income offered them was quite close to the wages and other benefits received by the graduates of engineering faculties. At the same time, only the young of *lower* socio-professional origin could be attracted by such a possibility, since, with an equivalent diploma, they could not hope for an income comparable with that of graduates from more fortunate circles.[15]

The income difference between the two socio-professional categories after a long education explains why the young of modest socio-economic origin sought an intermediate career, with remuneration at a rate scarcely lower than that which they would have received had they chosen conventional long-term education. In this way, after a shorter education (and thus a smaller loss of earnings) they could enter the labour market without suffering significant differences in their incomes.

In El Salvador a similar survey — precise and in-depth — had shown, at the beginning of the 1970s, the urgent need for higher-level short courses in the industrial sector. Hence was born the Central American Technological Institute, which trains higher technicians in two years after completion of secondary education. Recruited (as the above-mentioned Honduras study showed) from among the children of the lower socio-professional classes, after five years these technicians were being paid at a rate not far short of that offered to engineering graduates. Among the reasons for this success should be mentioned the fact that the potential employers take part in the drawing-up of the training curricula, and that the teaching is directly linked with the world of production. In addition, streams are opened — or closed — in relation to needs. Finally, the practical and up-to-date nature of the training, together with a strict control of the student's work, trains the type of technician that the industrial sector is seeking. Two further post-secondary institutes on the same model were opened in 1978.

Obviously, it should not be concluded from the foregoing that short higher-level courses are the most perfect instrument, necessarily and universally, for an economic function. The two examples cited are more an illustration of a *manner* of using the educational system to meet the needs of the economy than a demonstration of the value of one possible answer.

In reality, the two examples are intended to suggest that education *can* play a direct economic rôle by furnishing a specific 'product' demanded by the market when the education offered corresponds to a specific demand. If the preliminary surveys are meticulously carried out on a particular population (employers and students) in selected circumstances (Honduras, agricultural sector, 1977/78; El Salvador, industrial sector, 1972) it is possible to establish a *direct* economy/education relation. In this way it is possible to avoid generalizations, proceeding from universal laws (or justifying their formulation) which underlie the economic sciences but which apply only imperfectly to the very special conditions of educational systems.

Section 3. **Out-of-school education: for liberation?**
In spite of the attempt in the two previous sections to appreciate, in the

15. M. Carnoy, op.cit.

Central-American context, the significance of the rôle (value system) and the productive function of education, we are still unsatisfied. The question remains: how can education enable us to reconcile the exercise of individual liberty in the search for the 'self' (the Platonic ideal, the free man of Alain) or the eternal attempt to draw ourselves nearer to the 'perfection of our nature' hoped for by J.S. Mill,[16] with the demands of the 'society' of Durkheim[17] for the ideal of a human society,[18] or those of the Marxist state which will come to fruition under the dictatorship of the proletariat?[19]

The answer depends on a network of factors so rich, so complex and so shifting that we must concentrate our efforts on only one aspect of the problem: that concerned with educational institutions. For this purpose, we will start with the premiss that the more the educational response is institutionalized by a central authority acting in the name of the community (State, Government, Society), the more the latter will tend to reproduce the criteria of those who have brought it to power; conversely, the less the response is institutionalized and centralized, the more chances it has of lending itself to varied formulae adapted to a greater number.

The last half of this premiss should help us, where we can find it in operation, to see the direction in which we should seek the answer we need. This notion of an education distinct from the school has very old and widespread roots, which antedate the 'school' of today.[20]

It is worth beginning by rapidly sketching the backcloth woven by the history of education in Central America.

The historian of the Conquest of New Spain reminds us that among the 'benefits' bequeathed to Central America by the Spaniards 'in Mexico there is a Universal College where grammar, theology and rhetoric, logic and philosophy, and other arts and learnings may be studied; there are moulds and matrixes for the printing of books, both in Latin and in the Romance languages; bachelors and doctors there perfect their studies'.[21] For many years to come (the 17th and 18th centuries) education in Latin America was in fact to be the product of an 'imposed culture' in the words of the Argentinian historian Gregorio Weinburg,[22] imposed by a colonial power

16. Quoted by E. Durkheim, op.cit.
17. *Ibid.*
18. See P. Lengrand, *An introduction to lifelong education,* London, Croom Helm, 1975; E. Faure *et al.,* op.cit.
19. See, especially, K. Marx and F. Engels, 'Introduction on various questions to the delegates of the provisional Central Council', reproduced in *Selected works,* Moscow, Progress Publishers, 1970.
20. E. Faure *et al.,* op.cit., p.5, where examples are given of the earliest educational institutions in Africa, Asia and Europe.
21. Bernal Diaz del Castillo, *Historia de la conquista de Neuva Espana,* Mexico, Editorial, Porrúa S.A., 1974 (first edition: Madrid, 1682), p.583.
22. The three types of culture can be found in Gregorio Weinberg, *Educational models in the historical development of Latin America,* Santiago de Chile, Unesco Regional

which from the exterior determined the norms and values to be adopted, these reflecting the interests and the customs of the mother country. This, according to Weinberg, was the first stage.

The movement for independence and the directing of the economy towards the exterior characterized the second stage (the first half of the 19th century), called the stage of 'admitted and accepted culture'. Referring to this, German Rama[23] points out that being associated with the creation of an independent society, its focal point was the citizen. 'The political society is the expression of free citizens, who must be educated for the future. . . The unforeseen and unforeseeable participation', Rama goes on, 'of popular social groups in the struggle for the new political order only strengthened the conviction held by those who were in power and who hoped for a stable order that, taking into account the conditions of the period, only the restoration or preservation of the social hierarchy characteristic of the Colony was capable of guaranteeing this order. Participation and exclusion were the twin poles of reference of the concept of order, which crops up more or less constantly throughout the history of Latin America. Education plays a central rôle in the debate, for throughout the 19th century it was regarded as an institution responsible for political training.'

Opinions diverged regarding its aim: the training of the élite or, conversely, the socialization of the masses so that they should integrate with the national 'project'. In Costa Rica, for example, coffee production gave birth to a class of small and medium agricultural enterprises. This social change could not fail to influence the rôle which these new full citizens wished to attribute to education. Conversely, in Guatemala, Honduras and El Salvador the opening-up to world markets did not produce a shift in the centre of gravity of the social organization, as happened in Costa Rica. The same landowners, the holders of power, gathered new sources of wealth (coffee, and later on sugar, cotton, stockbreeding, etc.), which did not for all that bring about a social mobility which would have resulted in the handing-over of power, especially as regards education, to new authorities.

It was not until Weinberg's third stage (the end of the 19th and beginning of the 20th centuries), marked by a 'criticized or disputed culture', that we find the beginnings of the rejection of the men and values formerly accepted.

José Marti, who was born and died in Cuba, passed the greater part of his life in exile, principally in Mexico and Guatemala. Struck by the unsuitability of the resources bequeathed by the colony for the task of building a nation and achieving greater social justice, he was led to formulate a definition of the ideal teacher, and consequently of the new education, which should

Office for Education in Latin America and the Caribbean, 1981. (DEALC/5), UNESCO/ECLA/UNDP Project 'Development and Education in Latin America and the Caribbean' p.5.
23. *Ibid,* Introduction by G. Rama.

be neither that of Spain, nor that of the 'creoles', another generation of 'colonialists'. In an historic essay written in 1884, entitled 'The wandering teachers',[24] he lays the foundations of this new education, of which it may be said that it is the source of the attempt that was later to be made to match education with the human condition, essentially rural in Uruguay, in Cuba, in Mexico and in the various Central-American countries:

'The only clear path to continuous and easy prosperity is that which leads to knowlege, to culture, and to enjoyment of the inexhaustible and indefatigable resources of nature. . .

Now is the moment to start the crusade which will reveal to men their proper nature and will give them, together with a knowledge of simple and practical science, that personal independence that will reinforce their happiness and awaken in them the price of being a loving creature and a being living in the enormous universe.

That is what the teachers should bring to the countryside. Not only agricultural demonstrations and mechanical contrivances, but also the affection which man needs so much and which does him so much good.

The peasant cannot leave his work and follow miles of tracks with the aim of seeing imcomprehensible geometrical designs, of learning the names of rivers, capes, African peninsulas, of burdening himself with an inane school-born vocabulary. The sons of peasants cannot spend day after day leagues away from home in order to learn Latin declensions and mental arithmetic. But it is precisely these peasants who are the leaven of the nation, its healthiest and richest element, since they receive fully and directly the fruits and the call of the land on which they depend. What happiness for these peasants to see, from time to time, the arrival of this kindly man who will show them the things that they know not. . . They will have something else to talk about — not just the cattle or the harvest, but now and then — until it becomes a full-time pleasure — what the teacher has told them, the strange applicances he has brought, easier ways of cultivation. . . There will be no need for lengthy discourses; fruitful ideas, thoroughly assimilated by the teachers, may be sown and may take root. The desire to know will be born. . . We shall not be sending pedagogues into the fields, but rather 'leaders of conversation' (*conversadores*). We shall not be sending learned doctors, but rather knowledgeable people who will strive to allay the doubts which trouble those who do not 'know', or to answer the questions which have been prepared for their visit. Seeing the mistakes made in the fields, or the lack of knowledge of exploitable riches, they will point out the former and reveal the latter, supporting their explanations with practical solutions.

To sum up: the need is to set in motion a campaign of affection and

24. J. Marti, op.cit., pp.260-264.

of knowledge, and to create a body of wandering teachers, which at the moment does not exist, in order to carry it out.

Regardless of what this text owes to positivism, or to any other concept of happiness, Marti's lines are, for their time, an original design for a conception of an apprenticeship to life, the communication of experience, mutual enrichment, the opening of the countryside to the urban world — and *vice versa*. All these lessons, and others, are what education should ideally offer to everybody, from primary school onwards. As we have seen earlier, the situation today does not yet correspond to the design of Marti.

With the exception of pilot projects and experimental schools, essentially reserved for relatively well-off urban populations, primary education has not yet become a means of sowing ideas that will bring forth 'the nucleus of liberty'.

Let us take up again the question already asked: if the State institutions, centralized and 'reproductive', do not provide this liberating education, is there a form of education outside the school, 'out-of-school' education as it is called, which could supply what conventional education is not equipped to offer?

Today, the 'de-schooling' of education takes many different forms: popular education, lifelong education, extension schools, open universities, etc. This collection of formulae is often referred to as 'out-of-school' education. By its very nature, this form of education should reflect the image that a community forms of its ideal of education. Is it a 'wind of liberty', that will enable every man and woman to contribute to an educating society? Does this non-institutionalized education lend itself to being manipulated by its creators? Is it just a variant, apparently de-schooled, of instructional education? Might it not be merely 'education on the cheap' for those who cannot embark on the 'royal road' of formal education?

At first sight, these new forms should represent a hope for those who have had no access to schooling, or who have attended so briefly that they have scarcely been able to profit from their brief stay. But each of the Central-American countries, in various ways and at various times, has tried to set up out-of-school programmes with the aim of 'recovering' those whom the system had neglected or rejected. Had the system been governed by criteria too different from those professed on behalf of education, in general? If so, 'non-structured' structures and 'nonformal' forms must be found, to embody more faithfully the principles that the school had not been able to defend while adding to them a cruder economic functionality.

A seminar of Central-American officials held in Panama in 1977[25] on Out-of-School Education, Rural Literacy and Adult Education threw useful light on the magnitude of the stake and on the volition of those in charge.

25. *Reunión de directivos de educación extrascolar y alfabetización en el medio rural del area centroaméricana,* Panama, 24-28 June 1977, Pazcuaró, CREFAL, 1978.

The official texts of each country bear witness to their desire to offer a 'really' democratic education, and to the apparent difficulty of doing so within the traditional educational system.

In Panama the Nonformal Education Programme (*Educación no regular*) was based on 'the need to encourage the process of liberation to which Panamanian society aspires'. This was to be done by the training of 'an active man', critical, aware of his actuality, so that he should be able to create, consolidate or transform this actuality'.[26] As part of this Programme the authorities set up Basic Education for Work (*Educación Basica Laboral*), in accordance with Article 19, Chapter V of the Constitution, as a 'nonformal (*no regular*) modality of the educational system' so as to 'strengthen the bases of lifelong education as the combination of means placed at the disposal of a person throughout his life, in the search for his own perfecting'.[27] Also in the same programme is found the bilingual training of an ethnic group of Indian origin, the Guaymi people, who number a total of 40,000 persons (5 per cent of the national population). This education will enable a Guaymi 'to be better qualified to take an active part in his civic capacity', since it is both 'an awareness and an immediate action whose object is to give the Guaymi the benefit of the educational policy promoted by the Revolutionary Government. . . The Community in its actuality is the foundation of a good school'. This will become a reality when 'young and old pay full attention to the development and progress of the community'.[28]

The language of this text reflects the ambition of the official in charge of the programme rather than that of his superiors. Nonformal activities and literacy programmes (these latter have a formal character in Panama) reached altogether some 35,000 persons in 1977, and mobilized about 1,200 promoters, teachers and instructors, over 40 per cent of them on a voluntary basis. The cost of these activities did not exceed 3 per cent of the Ministry's budget.

In 1977 El Salvador offered nonformal training to peasants in five programmes: artisanal crafts (leather, textiles, etc.), agricultural (soils, horticulture, pesticides, irrigation, etc.), food preservation, building (rural housing, carpentry, motors for electrical apparatus), rural economy (accounting, marketing, co-operatives, obtaining loans, etc.) and domestic economy. The programmes, conducted by non-professional instructors with the necessary experience, visited the villages and presented a complete 'course' (within each programme) covering a period of two weeks. The aim was to enable the peasant 'to become fully aware of himself and of his community, so that this might lead to a constructive attitude as regards community development'. The programme should also enable the Salvadorian to develop 'a positive

26. *Ibid*, Appendix, p.27, 'Report of the General Direction of Literacy and Adult Education' of the Government of the Republic of Panama.
27. *Ibid.*, p.57.
28. *Ibid.*, pp. 83-84.

attitude in respect of his family responsibilities' and so 'feel happy to be a useful and productive element, with ambition to improve the conditions of life for his family and for his community'.[29] To be effective, the programme required a measure of co-ordination with other Ministries (Agriculture, Health) and with the official body responsible for community co-operation, FOCCO. But the funds available for this activity amounted to 0.2 per cent of the Ministry's budget.[30] FOCCO, on the other hand, whose purpose was the financing of various communal investments (roads, school mains connections, etc.) had considerably larger resources available. Another project, 'National Network of Houses of Culture', had available funds four times as large as those for nonformal education, namely 0.8 per cent.

The two cases (Panama and El Salvador), while giving similar results as far as the budgetary impact of nonformal programmes is concerned, cannot otherwise be compared. The problems of literacy and of marginal schooling is merely residual (at primary-education level) in Panama, whereas in El Salvador it still dominates the scene.

The case of Guatemala is equally characteristic: it is the only country — with Honduras — to have set up a programme of out-of-school education to compensate for the limited activities of the traditional educational system. The Educational Plan 1976-1980, following the lines of the 1975-1979 Plan, divides education into three sectors: in-school education, out-of-school education, and science and technology.

The out-of-school subsector 'responds to the observed and demonstrated need to give simultaneous and extensive attention to all sectors of the population who, for one reason or another (socio-economic condition, geographical location, formal education), are in a marginal situation, as well as to all elements of society demanding a better preparation in order to integrate themselves into the productive system and thus participate as subjects, and not as objects, in the process of development'.[31]

The 1976-1979 Plan lays down the main lines of the out-of-school programme, described in the document submitted by the authorities[32] as 'the most innovative and fundamental aspect' of the document:

— The programme will be available to everyone aged 7 years or more;
— It will not be based on schools or other establishments;
— It is not bound to a fixed order of years of study;
— It allows flexibility in responding to study options;
— It uses modern communication media;

29. *Ibid*, Appendix, p.103, 'Programme of the Directorate of Adult Education and Lifelong Education', Ministry of Education, Republic of El Salvador.
30. *Ibid*, p.107.
31. *Ibid*, Appendix, p.121, 'Report of the Co-ordinating Secretariat, National Council of Out-of-school Education', Guatemala, January 1977.
32. *Ibid*, p.144.

— Its timetable and calendar are suited to the working hours of the
participants;
— It allows of a wide coverage of the population.

The Secretariat for Out-of-School Education co-ordinates the activities of
this nature carried out by a large variety of public and private bodies,[33] and
through a training programme 'The Basic Module of Out-of-school Education' it is bound to offer educational possibilities — in an organized form
— to any of the population who do not otherwise benefit from any other
out-of-school educational programme. It should ensure the extension of the
programme in the High Plains region (homeland of the majority of the Indian
population) 'in the perspective of a complete coverage of the country'. The
programme aims at co-ordinating all the public services directly interested
in out-of-school education in order to bring about the preparation and dif-
fusion of educational matter 'the content of which is concerned with
agricultural development' and encourages a rich development of the
'knowledge, capacity and attitudes of the population of the area'. This content will be based on the 'needs' of the population and on 'the manner in
which it perceives existential situations'.[34]

The 1975-1979 Plan forecast that the 'Module' would affect 600,000 people in 1980, and that nearly 12 per cent of the total Ministry budget would
be devoted to it. Actually, only some 30,000 people had been integrated into
the programme in 1979, thanks to State support equivalent to 0.9 per cent
of the budget.

In Costa Rica, where the enrolment rate for children of primary-school
age is close to 90 per cent and where illiteracy, as in Panama, is mainly residual
(10 per cent), out-of-school education is not the responsibility of the Ministry
of Education, which devotes only a very small part of its budget (less than
1 per cent) to a literacy programme. The National Directorate of Community
Development (DINADECO) has the main responsibility for out-of-school
education. The 1967 Law setting up the DINADECO lays down that its objectives include the following:[35]

— to foster the creation of opportunities for the integral perfecting of the
   human being, to discover his capacities and qualities, and to direct them
   for the benefit of the communities of the country;
— to create a favourable climate for the establishment of new values and
   the adoption of new attitudes, through a process of inner improvement
   of the population;
— to create, by recourse to an educational system of further individual training

33. The country had 5 public bodies responsible for various literacy programmes, 18 for
    domestic economy, 9 for community development, etc. (*ibid*, p.122).
34. *Ibid*, pp.131 and 132.
35. *Ibid*, Appendix, pp.166 and 167, 'Report of the National Directorate of Community
    Development', San José, Costa Rica, January 1977.

and democratic institutions, a collective consciousness of common responsibility to ensure national development in all its aspects;
— etc., etc.

DINADECO organizes courses, seminars, meeting, lectures, etc., on subjects connected with the concerns of the population covered by the programme, which is by nature 'continuous and indefinite' since it meets a demand which is not limited in time and which covers the entire national territory. In 1976 DINADECO trained 25,000 directors (the total population is about two million), organized over 1,200 different programmes, and set up more than 130 local training bodies (500 in three years). Its budget for the same year amounted to 0.7 per cent of that of the Ministry of Education.

The Government of Honduras (where complete illiteracy is of the order of some 40 per cent and where 70 per cent of the population is rural) founded in 1976, after a very serious cyclone which accentuated the already latent rural unemployment, a National Programme of Out-of-school Education (PRONAEH) with the aim of creating and organizing a system of out-of-school learning which would lead to 'the free and systematic development of a process of lifelong education of the population, training them both for an occupation and also to ensure for them an active, conscious, organized and responsible social participation'.[36]

This programme, which was at one and the same time to ensure education 'on demand' for the rural population (illiterate, or never enrolled, or simply dropped out) and to supply 'technical assistance' to public institutions working in rural areas, was able to finalize a technique of 'educational solutions to problems'. Its monitors and technicians formed a valuable professional 'asset' for the country and for the region.

The National Development Plan (1979-1983) confirmed the rôle of PRONAEH as the agency responsible for out-of-school education, with the task of promoting national activity which 'at the same time as raising the educational level of the population, will enable it to integrate itself consciously and effectively in development projects'.

In 1976 it was expected that PRONAEH would reach 70,000 rural inhabitants (out of a total of some two milllions) between 1977 and 1979; 10,000 in 1977, 20,000 in 1978, and 40,000 in 1979. The data available indicate that there were 1,000 in 1977, 4,800 in 1978, and 15,000 in 1979. The Programme's rôle in co-ordinating all the agencies at work in rural areas and carrying out educational activities has never reached the desired proportions. Its budget in 1977 was of the order of 0.3 per cent of that of the Ministry of Education.[37]

36. CONSUPLANE (Higher Council for Economic Planning), *Project: National Programme for Out-of-school Education,* Tegucigalpa, Honduras, August 1976.
37. CREFAL, op.cit., Appendix, p.222, 'Policies for out-of-school education in rural areas', National Programme for Out-of-school Education, Tegucigalpa, Honduras, January 1977.

Our description of the situation in Nacaragua (2,500,000 inhabitants) will not be based on the data supplied at the Seminar mentioned earlier, since it was held before the July 1979 Revolution. Instead, we will take as an example the National Crusade For Literacy, launched shortly afterwards, which has led to a reduction of at least a fifth in the illiteracy which afflicted 50 per cent of the population over 10 years old. This was nothing less than the mobilzation of the country, between March and August 1980, in a great ideological and political — in other words, educational — movement.

In the words of the Minister of Education:[38]

A cultural revolution does not take place independently of the political revolution. All revolutions, ancient and modern, bear witness to this. This is why the National Crusade for Literacy offers the other side of the same coin. Our revolution would be of little account if we had simply followed the old ideas inherited from Somozism[39] — namely, that literacy is a question of teaching, and nothing more. Such a statement is false, since for us, making a person literate consists in training, giving awareness, making political, modernizing and humanizing the sons of Sandino.[40] We do not want a half-finished man, big and strong but one-eyed like Polyphemus — but rather, a fully developed man, able in future to travel by his own resources along the many paths that will be opened for us by technology and culture.[41]

One of the five members of the Executive (the ruling Junta) defined the literacy mission of the Revolution in these terms:

We shall bring literacy to the peasants, the workers of Nicaragua, in accordance with their needs, with the aim of the Revolution, and with their involvement in the popular Sandinist Revolution. To make them literate without this political content would be senseless, since it would frustrate, after so many years of delays and forgetfulness, their real social and political motivations, which we wish to re-awaken in them so that they may become integrated in the revolutionary process, both from the productive viewpoint and from the cultural and social viewpoint.[42]

Shortly before the liberation of the country in July 1979, the future government had already decided on such a campaign, regarded as the first duty

38. 'En cada Rincon Liberado, un nino alfabetizo' (Special Number of the Review *Encuentro* published by the Central-American University, Managua), article by C. Tunnermann, 'Cruzada nacional de alfabetización — prioridad de la revolución', 26 February 1980.
39. Adjective derived from Somoza, surname of the family of dictators who dominated the national scene for more than 40 years, until July 1979.
40. Sandino was a 'national hero' who from 1927 to 1932 resisted the North American military occupation and was assassinated in 1934 by the 'first' of the Somozas, father of the last dictator.
41. C. Tunnerman, op.cit., p.9.
42. 'En cada Rincon. . .', op.cit., article by Carlos Ramirez, p.65.

of the new government. Detailed plans were therefore ready when the new team took office. Eight months later the Crusade was launched. Its organization relied on three sources of literacy teachers: the People's Literacy Teachers, the People's Army of Literacy Teachers (EPA), and the Workers' Militia for Literacy. It was the EPA (consisting essentially of students, volunteers as were the members of the other two groups) who provided the majority of the forces carrying out the Crusade. Working full-time for six months, secondary and higher education students offered their services to bring literacy to the people, chiefly in rural areas. This army was organised in 'Brigades', 'Columns' and 'Squadrons', attacking on the six 'fronts' where a year earlier their elders had fought against Somoza. More than 100,000 young people became the guides and instructors of a population at first incredulous, and then profoundly touched by this movement.

In all, there were 120,000 teachers for some 600,000 illiterates. The Crusade cost 20 million dollars (for infrastructure and food, since all the actors were unpaid volunteers except for a small central team at headquarters). This sum, which included contributions from foreign and international sources, represented 30 per cent of the total public expenditure proposed for education in 1980.

The results, published in August 1980, indicate that 70 per cent of those listed as illiterate in 1979 were no longer so. What is difficult to assess quantitatively is the 'mobilization' of this same population, for whom an organization was set up to ensure the natural practice of 'post-literacy'. It would appear that the majority of newly literate workers and their families became actively involved in trade union movements, civic groups, or — more simply — the courses and programmes organized in the 'People's Education Collectives' (CEP). The CEPs provide a nonformal type of education 'on demand', in a setting in which 'the people educate the people' in the context of 'an exchange of experience and knowledge'. In 1981/82 there were 17,000 unpaid volunteers in charge of the CEPs (conventional primary education employs 15,000 teachers), of whom less than 30 per cent were professional teachers.

Section 4. **Reflections by way of an answer**

This rapid general view of Central America seems to demonstrate three tendencies:

1. The aims of out-of-school education show that it is perceived:
a) As the declared embodiment of an education ideal: at one and the same time a factor of cohesion and social integration on the one hand and, on the other, a privileged means for the individual to free himself and come to fruition. However, it should be noted that this education, this 'subsystem', is destined principally for the 'marginals' (often the majority of the population) from the traditional system of institutionalized schooling which has apparently ignored — or is still ignoring — their existence.

b) As the alternative to a system which seems to be — in contrast — élitist and centralizing, and therefore uniform and constructive.

2. Except in the case of Nicaragua, the financial resources provided for an out-of-school activity, whether under the Ministry of Education or some other administrative body, are extremely limited in relation to the proclaimed intentions and to the number of people who might hope to benefit. Nevertheless, even though other efforts are not wanting (activities by other public or private institutions, voluntary help, external aid and assistance, etc.), and even though it is not easy to arrive at precise figures, it remains true that the proportion of its budget that a State devotes to this activity is a clear expression of the political will to transform intentions into action. Except for Nicaragua, where it appears that 'political will' and 'public resources' complement each other, the other countries scarcely demonstrate in action what they proclaim in their rhetoric.

3. This lack of will is demonstrated in two ways:

a) Out-of-school education can provide an alternative, to reduce the pressure caused by all those who wish to receive the education offered by the school system, but whose numbers are incompatible with the selective and reproductive function of the system. This alternative (of which the structures, the methods and the curricula do not meet the criteria of the instrument for social reproduction that is formal schooling) is proposed as a solution for demands that are extremely popular — and extremely demagogic. These are often incompatible with the *de facto* political situation (Guatemalá, El Salvador, Honduras). 'But is doesn't really matter', one can imagine an official in these three countries thinking, 'since the only, the sole, education to ensure the reproduction of society in the direction we want is that offered by traditional schooling.' Any alternative is, by definition, a parallel track, probably a siding, and can only be an education 'on the cheap'. What does it matter if, in order to 'sell' it to those who are unable to follow the 'royal road' but who hope, in spite of everything, for 'an education', recourse is had to slogans which have neither foundation nor prospects in the social context, and that lip-service is paid to an out-of-school organization which — for greater security — is not given the funds to be effective.[43]

b) By definition, out-of-school education, if it is to match up to the ideal of an educational goal at once 'liberating' and 'developing', can be neither highly centralized nor separate from the productive context. In other words,

43. Conversely, in a country such as Nicaragua, in which there is (i) the political will to provide for the large number of children without schooling and of illiterate adolescents and adults with no vocational training, but (ii) a complete lack of means (financial and real) for satisfying this demand in the traditional way (schools and teachers), the out-of-school alternative becomes necessary and, therefore, credible. It leads in its turn to the necessary effort to seek and find the national, international and foreign resources necessary for the National Project.

the resources at the disposal of the Ministry of Education alone cannot be other than insufficient or incomplete:
i) *Insufficient,* since if the number of children to be enrolled in school is doubled, and an equivalent number of adolescents and adults are added, they cannot be offered a meaningful education, even if costs are reduced, unless matching resources are also doubled. For both in-school and out-of-school education there can be no increase in services without a corresponding increase in means. This latter, therefore, is a condition *sine qua non.*
ii) Incomplete, since even if substantially increased resources become available, the *programmes* of out-of-school education must not be the product of the authority and competence of schoolteachers alone. We are dealing with an education that must *exist in active relationship with the centres of production.* For this, the active participation of other administrations and of the private sector is essential. In the words of the Panamanian Minister of Education in 1977, when he opened the Central-American Seminar referred to earlier, pointing out that a great many educational problems are not the responsibility solely of the Ministry of Education, 'these many problems . . . demand the mobilization of many other resources; this explains why we think that the problems of literacy and out-of-school education . . . require for their solution a union, a conjunction of efforts made not only by the various government bodies but also by other civic bodies so that they too can participate in such a system.'[44]

In other words, out-of-school education needs a loose structure, decentralized, having a function of support and co-ordination *vis-à-vis* the Ministries and public and private bodies that are in direct contact with the population which is already, or is becoming, economically active.[45] This being so, it could not depend exclusively on the Ministry of Education.

These, it would seem, are the necessary and sufficient conditions for making out-of-school education an instrument of economic growth and of participation. And, as we have just seen, it demands *sufficient resources and a decentralized structure.*

In these two conditions we see once again the concurrence of the two factors:
— the political expression of the collective determination, which will mobilize the resources;
— the individual expression made possible by direct participation in the selection and orientation of the content of education.

So we have come nearer to answering the original question regarding the capacity of education to react in the face of these two social forces, often unequal and sometimes contradictory. Out-of-school education is rarely provided with means compatible with the people's aspirations or with the official

44. CREFAL, op.cit., Appendix Panama, p.13.
45. From the age of about 7 years the children of seasonal workers on the High Plains of Guatemala accompany their parents for the coffee and cotton harvests.

rhetoric. In other words, this 'liberating' education, which by the very nature of out-of-school educational forms should be available to everybody, is scarcely ever made general. Regarded as too supple, too flexible, might it not take away from the central political authority the mastery of the 'educational thing' which — as long as it is confined in perfectly structured institutions — can easily be subjected to permanent supervision?

CHAPTER III

Education as machinery

Education, regarded as a system of values or as a *function* of society, has not failed to develop a corresponding organism. This structure, by the importance of the mission with which it is entrusted, has acquired over the years in most Central-American countries an extent and a volume close to — and even surpassing — those of the State's apparatus for internal and external security. Its share of the national budget in 1978 varied from 10 per cent (Guatemala) to 12 per cent (Nicaragua), 15 per cent (Honduras), 20 per cent (Panama and El Salvador) and 32 per cent (Costa Rica), as shown in Table 1.

TABLE 1.
Educational budget in relation to GNP and to national budget, 1978 (percentages).

Country	Education GNP	Education National budget
Costa Rica	5.0	31.8
El Salvador	3.6	19.9
Guatemala	1.3[1]	9.6
Honduras	3.5	15.2
Nicaragua	2.6	11.5[2]
Panama	3.5	19.2

Source: Document prepared by the Coordinación Educativa Centroamericana (CEC), *Algunos aspectos relacionados con el financiamiento de la educación en Centroamerica,* Guatemala, CEC, 1980, (DOC-CEC-8-80), Section 4.2.3, Table 19, for the Seminario Latinoaméricano sobre Financiamiento de la Educación, San José, 7-11 de Julio de 1980.

However, the major part of this expenditure is not on investment (buildings, equipment, land, etc.) but on the functioning of the educational machinery (85 to 95 per cent, depending on the educational level), consisting for the most part of the salaries of the civil servants employed by the structure.

1. Author's estimate based on the principal source, Tables C.3, C.4, C.6.
2. Public expenditure in the second half of 1979 (i.e., after the Revolution) and in 1980 shows an increase of more than double compared with that of 1978.

Thus, although it is difficult to arrive at precise figures, one estimate[3] has indicated that 30 per cent of public service employees in the six countries are either teachers or Ministry of Education officials (see Table 2). A rough estimate based on the age of entry into the public service and the length of effective service in the various Ministries would appear to indicate that nearly 50 per cent of retired public servants receiving State pensions come from the Ministry of Education.

The public service is of particular importance in the tertiary sector, since it is the most 'attractive' part of that sector for the classes 'on the way up'. The European tradition — Spanish and French for the main part — of a central and centralizing administration of formal legality offers stable employment, higher remuneration than in the rural world or in the urban artisanal or marginal world, and a prestige and above all an authority which are not devoid of possible lucrative inducements. . . The public sector in countries such as Guatemala or El Salvador, where the Administration is not coveted by the sons of the 'established' families whose authority and power depends on their economic situation, represents 'a world apart' in which political influence, personal contacts and services given and returned prevail.

It is obvious that this closed world, humming with interior activity, tends to become a stake in the game itself, enabling, for example, polticians to exert their influence in obtaining appointments for teachers in the capital, at the heart of the central administration. Social promotion, economic improvement and exercise of power combine to form an *end* in themselves. Thus the educational machinery created to fulfil the functions assigned to it by society becomes an objective to those who control it. This 'bureaucratic phenomenon' should not surprise us, since it takes place without jeopardizing its reproductive purpose.

On the contrary, the rich variety of its make-up (persons and goods), its inertia, its secret language, its methods of co-operation and interior reproduction do not contradict — in fact, they even strengthen — the reproductive function which society wishes to see it exercise.

We propose to examine this statement by analysing three particular aspects: the place of the educational subsystem in the political system; the functions and structures of the machinery; finally, the pressures and alliances which, balancing each other, lead to an inertia in the public administration of education which is hard to overcome whatever the political 'colour' of the government in power.

Section 1. **The educational subsystem in the political system**
The first thing we notice is that the portfolio of education is not necessarily given to that member of the political constellation in the ruling cabinet who is most in the public eye — unless it be to ensure the eclipse of a star that

3. Instituto Centroaméricano de Administración Publica, *Bases para una estrategia de cooperacíon del ICAP con los países del istmo centro-américano,* San José, Costa Rica, 1980, p.22, Tables 1 and 2.

TABLE 2.
Ministry of Education personnel in the public service, Central America, 1976/77.

Country	1 Public sector[4] (number)	2 Teachers[4] (number)	3 2/1 (%)	4 Administrative officials (number)	5 4/2[5] (%)	6 2+4/1 (%)	7 Other officials (part-time or contract) (number)	8 Total (number)	9 8/1 (%)
Costa Rica	91 500	20 000	21.9	3 000	15.0	25.1	15 000[6]	38 000	41.5
El Salvador	66 600	13 300	20.0	1 900	14.0	22.8	9 500[6]	24 700	37.1
Guatemala	109 400	14 000	12.8	1 600	11.4	14.3	7 400[7]	23 000	21.0[11]
Honduras	41 400	10 500	25.4	900	8.6	27.5	3 200[8]	14 600	35.3
Nicaragua	42 100	8 700	20.7	500	5.7	21.8	22 200[9]	31 400	—[12]
Panama	89 000	19 000	21.3	500	2.6	21.9	4 500[10]	24 000	26.9

4. Instituto Centroaméricano de Administración Pública, op. cit., p.22, Tables 1 and 2.
5. L.F. Crespo y A. Gutierrez, *Informe provisional sobre la situación del Subproyecto Formación de los administradores de la educación en Centroamérica*, Guatemala Unesco, 1977. (Documento técnico no. 12), Proyecto Regional PNUD/UNESCO RLA/72/100 Red de Sistemas Educativos para el Desarrollo en Centroamérica y Panamá, p.11, Table.
6. Estimation de l'auteur basée sur moyenne pondérée du Guatemala, Honduras et Panama.
7. Guatemala, Consejo Nacional de Planificación Económica, Secretaria General, *Primer Censo Nacional de Funcionarios y Empleados Públicos: 1977, Informe preliminar*, Guatemala, SEGEPLAN, 1978, Proyecto 'PRODASP', p.54, Table II-1.
8. Dirección General de Servicio Civil, Informe General Estadístico del Censo.
9. Dirección de Planificación Nacional, 'Los Servidores Publicos . . . quienes y cuántos son? Datos Iníciales del Censo Inventario de Recursos Humanos del Sector Público', p.14, Managua, 1978. This figure seems abnormally high.
10. Ministeria de Planificación y Política Económica, Unidad de Investigación administrativa 'Los Recursos Humanos del Sector Público en Panama (1977)', p.125, Appendix Table II-1, Panama, 1979.
11. A study by the Direction du Développement Administratif du Secteur Public (DISASP) au Plan (SEGEPLAN) gives higher relative figures for 1979, giving a proportion of 29 per cent and not 21 per cent.
12. See Note 6 above, which suggests that the percentage (74.5) is meaningless.

shines too brightly. And yet, judged by the number of civil servants under its authority (teachers, administrators, various professionals) and by their level of education in countries where illiteracy is often predominant, this government department plays no small rôle in the inculcation — or maintenance — of political attitudes at the local level. In Guatemala a study which appeared in a classic work published in 1970 by the University of Texas[13] shows that with the exception of the secretariats of the President, of Finance and of Defence, whose rôle is overtly political and whose principal function is that of inspection and control, the only State institution effectively present at departmental, cantonal (the *municipios*) and communal levels is that of the Ministry of Education.[14]

It is this privileged position which underlies the importance of the part played by its officials at times of elections or, more generally, of any political manifestation. This explains why in highly centralized countries of relatively small area, such as those of Central America, the greater part of the time and attention of ministers is taken up by appointments, retirements, transfers, promotions and movements of teachers. In addition to the political rôle that the Minister can play in order to satisfy the demands of his political party or of the ruling coalition, in disposing of his personnel in accordance with the wishes of 'higher interests', he must not fail to maintain 'good relations' with his colleagues in charge of other ministries, who either for themselves or to meet the wishes of their own 'clients' intervene unceasingly to influence the future of a teacher, or of several teachers, or — sometimes — of a large number of teachers.[15]

A second political trump-card at the disposal of the Minister is his rôle as a 'builder'. Even though the investment budget of the Ministry of Education represents no more than a fraction (rarely exceeding 5 per cent) of the total annual budget of the department, the siting, the construction, the modernization or the extension of scholastic establishments confers on the Minister a certain political power. In addition, external aid for education is given for investment purposes only. Nevertheless, the size of this contribution can have the effect of multiplying by three — or even five in some cases — the national budget for investment (AID and the World Bank in Guatemala, BID and AID in El Salvador and Panama, BID in Costa Rica and Panama). But the choice of sites and of the type of school depend on a discretionary power

13. R.N. Adams, *Crucifixion by power*, Austin, University of Texas Press, 1970.
14. Ibid., p.108.
15. A notable exception could be found in the Nicaragua that emerged from the 1979 Revolution: the members of the Ministerial Cabinet of the Junta (the 5-member executive) and of the Directing Committee of the Sandinist Front (the highest political organization) pledged themselves to disregard any canvassing on behalf of individual candidates for State employment. The system seemed to be working perfectly in August 1980, when the Minister of Education informed visitors that he had not received any requests to intervene from his ministerial colleagues or from members of directing organizations since taking up his duties immediately after the Sandinist Revolution.

that a Minister anxious to capitalize on his influence will know how to use. Even if the international or bilateral financing bodies succeed in imposing certain 'objective' criteria for the selection of sites, the size and quality of the buildings, etc., it is still a fact that in the last analysis, since it is basically a question of loans, even at long term, the government — that is, the Minister — often has the last word. Finally, even if certain conditions limit the choice of the decision-maker he can always fall back on the national credits, freed to the degree that external aid takes over some of the expense, and allocate them according to this or that political criterion (for example, a constituency that is loyal to the party, or one which it is essential to win over) or a general one (for example, the building of schools in a sparsely populated frontier area).

The political power of a Minister of Education is not measured only by his capacity for playing with the pennies. It also depends on his ability — or cunning — in dealing with the pressure groups who 'represent' education: teachers' unions, students' unions or federations, parents' associations. Here his political repute is inversely proportional to the importance which is attached to his interventions. What Minister, at one of the periodical meetings of the six Central-American ministers, has not said to the Head of State of the host country, 'We are basically firemen, whose job is to put out every little flame before it develops into a fire'. In the context of this part of the world, this authority could not be accused of a lack of realism.

The Central-American teachers' unions are strongly politicised, at the level of both words and actions — as witness the events in El Salvador, where the National Association of Salvadorian Educators (ANDES), with a membership of 21,000 teachers (95 per cent of the total) formed the nucleus of the opposition to the government consolidated around the People's Unity Front (FUP). In some countries unions with opposite views are face to face (Panama), while in others (Costa Rica) the unions know how to ally themselves in defence of common positions. All the same, in every case the Minister must distinguish the revolutionary language (usually anti-government) of the leaders from the real motivation of the rank and file on whom, most of the time, the rhetoric has little or no impact (El Salvador, in the course of 1980, was the exception).

The Minister must know the points on which he will be bound to negotiate if he does not want all the forces of the unions ranged against him, and those where he can — with less difficulty — demonstrate the incompatibility between the arguments of the leaders and the motivation of the rank and file.

As regards the secondary students' federations (the movements of higher-education students are the concern solely of the Universities, which enjoy an autonomy that the Minister of Education cannot violate), the Minister must know how to avoid bringing about either police intervention, or an alliance with the teachers' unions. In either case public opinion would be aroused, the spark would develop into a blaze, and the Minister would not have played his part as 'fireman'.

Within the Cabinet, the Minister must continually hold his own *vis-á-vis* his many colleagues: the size of his budget brings him up against the Minister of Finance, his building programme against the Minister of Public Works; his specialized courses involve him with the Ministers of Labour, of Agriculture, perhaps of Health; he will be in quasi-institutional conflict with the Rector of the University; and above all, he will be a potentially deciding factor in the structure and orientation of the public service (especially as regards retirement and leave). Given the size of the forces under his control, all these responsibilities imply that the Minister must frequently put his political future at risk.

'Political future' — the secret is out. This unenviable position often puts to the test the man in charge of education. If he emerges from it showing evidence of his ability to make use of a subtle political sensibility, this means that he will have the chance to apply for, and obtain, ministerial posts of much greater 'consequence' — even of Head of State.

It would seem from what has been said that the nature of the Minister's function is, all the same, essentially conservative: he defends his prerogatives and his budgets, and avoids conflicts. That seems far removed from the goal of his nominal function: to watch over the education of pupils and students. However, he does not appear to make any moves in this direction unless 'pressured' into activity by the various interested parties. Among these, the parents' associations are by no means the least active. But in countries where primary education is a long way from being universal, especially in the rural areas, parents do not generally intervene except to obtain the appointment or dismissal of teachers, the building of a new school or additional classrooms — or to protest against reforms.[16]

And so? Is the Minister of Education nothing more than a Minister of Schools — or, even more exactly, a Minister of Teachers?

Admittedly, there are always attempts at reform or innovation in the 'system', and it is precisely these that will be examined in the second part of this work.

What is really the import of four or five years spent in a Ministry that is either a trampoline or a trap? Is not the function of reproduction most firmly guaranteed by the absence of continuity of the decision-maker and by the permanence of the machinery which — in reality — is his master? In fact, during his short stay in the Ministry, only very rarely will he have been able to disturb the structures and the men who, in truth, carry out in the name of 'society' the task of forging and adjusting the instrument which will guarantee longevity to this same 'society'.

The functions and structures of this machinery should throw an additional light on certain aspects of this function of reproduction.

16. See below, Part II, Chapter 1, section 2.

Section 2. **The practices and forms of the machinery**

Expressed in simple form, educational administration in Central America takes place at three levels: at the centre, at the bottom (in the schools themselves), and at an intermediate stage — regional or departmental — where a certain measure of deconcentration is the rule (though some people use the word decentralization, either as a metaphor, or optimistically, or in ignorance).

Given the size of the six countries and their centralizing tradition already referred to, this intermediate stage can be largely ignored, since the regional or department directors are merely a territorial rank of the central administration. They have practically no discretionary power to modify directives to suit the particular conditions of the geographical regions they control.

A brief glance at the functions and structures of the central administration will show the nature of its constituent elements, its history, and its ambitions.

At a meeting[17] called by Unesco for Central-American specialists in educational administration, the following functions were identified, in a synthetic manner, as belonging to the Ministry of Education:

a) planning and preparing policies for decision-making;
b) administration of resources (finance, construction and maintenance, personnel, projects carried out with external assistance);
c) administration of services (school plans and curricula, pedagogical research, inspection, outside technical assistance);
d) development of the administration (continuous analysis and evaluation of the system, 'horizontal and vertical' inter- and intra-structural co-ordination, research and studies).

If the function is assumed to create the organ, the structures of Ministries should represent in broad lines the four main tasks described above, if not exactly at least in their relative importance.

As an illustration of a particular but not unique example, the organigram of the Ministry of Education of Guatemala in 1974 (reference period for the analysis of it in Part II below) shows some interesting features (see Figure 1).

In essence, it consists of two main General Directorates: Education and Culture and Fine Arts.

In view of its predominant importance (94 per cent of the Ministry's budget), we can limit our examination to the General Directorate of Education, which deals with the essential activity of the Ministry. In addition to the two General Directorates there are thirteen units or services and five liaison structures directly dependent on the Office of the Minister, assisted by the vice-Minister.

17. Regional seminar on the training of educational administrators and inspectors, Caracas, 28 November-2 December 1977, organized by the Unesco Regional Office for Education in Latin America and the Caribbean. See the Final Report published by that Office, Santiago, 1978.

These latter are not concerned merely with secondary activities, since among the service units can be found the Technical Council (a body with power of decision on any non-administrative matters entrusted to it by the Minister), the Planning Office (OPIE), the Legal Adviser, Liaison with international bodies, the Directorate of Personnel, the Personnel Qualification Council (independent of the Directorate of Personnel), and various services — as, for example, Account, Budget, the Secretary-General of the Ministry (without structural authority), Public Relations, the Special Lottery (certain of the profits from which are devoted to literacy activities), Records, etc. The liaison structures, for their part, form bridges between the Minister and the Plan, the University, External Technical Assistance, Unesco, etc.

The General Directorate of Education is divided into two 'substructures':

— a General Subdirectorate of Education, and
— a General Inspectorate.

The Subdirectorate has nine divisions:

— Rural socio-educational development (rural primary education);
— Urban pre-primary and primary education;
— Middle-level education;
— Literacy and Adult Education;
— Student affairs (counselling, evaluation, social service);
— Aesthetic education (music, plastic arts, dance, theatre);
— Physical education and health;
— Publications and production of teaching materials;
— Audiovisual centre.

Not shown on the organigram, two 'satellite' vertical substructures still existed: the PEMEP (Programme of extension and improvement of primary education, financed by bilateral aid from the United States) and the PEMEM (for middle-level education, financed by the World Bank), each with a staff covered by rules which reflect the criteria of the financing bodies rather than those of the Ministry. This anomaly resulted from the hesitation on the part of the external agencies to entrust investment and modernization programmes to a machinery 'split up' among its various units and governed by administrative procedures and habits considered poorly adapted to programmes with a limited time-span.

The General Inspectorate, for its part, was split into two groups: inspection of pre-primary and primary education, and inspection of middle-level education. In both cases the inspectorate had direct access to the directors of schools at the respective levels.

An examination of this structure shows its manifest incompatibility with the functions enumerated above. Thus, for example:

a) While planning is the responsibility of the Office (OPIE), the setting of

Organigram of the Ministry of Education, Guatemala

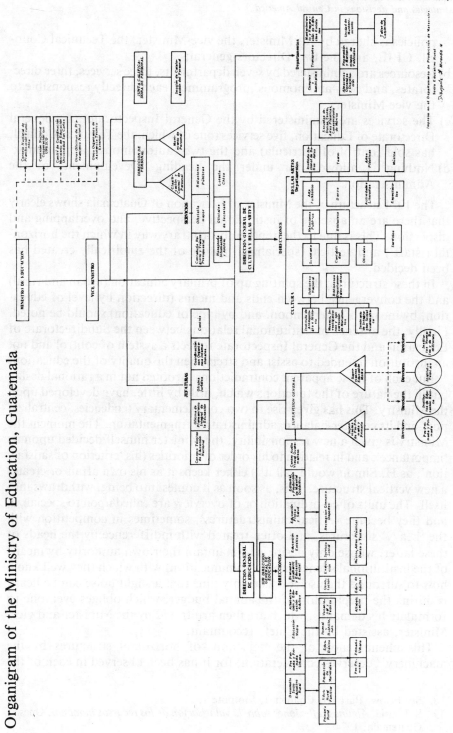

policies is shared by the Minister, the vice-Minister, the Technical Council, OPIE, and the two Directors-general;
b) Resources are administered by seven departments, three services, three directorates, and two 'autonomous' programmes, each directly responsible to the vice-Minister;
c) The services are administered by the General Inspectorate, the General Directorate of Education, five services (one of which, the Technical Council, has sole control of curricula) and the two 'autonomous' programmes;
d) Nothing is allowed for under the heading 'Development' of the Administration.

The 1974 structure of the Ministry of Education of Guatemala shows clearly that there are an absence of institutional perspective, and overlapping and dispersion. This is due to the apparently arbitrary way in which the horizontal ('staff') and vertical (specialized) nature of the empirically-created has been decided.

In these structures, the splitting up of primary education (urban and rural) and the convergence between ends and means (direction by level of education, by means of intervention, and by type of education) should be noted. Finally, the absence of institutional relations between the Subdirectorate of Education and the General Inspectorate reflects a system of control and not an institution intended to assist and strengthen the quality of the education.

But each of these apparent contradictions is rooted not in a rational design but in the nature of the functions which, little by little, have developed upon the Ministry. This has given rise to two complementary tendencies: centralization, and its counter-balance, administrative fragmentation. The moment the Ministry is given a new responsibility, the Minister himself decided upon its 'importance', and in relation to his order of priorities (his 'criterion of satisfaction', as H. Simon would call it[18]) either keeps it as his own affair or creates a new vertical structure. This, as soon as it comes into being, withdraws into itself. The units of co-ordination or of overview are called upon to specialize, and they become vertical 'ministructures', sometimes in competition with the 'heavy' structures, and often treated with indifference by the heads of these latter, whose only desire is to maintain their own authority by means of the institutional silence (non-communication) with which they well know how to surround themselves. The only time that a slight noise can be heard is during the preparation of the annual budget, which obliges everyone to formulate his demands, which are then arbitrated by the Minister and vice-Minister, assisted by the Chief Accountant.

This phenomenon of the 'rejection' of horizontal structures by the machinery[19] deserves consideration, for it has been observed in each of the

18. See below, Part III, Chapter 1, footnote 1.
19. S. Lourié, *Algunas reflexiones sobre la valorisación de los recursos humanos,* Unesco, Guatemala, 1974.

six countries studied. When a Minister sets up a planning unit in order to predict the 'medium term' or even the 'long term' future of his Ministry in an integrated or overall manner, he assumes that a communications and information network will set itself up between the structures which are rooted, basically, in the reality of the actual schools, and that this consultative body will provide him with an overall view. Since the sharing of information is equivalent to loss of power, it is rare for a conventional structure (urban primary education, for example) to accept the sacrifice of a part of its authority for the profit of an organ which, by collecting the many and varied 'parcels', would thus acquire a new 'territory'. The game is played both ways: communication is minimal, demands are maximal. And so the 'horizontal' planning unit is given all the new responsibilities which are slightly delicate (external-aid project, presentation of budget, relations with the Ministry of Planning, special courses), with two consequences:

— the activity of the vertical structures 'purifies' itself, consolidates itself, and withdraws even more into what it regards as vital to its existence;
— the planning or homogenizing activity of the horizontal structure becomes more fragmented and confused, getting further away from the medium term and nearer to the day-to-day. The horizontal structure's field of activity, in fact, is not *space* — which is the concern of the vertical structures which have authority 'locally' (the county, the scholastic region, the inspection, the school itself) — it is *time*.

Once this structure can no longer have the necessary perspective, it cannot have an overall view. By overloading it with *'ad hoc'* activities — for example, meeting the demands (often technocratic) laid down by external aid sources in the drawing-up of projects — it is prevented from acquiring too much power. It thus becomes an artificial superstructure, more useful to external aid agencies (who finally becomes its sole *raison d'être*) than to the units of the Ministry, who combine momentary annoyance with a concealed smile whenever anyone mentions the 'plan' or the medium-term perspective.

Thus we have seen that these structures, taken as a whole, reflect a series of decisions[20] each of which is embodied in an institution or an organ which identifies itself formally with that decision. The dynamic current which, by uniting them or reconciling them, would make of them a whole (which, even if not logically coherent, would at least be operational) is lacking. Spontaneous horizontal communication is deliberately avoided, and the organs created to make it possible are paralysed. It is tempting to compare the structure

---

20. Underlying certain decisions we often find either the imitation of a 'fashion' (scholastic tendencies, audiovisual, etc.) or the reflection of an endogenous social reality (a complete gulf between rural pupils and teachers on the one hand, and urban ones on the other; distrust of over-complicated administrative structures and a preference for breaking them down and attaching the separate parts directly to the Minister, etc.)

of the machinery to a 'museum of fossilized decisions': one floor of 'ancient' products (galleries of primary and middle-level education, inspectorate room, etc.); one neo-classical floor (teaching/materials production room, school counselling display, etc.); and one modern floor (public relations stand, international co-operation gallery, audiovisual centre room, etc.). This museum would have many keepers, no staircases between the floors, few corridors between the rooms, and no lighting. It can easily be understood why it is practically unthinkable for a student or a parent to enter or circulate in such an institution.

The selected illustration does not appear to show any exceptional features. The isolation of the Ministry (by the management standards generally applied in other administration) on the one hand, and its inability to meet the growing demands for an education adapted to the world of today, its isolation from the 'users' of educational services, and the 'static, routine-ridden and rigid' nature, as well as the 'small stability of its staff and the incompetence of its managers' on the other, are the faults of educational administration not only in Central America but in many Latin-American countries.[21]

If 'the lack of dynamism, innovation, foresight, stability and participation'[22] is the trademark of the machinery, we cannot evade the final question: who are the custodians of this institution who have substituted themselves for the purposes which it is supposed to serve?

Section 3. **Pressures and alliances**

3.1. *Bureaucracy*

The lack of articulation between the structures and functions of the Ministries of Education in Central America is partly accounted for by the qualifications of the staffs of these ministries. Applying the classiciation system of the categories of educational civil servants approved by the six governments,[23] it is of interest to ascertain the professional background of those who occupy the executive positions and thus to assess the degree to which they are trained for the job to be done.

i) Political direction: This accounts for 5 per cent of the total of executive positions, and includes the vice-Ministers in charge of administration and the Directors-general, these latter often allying themselves with the political

21. See the conclusions in the Final Report of the First Spanish-American Seminar on Educational Administration, organized in Madrid, 13-17 February 1978, by the Secretary-general of the National Institute of Educational Sciences of the Spanish Government.
22. Ibid., pp.25-26.
23. See UNDP/Unesco Project *Network of educational systems,* sub-project 'Training of educational administrators in Central America', Technical Document No.12, Consultants' Report by Crespo and Gutiérrez, pp.12-20. The total percentage exceeds 100% as principals or heads of institutions also belong to the technico professional category.

activity of the Minister. Even though four of the six countries do not count these as positions in the civil service, they nevertheless have regulations relating to the teaching profession which define them as the highest positions in a *teaching career*. Thus in Nicaragua in 1975 everyone becoming a Director-general had to have been a teacher for at least ten years; in El Salvador, five years. In Guatemala only graduates of the teacher-training college or holders of a degree in pedagogy can occupy these positions.

ii) Directors or Heads of services: The great majority of these posts (3 per cent of the executive positions) do not require any particular training. In Guatemala, the primary-school teacher's diploma is the sole requirement. Only in Nicaragua is a university diploma required. In general, it seems that the only qualification demanded is that of being a teacher, and that teaching experience is the only condition stipulated. There is no mention in the requirements for access to any of these positions of any experience in positions or functions of direction or management. The only exceptions concern two posts in Costa Rica and in Honduras, and one each in Guatemala and El Salvador.

iii) Directors of regional services: In reality this category (4.6 per cent of executive positions) is practically non-existent, given the degree of centralization and the size of the six countries. However, the authorities include under this classification the inspection services, whose members have all started their career as teachers — which shows yet again the convergence between the rôles of pedagogic adviser and administrative controller and supervisor.[24]

iv) Principals of schools: Making up 58.3 per cent of executive positions, they are naturally recruited exclusively from the teaching profession. It should be noted, however, that with the exception of Panama, which requires supplementary administrative training, none of the countries demands for appointment to such functions (at least for certain urban schools, whose size places them in the class of 'enterprises') knowledge of management or administrative techniques.

v) Technico-educational staff: In this group (11.7 per cent of executive posts) are found vocational advisers, pedagogical advisers and certain inspectors, and specialists in audiovisual and in pedagogical research. The variety of conditions laid down for these positions is so great, both as regards their nature and their level, that no definite conclusions can be drawn, even though it is clear that the holders of the great majority of these posts had been teachers, even in the case of such specialized functions as audiovisual techniques and psychopedagogic research.

24. Op.cit., p.15: 'The concentration in a single job description of such heterogeneous functions, which call for very different qualities and for types of relationship which are incompatible with each other, causes great difficulties both in the functioning of the educational system at the regional level, and in the relationships between the central services and the schools themselves.'

vi) Technico-administrative staff: This category (19.4 per cent of executive positions) includes those in charge of the smaller administrative units (offices, sections), accountants, editors, office staff. Posts requiring training at higher-education level are very few. In the majority of cases there are no 'professionals' specialized in staff or budget management. The situation common to nearly all the countries is that such posts are occupied by former secondary-education masters and by teachers 'who find themselves obliged to compensate for the lack of adequate training at the start by mastering the intricacies of routine and by an empiricism full of good intentions'.[25] As an illustration, in Guatemala entry into the Planning Service (OPIE), which consisted in 1977 of ten civil servants, was open to all graduates of secondary education, and closed to. . . all non-teachers. Three of the five employees of the Planning Unit in Honduras had been teachers. In Costa Rica it is required that planners possess a higher-education diploma and experience in school inspection (which assumes at least ten years teaching or direction of a school), but nothing is laid down regarding training of a strictly technical nature (economics, statistics, sociology, etc.).

vii) Various professions: This mixed group (2.5 per cent of executive positions) includes librarians, lawyers, engineers and technicians, etc. Generally speaking, there are no clearly-defined criteria governing the recruitment of this category of staff.

The difficulties encountered in carrying out the study on which the above classification is based reveal, according to its authors, 'the weaknesses of educational administrations which are a reflection of the traditional idea of Ministries "of and for" teachers, and which prevent their adaptation to the needs of a modern educational system'.[26] Both the Unesco seminar at Caracas mentioned above and the Madrid seminar show the virtual monopoly which teachers exercise over educational administration, and deplore the lack of administration and technical executives in posts which do not require the lengthy pedagogic training which has been undergone by almost all the officials occupying the various levels of the administrative hierarchy of Ministries of Education.

In the opinion of the six governments, 'the educational situation in the region' (Central America) 'is an alarming one.' There is 'an almost generalized absence of or indifference to staff trained for the administration of the educational system . . . recruitment of staff for this sector is carried out without any technical or scientific criteria . . .'[27]

25. Op.cit., p.18.
26. Op.cit., p.23.
27. See Seminario-Taller sobre Formación de Directores de Centros Docentes, Panamá, 28 de Junio-9 de Julio de 1976, *Informe final,* Guatemala, Unesco, 1976, Proyecto Regional PNUD/UNESCO RLA/72/100 Red de Sistemas Educativos para el Desarrollo en Centroamérica y Panamá, pp.3-4, Section 2.

This, then, is the most striking aspect of the scene in Central America and, more generally, in Latin America: the 'colonization' of the administration by the teachers. The attraction of positions that are appreciably more highly remunerated, thanks to various allowances, and the impossibility of going beyond the highest rung on the ladder of seniority in the hierarchic and salary scales of teaching, lead teachers to seek posts in the central administration. In addition, there is the desire to have a post in the capital, and the satisfaction of exercising a 'parcel' of power.

From the Public Service viewpoint, the regulations[28] — and even the laws[29] — have adapted themselves to the state of things as they are: the Ministry of Education 'belongs to' the educators.[30] Thus the indices laid down by the public service on the basic of the training and payment of teachers discourage entry into the Ministry on the part of anyone outside the teaching profession.

In these circumstances, two facts stand out clearly. First, the relative inefficiency, incompetence and inertia of the administrative machinery results from the fact that it is in the hands of officials, relatively numerous, representing on average 10 to 15 per cent of the total staff employed by the Ministry, and who have had in essence only pedagogical training and teaching experience. Second, this situation, regrettable though it may appear from the standpoint of the rational use of State funds and the quality of the public service, is not in contradiction with the social *function* attributed to the machinery which is the Ministry of Education.

Certainly, if it is assumed that its object is essentially that of ensuring the maintenance and reproduction of the existing social organization, it can be deduced from this that the machinery will contain within itself the means of ensuring its own permanance. This takes shape in practice through the system of 'nomination-co-opting' — among fellow-teachers — ratified by a complaisant Minister. Thus all the elements are there for a perfect accord: society relies on the machinery to maintain a relatively unchanging system, the whole of which has the duty of selecting its élite, and in exchange society leave the machinery free to consolidate itself. However, as we shall see in

28. The posts of Director of Primary Education in Guatemala and Honduras are established at the salary level of a top-level primary schoolteacher.
29. See Part II, Chapter 2, sections 3 and 5.3. In Guatemala a Law had to be passed so that the Secretary-general of the Ministry could be recruited from university personnel and paid at the same rate as the Secretary-general of the Ministry of Public Health who, as a doctor, and therefore a university graduate, earned twice the ceiling payment authorized for the Ministry of Education, where such a post could be filled only by a graduate of a teacher-training college (end-of-secondary level).
30. University graduates in public administration, in commercial administration, in the social sciences and in economic sciences 'in each of the six countries countries do not amount to 1 per cent of the total technical and directing staff in the Ministries of Education', L.F. Crespo y A. Gutierrez, op.cit., p.19.

the case of Costa Rica,[31] it often happens that individual ambitions and the aims of the community merge into one another: the teacher, having become an official in the central administration, knows that he is one of the chosen few in the rank and situation in which he can act in the name of the directors of society. He has been allowed to enter the 'holy of holies' in order to perpetuate the system which has been the agent of his promotion. The actor and the 'reproducing' society find there the fulfilment of their intentions. The structures with which the teacher-become-bureaucrat identifies himself throughout his career become even more hermetically closed and inviolable as he carries out the conservation functions assigned to the machinery of which he is in charge and which at the same time enable him to defend his own privileges.[32]

One question remains: is there not a risk that the preponderance of teachers at the heart of the machinery will by-pass the users of education? The permanent communication between teachers exercising their profession and those who have opted — or been co-opted — to 'manage' their colleagues — is this not what in electricity (or in medicine) is called a 'shunt' (or a 'counter-irritant')? If so, is there not a risk that the stage may be reached where only an extremely limited part of the politico-administrative current will be fed into the circuit that feeds the pupils, while the greater part of the energy of the machinery will be channelled towards those who should be only a relay for it, and not in any case its principal recipients? A brief glance at the political activity of teachers will enable us to begin to understand which of the two — the machinery, or the user, of education — determines the behaviour of the teacher.

3.2. *Teachers and unions*

The teaching profession alone represents some 25 per cent of those employed in the public service (except in Guatemala, where the school enrolment rate is the lowest of all the six countries). Within the Ministry of Education it is usually they who turn the wheels of government and appear, by their physical presence, to be the only real clients of this administration.

31. See Part II, Chapter 1, section 3.2.
32. This true, however, only as long as he considers that his treatment conforms to the privileged position he has given himself in function of the apparent autonomy of action entrusted to him. If the Minister introduces changes which would affect his powers or his salary, the solidarity which resulted from the fusing of his various ambitions is broken. To assert his 'rights' the central-administration official will then turn to his 'collectivity', that of the teaching profession, thus turning his back on the 'collectivity' of the other State officials. Such cases are rare, but they exist (Peru in 1973 - Part III, Chapter 2, section 1.2.).
33. C. Olivera, *Diagnóstico del cuerpo docente de la enseñanza básica en Centroamérica,* Guatemala, Unesco, 1976, (Documento de trabajo no. 3), Grupo Formación Permanente del Docente, Proyecto Regional PNUD/UNESCO RLA572/100 Red de Sistemas Educativos para el Desarrollo en Centroamérica y Panamá, p.38, Table 13.

Their distribution throughout the countries is dense. More than half of them teach in rural areas,[33] even though rural education is far from reaching the total of the age-group concerned (except in Costa Rica and Panama). It can be assumed, therefore, that their political weight is far from negligible.

We now need to estimate their capacity to organize and structure themselves in order to transform — by constituting a pressure group — their potential power into an instrument for action. Obviously, the existence of a pressure group is not in itself enough to identify the teachers' political rôle. The general political climate, and the freedom allowed to unions in particular, are the factors enabling teachers, more or less successfully, to have an effective influence on the decisions of the State.

Data are not easy to come by,[34] but some of the information available regarding the organization of teachers' unions in some of the countries of the region may provide the elements for an answer.

3.2.1. *Symbiosis or confrontation*

In Costa Rica[35] the National Association of Educators (ANDE) was formed in 1943, consisting mainly of primary-education teachers. Its statutes define its objectives as the improvement of the 'economic, social and cultural' conditions of its members, the encouragement of a spirit of co-operation among the educators, the guarantee of the professional and human dignity of the teacher, and the creation of links with fellow-teachers in other countries. Only this last paragraph (out of five) makes any reference to promoting 'the progress of the education of the Nation'. Subsequently, branches have been created at grass-roots level, consisting of cells (of at least fifteen persons) enabling the teachers of all levels (including the University) as well as those 'employed in the central office of the Ministry of Public Education' to meet together in a decentralized manner.

Together with APSE (Association of Secondary-education Teachers), it is ANDE which negotiates the major salary agreements and conducts the political battle (either on the side of or against the authorities). The two associations thus practically control the teachers' union movement. In a liberal country with a representative structure, in which the rights of unions are fully recognized, these two organizations play a political rôle which is sometimes decisive in the world of pressure groups which dominates the political scene in this country. Their attitude is mainly — though not exclusively — dictated by the working conditions of teachers (based mainly on salaries and working hours). Given their importance (the two unions together represent

---

34. It is an interesting fact that in no official publication of the six Ministries of Education in the years 1974-1980 is there any reference to or description of the trade-union organization of teachers.
35. In 1975 37 per cent of the economically active population of Costa Rica was unionized (see Proyecto Regional PNUD/UNESCO RLA/72/100 *Red de Sistemas Educativos para el Desarrollo en Centroamérica y Panamá*, Monograph No.2, Series V.)

more than 80 per cent of the primary and secondary teachers) and their influence on the elected members of both the principal parties, no legislation which directly or indirectly affects the nature or exercise of the teaching profession can be passed without their seal of approval.

Admittedly, there are three other unions (the College of Teachers of Letters, Philosophy, Science and the Arts, which consists of secondary-school teachers who are university graduates; the Union of Costa Rican Educators (SEC), founded more recently and reflecting a political affiliation more progressive than that of the other unions; and finally ADEM, the Association of Middle-level Headmasters, founded in 1966), but apart from the fact that their membership is also open to members of ANDE and APSE they have neither the resources nor the prestige of the two major unions.

The Unions are represented in the Higher Council of Education and thus have their part in the drawing-up of national policies. Given the importance of the Public Service as guarantee of positions or employment to officials of the Ministry, these latter — though they can no longer be members of ANDE as teachers — can join the ranks of the branches which exist within the administration itself. In this way the line of cleavage between members exercising their profession and those who have entered the administration disappears. In fact, the defence of professional interests by the unions is interpreted by them as being concerned with all those whose origin lies in the teaching profession.

We shall see later[36] the extent to which this alliance — collusion or complicity — between teachers 'outside' (those engaged in actual teaching) and the large number 'inside' (officials of the central administration) has been able to 'block' the government's projected changes in the nature and forms of school education. Clearly, any attempt to change the machinery or to alter the conditions of the teaching profession can be viewed by the unions as a threat to the power of that profession.

The teachers' unions in Costa Rica play such a direct part in the definition and application of educational policy that it is practically impossible to distinguish between their influence and that of the administration.

The situation of the teachers' unions in El Salvador is very different.[37] In this country of four million inhabitants the teaching profession was until 1964 a sector entirely dependent on the government. The 'teachers' fronts' (*frentes magisteriales*) emerged at time of elections and disappeared as soon as the results were announced. It was not until December 1965 that the *Asociación Nacional de Educadores Salvadoreños* (ANDES), the National Association of Salvadorian Educators was formed and its statutes were not approved until June 1967 (giving rise to the name 'ANDES 21 de Junio'). This union,

36. See Part II, Chapter 1, section 3.
37. Valuable information on this subject can be found in a study by F. Rivero (at the time Adviser to the Ministry of Education, El Salvador), on 'ANDES June 21', written in May 1980.

resulting from the amalgamation of two associations (the Salvadorian Teachers' Union and the Association of Teachers Trained in the Higher Teacher-Training College) began life as a Committee for the Defence of Teachers' Rights. Its foundation, supported by the Costa Rican ANDE, was mainly inspired by the wish to present a united front to the authorities in order to obtain satisfaction of their demands concerning salaries and administrative matters.

By 1972 the organization of ANDES already covered the whole country and numbered 10,000 members out of a total of 14,000 primary-school teachers.[38] In 1980 it represented 95 per cent of primary-school teachers and 70 per cent of the total number of primary and secondary teachers.

The position of the union was greatly strengthened by two events. A strike declared in October 1967 and twice repeated, in January and February 1968, caused by the teachers' demand for the setting-up of an Institute of National Insurance, demonstrated the authority of the union and its ability to conduct an organized struggle, which identified it in the opinion of the public as a structure of 'resistance' to State authority. In 1971 ANDES declared a strike which lasted 58 days, to obtain a new salary scale and the improvement of the 'economic condition' of the educators.

This second act of 'resistance' encountered very strong opposition from the State, which did not want to change the conditions for teachers lest this have repercussions in the form of demands from other sectors of the public service. It should be added that these demands by the teachers coincided with their opposition to the possible results of the decision (by an energetic and strong-willed Minister of Education[39]) to reform the content (new curricula), the structures (nine years of general education) and the methods (educational television for the middle level) of education. If the criticism of the reform had overtones more political than technical, two facts must be emphasized: the first is that, on the whole, the officials in the central administration were on the side of the Ministry, and thus allowed a gulf to appear between the teachers 'inside' and those 'outside'. It should be stressed that the reform team was a small group concentrated within the Ministry's Office of Planning, composed in the main of engineers, economists and architects not closely linked with the teachers. The second fact is that the repressive measures taken against the teachers were severe (prison, torture, assassinations) and caused a spontaneous popular movement of support: second-level and university students, as well as unionized workers, showed their sympathy during the strikes and demonstrations. For the first time for many years peasants came

38. This figure of 70 per cent should be compared with that of 3 per cent of the profession unionized in the PEA (compared with 37 per cent in Costa Rica).
39. This Minister, after introducing his reforms (El Salvador is one of the few countries where teaching by television in secondary education is general) was forced to return to private life in 1974. In 1980 he was assassinated.

to the capital to show their sympathy with the ANDES demands (the March of the People's Will included more than 50,000 demonstrators).

Neither in 1967 nor in 1971 did ANDES obtain satisfaction of its strictly union demands. On the contrary, faced with the systematic opposition of the State, and as a result of the movement of support which it had generated, its character gradually changed. Whereas in 1967 half of the leadership belonged to the Christian Democrat party, and the other half to various groups with marxist-leninist tendencies and in particular the Salvadorian Communist Party, the rank and file for its part owed their allegiance almost entirely to Christian Democrat tendencies. By the end of the 1971 conflict ANDES became the nucleus of the People's Unity Front (FUP).[40] The FUP in the next few years (1971-75) asserted itself as a credible alternative to replace — or at least challenge — the traditional political parties.

In 1974 the leadership passed into the hands of members who favoured a marxist, pro-Peking attitude, and in 1975 ANDES joined the People's Revolutionary Bloc (BPR). This change of political orientation caused an internal restructuring, which led to activities more partisan in nature than trade-unionist. A new institutional period began: ANDES was an active partner in the BPR, supporting its decisions and its political activity, and in particular allying itself with the demands of the Christian Federation of Salvadorian Peasants (FECCAS), likewise affiliated to the BPR.

The activity of the leaders became more and more clandestine,[41] and could not be subject to any pretence of consultation with the rank and file. This caused trouble — and even resistance — on the part of a number of teachers, the majority of whom were not yet 'radicalized' but still clung to their Christian Democrat tendencies. Nevertheless, most of them supported the leaders and followed, in a disciplined manner, the orders to strike or to mobilize — which enabled them to reap some new advantages.

Thus, the Molina government (1973-78) and that of Romero (1978-79) gave way to the teachers' demands for the restructuring of the Retirement Fund, for a more generous medical and hospital coverage, for the founding of a 'House of Teaching', and so on. These concessions were made by the government in the years that preceded the armed clashes between the authorities and dissident groups (including the BPR), in the hope of avoiding an ag-

40. ANDES was joined by the General Association of Salvadorian University Students (AGENS), the Association of Secondary Students (AES) founded at the National University at the time of the 1971 conflict, and various trade-union headquarters and independent unions.
41. The political repression throughout the country in 1979-80 did not spare the directors of ANDES: in 1979 alone 35 teachers met with political assassination and 19 others were arrested and subsequently tortured. From January to April 1980 40 teachers among the leaders of ANDES are reported to have been assassinated (*El Dependiente,* 7 May 1980).

gravation of the political tension and the spread of opposition among the most important group of public servants.

This has similarities with the case of Peru and its educational reform of 1972, which came up against the fanatical opposition of the teachers' union (SUTEP — the Sole Union of Peruvian Educational Workers). The leaders of this union made use of extremely violent marxist language about the educational reform which, according to them, was to be identified with 'the interests of imperialism and of the *bourgeoisie*' in support of 'a corporativist economy, the basis of bureaucratic capitalism'. At the same time they demanded, with some success, improvements in their working conditions (salaries, hours of work, etc.). In this they were supported by the rank and file. But these latter could be most easily identified with the *petite bourgeoisie* and with the tradition of APRA, a political party with a 'labour' origin which had changed course to the extent of being clearly to the right of General Velasco's 'revolutionary' government. In a study of the teaching profession and its struggles in Peru, the authors explain this apparent contradiction by the fact that 'the consistency of the SUTEP leaders in the claims dispute, their ability to stand up to the State, and their means of presenting the teachers' demands in concrete terms, are the reasons which endeared them to the rank and file rather than their political thinking'.[42]

Similar terms can be used to explain the trade-union phenomenon in El Salvador. The teachers, exasperated by the systematic rejection of their demands and the contempt with which they had been received, closed their ranks behind the leaders who made use of a political rhetoric which, although scarcely reflecting feelings of the majority at the start of the movement, paid off. Gradually words became actions, and the trade-union movement in 1980 changed — after some noteworthy victories of a strictly trade-union nature — into a militant and political movement. This is not a unique situation in the Central-American region.

The politization of the trade-union movement in El Salvador is similar to the situation in Honduras, where the COLPROSUMAH (*Colegio Profesional de Superación Magistral Hondureño*) founded in 1963 was from the start in collision with a government directed by the National Party which, accusing the leaders and their followers of favouring the Liberal Party, branded them as 'enemies of the State' and 'communists'. Thus, although when it was founded, COLPROSUMAH set out to be non-political, pluralist and devoted to defending the professional interests of its members, the 'College' gradually identified itself with the left, though without affiliating itself to any political party whatsoever. The ideological position of the leaders changed COLPROSUMAH into a body offering practically permanent support to the demands of peasants, workers, local groups, etc. This involvement 'led it

---

42. C. Pezo, E. Ballon and L. Peirano, *El magisterio y sus luchas 1885-1978,* Lima, Desco, 1978, p.169.

to forget its active participation in the process of educational reform, the transformation of the national educational system, and the training of teachers — activities all of which would have enabled it to act as an agent of change within the Ministry of National Education'.[43]

Let us compare the two examples we have given. On one side is Costa Rica, where union freedom encourages the multiplication of organizations, the largest of which can *de jure* and *de facto* blend with the administration. It is hardly an exaggeration to speak of a symbiosis between the three poles: the profession, the legislature and the machinery of the Ministry.

In contrast, El Salvador appears to present a picture of a political power, which acknowledges scarcely any difference between the executive and the legislative and which dominates the scene in which the unions have scarcely any voice in the circuitous 'normal' sequence: demands — negotiation — agreement. In order to combat this relative weakness of union freedom the teaching profession is less dispersed than in Costa Rica and gives the impression of presenting a common front. Nevertheless, there is no symbiosis between the three poles: the profession is isolated in the face of the political power and the machinery, which far from intermingling with the union is in fact the tool of the political power. There is confrontation.

It would appear therefore that the differences that separate the two cases, as regards both the political climate and the power of the unions — the latter judged by its ability to negotiate and its ability to achieve results that satisfy the wishes of its members — cannot supply a coherent answer to the original question (is there a shunt of current that favours the teachers?). In the one case, symbiosis: in the other, confrontation.

3.2.2. *The tool and the machinery*
Nevertheless, even though the tactical relationships between the teachers and the political power follow different patterns, for reasons already outlined, does it follow that the strategy followed by the unions and its consequences for the state of education of the population are equally different?

In educational matters the teachers (intermediaries between the government, which puts its educational project into practice, and the citizens who hope to benefit from it) have become, in Central America, the only people who take part in a dialogue with the State. In the industrial production sectors the workers' unions directly represent the producers of goods. In the Education sector, as in that of Health, the same is true. 'The 'good' is education, and, in addition, the quality of the product offered is something which is judged not by the consumer but by the same producer. By negotiating with

43. Quoted from a very useful note entitled 'The trade union movement among Honduran teachers', written in May 1980 by M.N. Morazan, former National Co-ordinator of the Honduran National Programme for Out-of-school Education and former Director of COLPROSUMAH.

the producer rather than with the consumer of the services it offers, the state resembles somewhat the man in Plato's myth of the cavern, confusing the shadow (the educator) with the reality (the education offered). But it is precisely this closed game which reveals the exercise of power on the part of those who hope to use it to protect themselves, to maintain themselves — and to reproduce themselves. The teachers' shield is finally a protection for the State, through the collusion already referred to.

In the one case as in the other, we have noticed that the essence of the changes which the teachers want to introduce in the educational system, and which give rise to their demands (which justify the creation of their pressure groups) are connected with the teaching conditions themselves. Thus we noticed in El Salvador, as in most of the other Central-American countries, the way in which the teacher identifies himself hardly at all with the rural commune in which he teaches. The short distances which separate the country from the town explain that a very great number of teachers, gathering round the taxi which delivers them at the village or hamlet in the morning and takes them back to their homes in the afternoon, are better known under the name of '*taxistas*'. And yet these systems of which the teachers are a part, and for the functioning of which they are responsible, are all the same intended to offer a service — a public service — to the population and ensure a sufficient education by teaching and instruction.

Is there not good reason to ask whether, besides the legitimate defence of their interests, the future of education should not become one of the chief concerns of those responsible for the service when they organize and unite themselves? And yet we have noted that not one of the unions we have described gives much importance in its statutes to the improvement of the chances or conditions of the pupil. Admittedly, this problem is the concern of the authority, but should not the 'mission' — the 'vocation' of the teacher (at the same time as other professional claims) be defined in terms of its true objective: improving the well-being of the pupil, of the student, of all learners, whatever their origin, age or home?

In Costa Rica, in spite of the quantitative expansion of the network of schools — and of teachers — there are still very high drop-out rates which indicate, among other things, that the teaching is not in line with the real needs of the rural school-age population.

In the neighbouring country of El Salvador the 'condition of the taught' is much worse than in Costa Rica. Some 50 per cent of the children in the primary-school age-group were not enrolled at the time of the 1971 census. The high repeating and drop-out rates show the absence of universal complete primary education, and the strict application of administrative standards in the selection and promotion of pupils.

Yet, in both countries, the chief concern of the teachers has been to negotiate with — or clash with (different tactics) — the State in the name of *their interests*. In the case of Costa Rica the teachers' unions appear to be included in the process of decision, while in El Salvador they are excluded. But in neither country does the dialogue lead to an improvement in the condition of the taught, the 'great absentee' in the public debate — or dispute — on the subject of education.

We can see clearly here that there is indeed this shunt for their own profit of the power of the teachers (either for negotiation or for conflict). Teaching would appear to be a profession whose only and chief concern is the safeguarding of its own interests. Those responsible for it have no desire to take the initiative of participating in defining the social, political or cultural purposes of the educational phenomenon. To do so would be, in the eyes of many union leaders, to interfere in affairs of State.

The relations between teachers' unions and the State are a function, not of these purposes, but rather of a single one of the many ways of action that tend toward such purposes: the position of the teacher and the image he wishes to impose, or modify, of his place in the social organism.

As far as the material conditions of the teachers are concerned — and they are, it is true, always open to improvement — it might perhaps be asked whether the nature of their mission justifies such a marked difference from the living conditions of other workers. In Costa Rica, for example, the lowest monthly salary of a newly appointed teacher[44] is six times the minimum salary in the transport sector[45] and ten times that paid in agriculture.[46] And yet officially the primary-school teacher works only some twenty hours a week, for less than 35 weeks in the year, whereas the employees in transport or agriculture must supply some 50 hours a week, and this during 50 weeks of the year. In comparing these figures it is not without interest to note that union membership is about 12 per cent in agriculture, while it is 38 per cent for the public service as a whole and over 80 per cent for the teachers alone . . .

In El Savador the average hourly wage of a primary-school teacher in 1978 was of the order of 6.7 colones, whereas the highest average in the manufacturing industry (chemicals) at the same period was 1.69 colones[47] and the lowest average (lumbering) was 0.88 (the weekly working hours are 43.6 for the chemical industry and 44.4 for the lumbering industry).

While the material conditions of the teacher are considerably better than those of practically all workers in the industrial sector, matters are hardly

44. *La voz de ANDE,* no.70, May 1980 (Journal of the ANDE Union, San José, Costa Rica).
45. Op.cit., Costa Rica, Monograph No.2, Table 47 (updated).
46. On the basis of 35 weeks of 22 hours, and assuming that 90 per cent of the current expenditure at the pre-primary and primary levels of education represents salaries. In 1976 there were 19,014 teachers and directors in pre-primary and primary schools (op.cit., C. Olivera, Appendix, p.1, Table 1A) for a budget of 109.5M colones (op.cit., CEC, Seminar on Educational Financing, Table B.7).
47. Op.cit., El Salvador, Monograph No.3, p.77, Indicator No.61.

the same when the comparison is with those of employees in the tertiary sector, whether public or private. This difference in the criteria of comparison may well be the reason both for the bitterness of the unions' conflict and for the State's reactions.

Behind these concepts, in fact, lies hidden the delicate — because subjective — question of the social status of the teacher. We will try to draw a rough sketch of this, inevitably somewhat of a caricature, which, while it may not lend itself to application systematically in every case, is not devoid of resemblance to a considerable number of examples in the region.

Whether in Costa Rica, in El Salvador, or in the other countries of Central America, the primary-school teacher's social origin is rural and/or from a family having a very modest level of income. In the countries where the average duration of schooling per inhabitant varies between one and four years, a child who overcomes all the obstacles presented by the selectivity of the system and reaches the final year of the teacher-training college (a total of 9-12 years (not counting repetition) in El Salvador and 14 in Costa Rica) is the exception. To achieve this, he has been helped by sacrifices and has given proof of capacity for 'success', both of them exceptional.

Sacrifices: firstly on the part of his parents, who were willing not only to forego the income which a child not at school would represent, but to shoulder the additional cost which schooling involves (clothes, shoes, food and even transport, as well as schoolbooks and materials). Sacrifices also on the part of the student, who will have to work in order to pay for his studies, the cost of which cannot be borne entirely by his parents, or who may wish in turn to share his privileges by paying the whole or part of the cost of studies for a younger brother or sister. And more sacrifices when he — or she — takes up his first appointment — in a rural school in an area several days' journey from home (on foot or horseback or in a canoe).

Success: since the diploma awarded by the teacher-training college is the proof that his twelve years of studies have placed him among that fraction of the age-group who entered primary school with him (1 in 8 in Costa Rica, 1 in 14 in El Salvador — and 1 in 80 in Guatemala). Success at having finally entered the profession while others in the training college failed to obtain their diploma. Personal application, extra studies, useful 'contacts' — all help to select a fraction of the fraction.

Success, above all, because once appointed the teacher will have taken his leave — definitely — of his origins and entered the world of his new ambitions. Certainly, as far as ambitions are concerned, the first twelve years of his life in rural surroundings are quickly forgotten during the six to eight years of secondary studies in a teacher-training college, frequently in the town, with many of the features of modern living (electricity and running water, of course, but also modern — unneccessarily so — classrooms). His whole aim, once appointed, will be to do everything possible to 'emigrate' to the town. This explains the fact that, concerned for his career and for his possible promotion to the town, he is scarcely likely to argue with his superiors. He will feel above all that he is the agent for transmitting orders, directives and instructions which he will carry out as a good civil servant, and that he will regard any attempts to change his relations of authority — either towards his pupils, or towards his hierarchical superiors — as a threat to the order he hopes to preserve. Both in his institutional and in his professional contexts he will be essentially a conservative.

Once appointed and relatively assured of a career,[48] the teacher who has turned his back on the hard and distant world of the countryside identifies himself with the urban way of life in which he finds his place naturally, classified in the 'white-collar' category of the tertiary sector.

But, in the same way as all the other categories of tertiary-sector employees, he will be obsessed by his status and by the 'consumer' features of urban society in the late twentieth century. His aim will be to improve (or, in times of inflation, to maintain) his purchasing power and to reach, by a natural upward movement, the higher rungs of the teacher-profession ladder. One of the many reasons put forward by Central-American teachers in favour of a transfer to the town is the possibility of following higher studies in the evenings, in order to acquire a diploma in pedagogy or in 'educational science', a probable guarantee of administrative reclassification and an increased salary.

Comparing himself with other public servants who, through possessing a university degree, have higher salaries, or with employees in the private sector whose earning are generally higher, the teacher will consider his condition hard[49] and will be attracted towards a union which will fight to improve it, at the same time giving him mutual aid, friendship and solidarity. These will be all the more welcome to him since his professional life will not always have allowed him to settle in one place for an extended period, or in an area where he has family connections.

Thus, little by little, the teacher — already classified as a civil servant by all the enumerators of statistics, censuses, employment surveys, etc. — will fight in the ranks of his union to preserve and improve his status. It is perhaps a paradox — though not completely erroneous — to suggest that the social

48. In Costa Rica a teacher, under the Law relating to Public Office, is appointed for an active period of 20 years followed by retirement at over 70 per cent of salary. In El Salvador a teacher on retirement receives almost the equivalent of his salary at retirement.
49. Some find it difficult not to take account of the length of school holidays. For those critics who point out that a teacher works only 22 hours a week for an average of 30 weeks in the year, the argument (justifiable in itself) concerning the stress of teaching, and the hours of preparation that involved, is not systematically tenable. There are many teachers, especially in secondary schools, who hold down two posts (one public and one private) and apparently have sufficient resistance to stand the doubling of stress and of hours of preparation, though this probably detracts from the quality of their performance.

mobility which education should give to the enrolled school-age population is beneficial above all to the teachers themselves.

These latter, for all that, do not usually repudiate their own social origins, and often fight in the ranks of unions, political parties or groups called 'left' or even 'progressive'. They do this in their capacity as citizens employed in the tertiary sector and preservers of professional order, while calling themselves 'men of progress' in politics whereas in fact they are in the process of becoming *petit bourgeois*.

But in that case, why compare a teacher's salary with that of a worker in the productive sector? This is the core of the misunderstanding, born of the contradition between the *status* of the teacher and his *vocation*. If the teacher must work in the whole of society, and particularly among the most deprived — or most penalized — classes of the population, to enable the advancement of the maximum number of *citizens*, such comparisons are more convincing than those which maintain the teacher in the most privileged sector.

Let us widen this concept of the cultural, spiritual and social 'aspiration' of the educational phenomenon in one of the Central-American societies. Let us look at this society in its overall political context, not limited to the groups or levels which have appropriated and constructed their instrument of reproduction, and examine its activity throughout its modern history (since independence from Spanish rule, for example). We shall be forced to admit that, apart from a few apostles who lived in the second half of the 19th century and at the beginning of the 20th, particularly in Costa Rica (whose disciples have in turn brought about a few exceptional moments in the contemporary educational history of the six countries), this concept of 'aspiration' has not found its advocates among the mass of Central-American teachers.

Perhaps a historian could explain why the élitism of Central-American societies has not allowed the teachers to play the part of 'ambassadors' of science and republican secularism which was played in Europe and particularly in France, at the end of the 19th century by the teachers in the communal schools. Perhaps, too, it should be admitted that the teacher-training college in Central America is not overflowing with political culture, and in fact is no different from what a number of sister institutions have become in this same Europe and France a century after Jules Ferry. It can be deduced from this that the structures have proved stronger than the cultural and social aspirations, and that they have prevented the Central-American teacher, at a given moment in history, from carrying out his mission (except, once again, in the clearly exceptional case of Costa Rica) by transforming him, directly he graduates from the teacher-training college, into a civil servant rather than an activist.

In order to play this emancipating rôle of social activist or ambassador of modern society, it would have been necessary that the society in and for which he works be sufficiently flexible to allow him to do so. Instead, it has enveloped him in bureaucracy and he, to defend his interests, has withdrawn into the collective activity of his professional group.

Admittedly, it can be said that the struggle of ANDES in El Salvador is political, and that in this respect it works indirectly for a society which will produce a fairer and more modern education. Unfortunately, such unions in neighbouring countries of the Central-American region and the Caribbean that have eliminated or are in the process of eliminating, one form of social élitism, are not necessarily a good example. Here too there is an approach which cannot be put into reverse: once the union structure has been created and the acquired rights confirmed, the activity which consisted in individual devotion to a community to help solve its problems and meet its aspirations becomes an extremely difficult task. As for the 'cultural revolution' of a whole community, it appears that that is not sufficient to moblilize — and therefore change the basic attitude of — traditional teachers, as the current experiment in Nicaragua would seem to suggest.

Coming back to Central America as a whole, there was a perhaps unique opportunity (before the urban explosion, and the development of the tertiary sector and of unions who have tried to defend its victims) which, once let pass, never again returned to allow the teacher to play fully the social rôle to which he might have aspired.

* * * * *

Our *first* consideration led us to the conclusion that pre-1979 education in Guatemala, El Salvador, Honduras and Nicaragua was not a means at the disposal of everybody but on the contrary an instrument at the service of the few, and that even though there were hopes of some types of out-of-school education there was not, except in the case of Nicaragua after 1979, an intention on the part of the State to transform such weak impulses into a living, moving and sufficient network. Education continued to transmit acquired values, unchanged since rarely questioned, and thus performed essentially a process of reproduction. Admittedly, for some people, any kind of education is better than none at all, since every kind of education brings with it the hope that one day both its form and its content may be changed. Besides the values which favour social reproduction there is the knowledge which is useful for the productive function. The new forms and conditions of production, possibly intensified, will eventually influence the values of that society which originally produced and has preserved an educational system in line with its criteria or its beliefs. Thus we shall find that there will in turn be changes in the educational system which is to serve the 'new society'.

Assuming that there *is* a solution to the problem presented by the fact that every system gathers together all the means of exercising power — and education is one of the most spectacular examples of this — let us see where our *second* consideration, regarding the educational machinery, leads us. First and foremost, we must take note of the importance of the two forces which — even in a situation of social change such as we have just outlined — can block whatever innovations might otherwise be brought about by new values and functions. These two forces are the teaching profession and the administration of the system. We have seen that in Central America, collusion between the teachers' unions and the officials of the administration is not exceptional. We have learned to appreciate to what point the social origin of the teachers, the political climate that surrounds them, the gulf between town and countryside, all work in favour of a *status quo* of the educational phenomenon and thus strengthen the reproductive tendency.

Such generalities, even at the level of very similar countries, very near each other and relatively small in size, do not seem to lead to any easy or obvious conclusions.

The study in Part II of this book will try to be more precise, by concentrating not only on one country at a time but also on one event, limited both in its time span and in the number of actors involved.

PART TWO

The system, the game and the actors

Introduction

In Part I we presented an impressionistic but static picture of the educational stage and its scenery. We now turn to the movements on this stage and concentrate on two different situations and on the actors involved in them.

We have chosen two Central-American countries, Costa Rica and Guatemala, both already mentioned more than once. Their educational decision-making structures and the actors who play a part in the realization of the ideas, the intentions or the promises will receive particular attention. In each case, after a description of the country, a decision will be analysed. This may be the outcome either of a political, even ideological, vision (Costa Rica) or of a tactical, even opportunist, intent (Guatemala). As far as possible, we shall take account of the socio-cultural context and certain outstanding economic features which characterize the tensions and struggles in the forefront at the time we are studying.

The analysis of the 'game'[1] and of the actors will attempt to give movement and new dimensions to the area or the system studied, as distinct from the instantaneous, static and linear picture given by the 'diagnosis'. This diagnosis, based on certain indicators (in practice insisted on by the consumer who is also the analyst) does not enable any relationships to be established between the vectors which make up an event. But it is only by examining the nature of their relationships that we may arrive at an understanding of the process of the decisions which gave rise to the event studied.

If the analysis of the game may suffice to define an 'area' which scarcely changes within a limited time-span (a particular enterprise or administration at a given moment) this is by no means the case for a political system situated in a changing historical panorama.

This study, which concentrates on the meeting-place of political systems and administrative organizations, will therefore try to determine the game

---

1. The terminology is that of M. Crozier and E. Friedberg, op.cit., and is used here since, from the start, it facilitates the presentation of events regarded as resulting from several games. We shall define these concepts later, to the extent that they can be given a concrete meaning.

and the actors either through a historical current, or in the socio-political current which characterizes the period studied.

The events reported took place between December 1973 and December 1978. The decisions studied have been selected by reason of their familiarity to the author.

In the case of Guatemala, the decision chosen for study does not necessarily represent the event which might be considered the most significant in political terms. In the case of Costa Rica the event selected, the Educational Reform, was the central point of the government's educational effort. In both cases the selection of facts considered pertinent, since it depends on personal experience, cannot be other than subjective — and probably more arbitrary than is desirable — and does not pretend to cover or summarize everything that happened in connection with these 'events' during the period concerned.

For Costa Rica, this period is between 1970 and 1974. The perspective of the last ten years should enable us to take a more general view of the various aspects of the situation described.

In the case of Guatemala, the selected period (1974-78) coincides with the life of the government elected in March 1974 for a four-year term.

From certain viewpoints the two countries chosen represent, during the periods under review, two opposite poles. Costa Rica is a democracy based on the very wide and free participation of various forces organised in parties, trade unions or 'pressure groups'. The political climate is one of periodic elections, entirely free, untroubled by military pressure since there is still no army (though there are City Guards and Rural Guards). The social climate is marked by a middle class mainly but not exclusively urban, a result of relative social and geographical mobility.

Over the last fifty years Guatemala has known only two governments headed by civilians. A succession of military leaders has governed, and still governs, this most populous Central-American country. These military governments, which have preserved the outward forms of parliamentary democracy (periodical elections of the Executive and of the Legislature) are closely linked with a landowning class, exporters of basic products, which maintains a social stratification not easy to penetrate. The government maintains order against all opposition to the system; the landowners rely on a labour force which is abundant, illiterate or under-educated, under-employed, and living on incomes which barely permit survival in material conditions comparable to those of the poorest developing countries.

In such conditions the rôle and importance accorded to education in each country are obviously not comparable. The effort made by the State for education is directly proportional to its desire to increase the people's participation in decision-making. For a democtratic government, schooling for all. For an oligarchic government, schooling for some.

This difference in the very essentials makes every comparison between the two countries extremely complex. This is not our purpose in describing the educational 'events' which took place in them. On the contrary, our aim is to situate a decision-making process in the particular 'micro-structure' of each country. Some reference to other countries, either of the region or the continent, will be made in order to support the selected illustration but, once again, not in order to compare but with the aim of analysing a process in a given context.

When we reach the end of the story we may perhaps wonder whether, in spite of these precautions, there are not some typical forms of behaviour which it is worth singling out in order better to understand what constitutes the 'area of indetermination' of the decision-maker.

In fact, of course, the decision-maker — in this case the Minister of Education — is a government agent who himself is the embodiment of a certain political theory or even ideology. He is therefore bound to remain faithful to the main lines of orientation which have been given him. But in the light therefore of both the intertia of the system and the limited duration of his mandate, how far does his real capacity to act upon events reach, whether for ensuring that a precise political intention is carried out, or for bringing into play his own discretionary power? It is the limits of this capacity, to the extent that they are significant, which will enable us to establish the 'area of indetermination' which he has for intervention.

CHAPTER I

Costa Rica

Section 1. **The historical 'scenery' and the rise of the curtain**

1.1. *Social and political characterists*

The population of two million occupies a country of 50,000 sq. km., and is a mainly rural society. Seventy per cent of the population are in communities of less than 20,000 inhabitants. While it is still true that the country depends to a great extent on its agro-export sector (coffee, bananas, sugar), the rapid increase of the tertiary sector over the past 30 years should not be ignored.

Unlike its Central-American neighbours, Costa Rica experienced a relatively gradual development, resulting from slow colonization which started very early. Coffee developed in a situation of shortage of manpower and available land. The lack of a workforce other than the few white settlers of humble origin, on the one hand, and the division of land for intensive cultivation into small and medium-sized properties on the other, gave rise to a wage system at a relatively high rate of remuneration.

The quality of life is singularly higher than that of the other countries, not only of the Central-American region, but also of the rest of Latin America, and its standards of health, social organization and education are close to those characteristic of Europe and the countries of the extreme south of Latin America.

Since its independence from Spain in 1821, and still more since its emergence as a sovereign state (after the break-up of the Federal Republic of Central America in 1829) Costa Rica has put into practice a highly democratic conception of society.

The chief characteristic of the country is the very high level of social integration, mainly due to the predominance of a European population from the beginnings of colonization, at a time when there were only a few small pockets of population with other ethnic origins on the Atlantic coast. It should be noted that this social homogeneity is reflected in the scale of income distribution, the spread of which has become even more narrow over the last twenty years (see Table 3).

TABLE 3. Distribution of incomes by deciles[1]

Income brackets	1961	1971
20 per cent lower (1st and 2nd deciles)	6.0	5.4
60 per cent intermediate (3rd-8th deciles)	34.0	44.0
10 per cent just before the higher decile (9th decile)	14.0	16.2
10 per cent higher (10th decile)	46.0	34.4
including 5 per cent of the highest	35.0	22.8
	100.0	100.0

While in the upper brackets there is a greater diversification, as a result of the concentration of wealth which has been still more accentuated during the years 1970-75, the intermediate brackets have increased in size and have improved their income, thanks to the existence of powerful professional organizations which publicize and know how to defend their demands. As for the lower brackets, some of them have been able to improve their situation to the extent to which they have been able to integrate themselves in the dynamic sector of the economy. Others still find themselves kept to a very low standard of living.

If we examine the breakdown of the labour market (see Table 4) we notice a complementary phenomenon: growth of all three levels of the secondary and tertiary sectors, whereas the three levels of the primary sector are on the decrease. This demonstrates the importance of immigration into the towns, a factor in the building up of the middle class.

The rapidly growing population of certain large towns is concentrated in the central plateau of the country. It is this trend towards urbanization, encouraged by the relatively rapid growth of the public sector, that explains (among other factors) the increase in the tertiary sector already mentioned.

TABLE 4. Breakdown of employment[2] (percentages)

	1963	1973
Middle and higher levels, secondary and tertiary sectors	19.5	22.6
Lower levels, secondary sector	18.2	24.9
Lower levels, tertiary sector	9.7	11.9
Middle and higher levels, primary sector	2.0	0.3
Lower levels, primary sector	44.3	35.0
Others	6.3	5.3
	100.0	100.0

1. Development and Education Project in Latin America and the Caribbean, 'Education and development in Costa Rica', Unesco, CEPAL, UNDP, 28.4.77, Table, p.44.
2. Op.cit., p.43.

1.2. *The history of education*

Three periods can be distinguished: the first, from independence to the end of the 19th century (1821-1900); the second until 1948; and a third period which led to the era which is the object of this study (1970-74).

1.2.1. *The first period: 1821-19.00*

From 1821 to 1849 the expansion of primary education in Costa Rica did not follow a well-defined and articulated national plan for education, but was rather a reflection of the regulations governing the rôle which the cummunes (municipalities) were to play in this field. The country still lacked a legal structure and an administrative machinery that could give direction and structure to schooling in Costa Rica. The ruling party, limited in both human and financial resources, set up learning centres for 'first letters' within the limits of their means in the few central towns of the country, in a purely empirical fashion.

It was not until 1843 that the University of Santo Tomas was founded. Despite its excessively academic nature, it took an interest in the spread of 'first letters', since this already contained the pupils who in due course would become teachers. But it was only in 1849 that an 'Organic Regulation for Public Instruction' was approved.

Costa Rica, unlike its neighbours at this period, had not experienced any confrontation of political parties, bloody civil wars,[3] régimes of terror, persecutions, or violent struggles between social groups for economic reasons. The development of a liberal, democratic political society, and of the economy, were the 'national project'. It was characterized by three currents: the creation of a republic, the impulse of education as the best instrument of democracy and, lastly, the development of an agro-export industry based on coffee.

Education in Costa Rica, then, played an eminently political rôle, since its primary object was that of integrating the entire population into a single national society. Whereas for other countries of the extreme south of America, which were witnessing at this period a rapid expansion of primary education, the national project consisted in integrating the flood of migrants and ensuring political pacification, what counted in Cost Rica was above all the establishing of a nation, with its individual characteristics, in the framework of Central America, which should be the expression of the participation of the 'lower' strata in the power system.

3. A North American diplomat-cum-archaeologist, John Stephens, describes the Costa Rica of 1840 as a country enjoying a level of prosperity unequalled by its neighbours since 'at a safe distance, without wealth enough to excite cupidity, and with a large tract of wilderness to protect it against the march of an invading army, it has escaped the tumults and wars which desolated and devastated the other States'. J. Stephens, *Incidents of travel in Central American Chiapas and Yucatan,* New York, Dover Publications Inc., 1969, Vol.I, p.359.

In addition, the fact that there was no essentially economic function attributed to the educational system, given the simple nature of the agricultural tasks, throws into relief the participation in the power game of the rural groups of simple settlers who were determined to reap, or see their children reap, the benefits of literacy and primary schooling, right from the time of their settlement in the country.

When the Constitution of 1869 was drawn up, Article 6 laid down that primary education for both sexes should be 'compulsory, free, and financed by the State'. It was to be under the direction of the municipalities, but inspection was the responsibility of the government. Article 7 insisted on the liberty of education, allowing any Costa Rican or foreigner to give or receive instruction. The first decree implementing these Articles appeared in the same year; it laid down that no child was to be excluded from the advantage of an education.

The dictatorship that was in force in the country from 1870 to 1882, in spite of being a period of repression of individual freedom, saw a rapid economic growth, due to the development of coffee cultivation. As the English market strengthened, a class of capitalists began to develop in a society which had hitherto been characterized only by the increase in the middle class of small landowners. It was at this time that the first groups of exporters and merchants emerged, to become in due course what is today called the 'coffee oligarchy'.[4]

It is interesting to note that it was during this period that the first practical schools of agriculture were founded, as a result of the need felt by the agricultural managing class to recruit the specialists and technicians required for the economic development of the country. It was also during this period that numbers of intellectuals and children of the middle classes went to Europe to complete their studies, returning influenced by the leading philosophical theories of the day.

It was from 1882 to 1888 that education in Costa Rica received a wholly new stimulus, one which still characterizes the 'myth of education' prevailing in the country today. The key figure of the period in the educational field was a lawyer, very much aware of the major cultural currents of the time and of the educational systems of America and Europe, and who had studied and written extensively in this field. As a result of his contacts in Europe and the United States he was profoundly influenced by the liberal and postivist thinking of the period.[5]

4. Monge-Alfaro and F. Rivas Rios, *La educaciíon: fragua de una democracia,* San José, Costa Rica, Editorial Universidad de Costa Rica, April 1978, p.15.
5. It was in 1850 that 'there was born in Costa Rica, as in all the countries of Latin America, a philosophic tendency, positivism, which influenced nearly all the struggles and many of the victories won in various sectors of national life and public service', *ibid.*, p.29.

95

Appointed Minister of Education, Mauro Fernandez realised that primary education — which had played a fundamental part in the development of a citizenship based on a population made up of the sons of artisans, day-workers, and persons of modest means starting to live in the urban centres — no longer corresponded to the new forms of social organization arising out of the general growth of the economy. The major structural changes had narrowed the field of this education, which had gradually been monopolised by the urban ruling classes. He believed that only a profound and rigorous reform could put an end to what he saw as an abuse. Fernandez, well grounded in French positivism, had very clear ideas regarding the methodology that should be applied in all processes of reform. He hoped to implement this by a 'scientific', not an improvised, method, in accordance with a clear philosophy of education and a general plan consistings of several stages which should follow each other in strictly logical order.

He announced that the first task for his country was the organization of primary education; only then would secondary education be dealt with. Not until later, in the general context of a completed system, would the University have a part to play. Don Mauro considered that the government should not concern itself with the University until after a 'complete reorganization of primary and secondary education, bases of higher education'.[6]

He intended to apply rational 'scientific' techniques, fully worked out and prepared in advance, in negotiating the great turning-point which he intended for education in his country. To this end he prepared a plan of action and strategy. The plan had been drawn up after consultation with all concerned, and was based on the experience of other countries. The reform itself would put an end to the administrative anarchy which reigned as long as the municipalities alone were responsible for the good functioning of the educational system. The Minister, on his side, would consolidate his power by becoming the sole national authority in educational matters.

All this was enshrined in the 'general Law of Common Education' approved in 1885. In accordance with this Law he set up a network of primary schools and tackled the structure and organisation of secondary education which, until then, had been left to the responsibility of urban colleges, usually in the hands of the Church or a few well-off families.

Two years later, inspired by the wind of positivism which was blowing over Latin America, came an event not in itself noteworthy but not unique in this region: Don Mauro *closed* the University of Santo Tomas, arguing that the people ought to have the full and entire benefit of universal primary education before the State could allow itself the 'luxury' of a University.[7]

6. I.F. Azofiefa, *Don Mauro Fernandez — Teoria y practica de su reforma educativa*, San José, Editorial Fernandez Arce, 1975, pp.21-22.
7. In Colombia, 'influenced by the French Revolution of 1848, some radical sections went so far as to sanction the utopian Law of 15 March 1850, which in the name

Perhaps we should not entirely exclude from his motives the wish to slow down the social cleavage which was beginning to appear, as a consequence of the gradual birth of a capitalist class whose sons, naturally, formed the great majority of the student enrolment.

1.2.2. *The second period: 1908-1948*

By 1908, new trends in pedagogy began to appear, and new reforms were made. These affected principally the curricula and the nature of the teaching. The aim was to provide education with a content which, while faithful to its national roots, would make it adaptable to 'a democratic and changing world'.[8] Contact was also established with pedagogical circles in Switzerland and Chile, who added the benefits of their own experiences to the modernistic trends of the period. In the words of the then Minister, 'we had to simplify the curricula of primary education, eliminating whatever had no practical utility or immediate application to life, so as to give greater solidity to the teaching of the principal subjects'.[9]

A few years later, in 1917, a second partial reform was carried out, based on the experiences of the 'active school'. In 1915 the first teacher-training college had been opened in Costa Rica, to train the teachers of the future. The chief feature of this reform was the wish in certain circles to give to the school a new responsibility for finding long-term solutions to the problems which affected the country and motivated the educationists of those years to give it a very special rôle. In the minds of those in charge of education at the time it became apparent that the school was not only an institution for developing the child's intelligence, but the place for training the minds of those who, one day, would be in charge of the nation's economy. In other words, the school should encourage an education for national development.

During the years following the first World War, European influence made itself felt, especially that of the Belgian educationist Decroly and the organizers of the 'active school' experiments. Another reform of curricula and content was drawn up in 1935. As a result of the conclusions of a Chilean mission which visited the country that year the University was re-opened in 1940, in the form of a State institution but autonomous, free to choose its policy, its structures, its faculty, its curricula and its students.

1.2.3. *The third period: 1948-74*

The civil war of 1948, resulting in the takeover of power by a left-wing junta headed by J. Figueres (who was to preside over the destiny of the country for two years) brought far-reaching changes. The political and social sector

---

of the most absolute freedom of education decred, simply and quietly, the suppression of the universities'. G. Weinberg, op.cit., p.27.
8. C. Monge-Alfaro and F. Rivas Rios, op.cit., p.42.
9. Quoted in *ibid,* p.45.

in power, while accepting the existence of an 'oligarchic' class, introduced deep-reaching institutional reforms tending to decentralize public administration and increase the rôle of the State in economic and social development, especially by destroying the monopoly held by certain groups over credit by nationalizing the banking sector. The aim was to introduce agricultural diversification linked with a reformist programme. Thus the principles of political liberty which had hitherto characterized Costa Rica were joined by new expressions such as 'social justice' and 'economic justice'.[10]

It was during the coming to power of the junta led by Figueres that the new Constitution of 1949 was approved. Under Title 7, this laid the foundations of a future educational reform. In the words of the junta's Minister of Education (who was to return to power some years later, and again for a third term during the period covered by this study), this Constitution 'is the first document carrying reform of the former educational system, and from this flows all that has been done in this field from 1950 to 1970 by five governments, all equally anxious to improve education both qualitatively and quantitatively'.[11]

As far as the state of education in the 1940s is concerned, Costa Rica had already reached relatively high enrolment levels in urban areas, having progressively included the majority of the age-group and at the same time beginning to open up secondary and higher education. As from the 1960s significant reductions in the marginality of schooling in rural areas make their appearance, and there is a gradual expansion of the first cycle of secondary education.

When Figueres returned to power as President, elected for the four years 1954-58, one of his first concerns (inspired by the impetus given to education by his Minister, who had already been at his side during the two years of the junta), was to define the principles, the objectives and the aims of a system considered to be an incrongruous mixture. It was necessary to give the officials responsible a philosophical concept of their rôle, in keeping with the demands of the times.

For nearly seventy years, in fact, no legal dispositions had changed, except in its purely formal aspects, the orientation of education. A new 'Fundamental Law for Education' was accordingly promulgated by the Legislative Assembly in 1957, after having been drafted by the Higher Council for Education.[12] This Law was intended to ensure a renovation of the school system, to bring it into conformity with the aims of the 1949 Constitution.

The Law extended the life of the constitutive document, thus avoiding a break in the continuity. In this document the emphasis was chiefly on secon-

10. Op.cit., p.111.
11. U. Gàmez S. and C.E. Olivera, 'Costa Rica: a national educational development plan', *Prospects,* Vol. IV, No.4, 1974 pp.503-511.
12. A consultant body under the chairmanship of the Minister, consisting of representatives of the University and of the teachers' unions, and also of former Ministers.

dary education, stressing preparation of the student to be a 'socially useful' individual able to integrate himself efficiently in the fundamental changes'[13] taking place in his country. In 1964 secondary education was consolidated by a revision of curricula, and 1968 saw the setting-up of the diversified *baccalauréat* and of the Higher Teacher-training College. Finally in 1970, a law was promulgated on the teaching profession, setting out the conditions for exercising the profession of teacher as part of the civil service, with all the guarantees attached to this status.

Section 2. The educational development plan

2.1. *Education in 1970*

In 1970, when Figueres returned to power for the third time (with the same Minister of Education), the educational system in Costa Rica, in spite of having made notable progress during the preceding years, was still a system of the traditional type. Neither its structure nor its results, according to the Minister, responded 'to the requirements of the moment and even less to those which could reasonably be foreseen'.[14] In spite of the measures taken to establish more firmly the generalization of primary education and the development of secondary, in spite of the redrawing of curricula and the diversifying of middle-level education, in spite of some reductions in the drop-out rate from primary school, the educational system in 1970, in the view of the government which had just taken office, was still far from perfect.

The illiterates made up about 5 per cent of the total population (7 per cent in rural areas). As for the age-group 20-29 of the active population, 20 per cent had not completed primary school, 44 per cent had, 24 per cent had received secondary education and 6 per cent higher. Ninety per cent of children aged 6-12 were enrolled, 40 per cent of the 13-18 age-group, and 10 per cent of the 19-24 age-group.[15]

These figures indicate that primary education was almost universal and that the general educational level of the population was more comparable to that of countries of the southern part of the continent (Argentina, Chile, Uruguay) than to that of Central-American countries (with the exception of Panama). Despite this initially favourable impression, while compulsory primary education was attended by 83 per cent of the children aged 6 and 7 and aged 11 and 12, and by almost all children of 8, 9 and 10, it is nevertheless a fact that '2,500 schools, mainly in rural areas, were too small and could not offer education of good quality.[16] The percentage of repeaters (mainly

13. C. Monge-Alfaro and F. Rivas Rios, op.cit., p.138.
14. U. Gàmez S. and C.D. Olivera, op.cit.
15. Costa Rica, Ministerio de Educación Pública. *Planeamiento del desarrollo educativo, Vol.I: Diagnóstico,* San José, El Ministerio, 1971, p.43.
16. U. Gàmez S. and C.D. Olivera, op.cit.

during the first two years[17]) was 11 and that of drop-outs during the course of schooling 35'.[18]

Secondary education consisted of five or six years, according to the section, and was divided into a common first cycle of three years and a differentiated second cycle of two or three years. About a third of the age-group concerned were in the first cycle, and some 17 per cent in the second. Four-fifths of the pupils followed studies of classical type, the remainder following technical studies (commercial, industrial or agriculture). In the words of the Minister, 'Elitist by origin and conception (though covering most regions of the country) this education aimed at providing a "general culture" which, in practice, consisted solely of accumulating particular facts, unconnected with each other, and which was torn between the ideal of the "universal man" of the renaissance and the mass of specialized knowledge dating from recent decades'.[19]

This education, which was attended by half the pupils who finished primary school, lost 53 per cent of its enrolment in the course of their journey (48 per cent during the first three years).

The abnormally high repeating rate at the beginning of primary education is mainly due to the application of 'objective' standards which oblige the teacher to refuse promotion of a child from the first to the second year if he is unable to read, and from the second to the third year if he cannot write. This is an indication of the rigidity of the system, which has its effect equally upon the training and the attitude of the teachers. In addition, the break between primary and secondary education is notorious (50 per cent of sixth-year primary pupils are admitted to the first year of secondary). On the other hand, pupils who successfully complete the first three years of secondary (some of them are pupils in urban private schools) have every chance of entering university.

Finally, it should be noted that in spite of the 'inefficiency' of this system, the cost of primary schooling (even though not all children completed the statutory period of six years) and of partial secondary education, together with the grant to the University, represented 35 per cent of total State expenditure and 6.4 per cent of GNP.[20]

Besides the qualitative difficulties already mentioned, the high rates of repetition and drop-out and the obvious connection between complete schooling and urban origin could not fail to raise the question of the proper utilization of public funds.

2.2. *The national plan takes shape and authority*

To cope with the difficulties we have outlined above the Minister, a few

17. *Diagnosis,* op.cit., p.69.
18. Gàmez and Olivera, op.cit.
19. Gàmez and Olivera, op.cit.
20. *Diagnosis,* op.cit., p.236.

months after taking office for the third time, drew up with the assistance of national advisers a short document entitled 'Integral Plan for Educational Reform', outlining a reform of all levels and structures of the national educational system. This document followed the basic principles of the 1949 Constitution and defined the field of application of the law passed in 1957.

Faced with a system which he considered unsatisfactory, ill-adapted to modern times, and not offering the future citizens of Costa Rica the necessary instruments to meet the changes in economic and social structures which were to be expected, the Minister hoped to undertake a complete remodelling after an analytical diagnosis of the situation. This analysis should concentrate on the problem of drop-outs and on the difficulty for the State to finance the linear growth of the school system in an inexorable sequence in which the justification of the first year of primary education is found in the ambition, transmitted by the system itself, to finish higher education.

The system offered no viable alternative for those who wished to enter the world of work earlier, perhaps returning to the educational system later in life. The Minister affirmed[21] therefore at the outset that he wished for a reform which would give an overall vision integrating the 'quantitative, qualitative, administrative, legislative and financial aspects'. It was no longer a matter of treating certain aspects of education as 'isolated questions'. What he wanted was 'treatment as a whole'. He wished to lay down policies aimed at offering a general education to the entire population — school-age or not — by modernizing the existing system and making rational use of the resources that were available.

Nevertheless, it should be noted that none of the Minister's writings or speeches justifying his intention of reforming the entire educational system was based on any explicit reference to a 'political project' of the Figueres government. Admittedly, there are general aims:

— 'these problems of structure and output arise in the first place from the obvious inequality of educational opportunities, strictly contrary to the assumptions of the political constitution. In the remote rural areas, and even in the marginal urban areas, educational opportunities are far fewer . . .'[22]

— 'in general, there is a marked absence of links between the school and society. For example, on the one hand little attention and little money is devoted to remedying serious problems of nutrition and health, factors of social origin which have serious repercussions on schooling, and on the other hand there is unanimous agreement that the results of formal education have little to do with the needs of society'.[23]

21. Report of the Ministry to the Legislative Assembly, *Memoria del Ministerio de Educaciíon Pública,* quoted in C. Monge-Alfaro and F. Rivas Rios, op.cit., p.151.
22. *Plan nacional de desarrollo educativo: memoria del Ministerio de Educatión Pública, 1971,* Part.I: Description of intentions, para. 1.3.1., p.130.
23. *Ibid.,* para 1.3.3., p.130.

— 'faced with a rapidly changing world, and particularly with technological progress in all fields, present-day education is satisfied to transmit knowledge which to a great extent will be out of date or useless in the world of the future. Such an education does not awaken the spirit of discovery, of observation, of analysis, of application of what has been learned to new situations. In a word, current education does not permit creativeness'.[24]

— etc., etc.

Thus, no explicit or direct links appear to exist between an employment policy (by the creation of regional industrial 'poles') or a policy of agricultural diversification (by increasing the cultivation of food crops) on the one hand, and the need to adapt the school system to the demands of greater specialization or greater regionalization, on the other. All the same, those first two objectives were part of the general policy of the Figueres government, and the reform hoped for by the Minister included developments which would have been, in effect, a response to them.

But it is still a fact that in none of the basic documents, including the proposed law presented to Parliament by the Minister, can any direct causal relationship be found between the precise expression of an economic or social policy and the objectives of the educational development plan.

If the Minister envisaged at the outset a complete reform of education, he was later forced to admit that this could not be carried out within four years, the term of an elected government. The problem was to change the educational system without tying it down to a 'reform' which would be too brief because too limited and superficial. Education must be able to develop over the years in line with the demands of society and the resources of the State. This did not exclude the possibility that a first series of measures, which he hoped would be irreversible, would coincide with the time-span of the mandate of the government of which he was a member. It was in this spirit that a 'Development Plan' for education was drawn up, and not a 'once-and-for-all-reform', as the Minister emphasized[25] in declaring his intentions.

In these preliminaries to a process of change the Minister decided to draw up his plan in different stages, so as to gather the maximum of information and surround himself with necessary precautions to arrive at a document that would be both precise and acceptable. As a first step he arranged for a general 'diagnosis' of the educational system, describing and analysing the national situation.[26] This was carried out between the beginning of 1970 and the beginning of 1971. Shortly after this, the 'Objectives'[27] of the Plan ap-

24. *Ibid.*, para 2.2., p.131.
25. *Ibid.*, para 2.1., p.134, in which it also made clear that 'an end must be put to the series of sudden shocks which kept happening in the past, interspersed with long periods of immobility'.
26. *Diagnosis,* op.cit.
27. *Planeamiento del desarrollo educativo: los grandes objectivos,* San José, Ministry of Public Education, 1971.

peared, and, finally, the 'Programming'[28] by sector, branch, level and cycle of the school system.

The Minister set up eighteen working committees, each dealing with one of the major educational problems. Membership of these committees included not only the various departments of the Ministry but also the University of Costa Rica, the Ministry of Planning, the National Apprenticeship Institute, representatives of the National Council of Retired Teachers, and of the Teachers' unions, the Inspectorate, etc.

The propositions put forward by these committees were, in effect, the first version of the Educational Development Plan. To explain it, a group of officials of the Ministry and of the University organized study seminars, round tables, lectures and discussions with heads of colleges, regional administrators and inspectors. At the Congress of the Professional Association of Secondary Teachers (APSE)[29] representatives of the Ministry explained various aspects of the Plan. In this way, within the timetable laid down by the Minister, the Plan was made known to the largest possible number of those who would be affected by its results.

The decisive phase of this process of consultation was the organization, in the fourteen regions of the country, of sixteen working sessions in which educators, students, fathers of families and community representatives took part. The groups trained by the Ministry to explain the Plan took part in these meetings and discussed the 'Diagnosis', the 'Objectives' and the 'Programming'. Finally, contacts were established with the University of Costa Rica and the second major national teachers' union, the National Association of Educators (ANDE),[30] with the aim of ensuring wider acquaintance with the content of the Plan. On the basis of these contacts and meetings the Minister invited the delegates of the various regional seminars and the national and international bodies to the National Education Seminar held in the capital, San José, in October 1971 under the chairmanship of the President of the Republic himself.

On this occasion the various aspects of the Plan were discussed in detail and modifications were made as a result of the discussions. The Plan was then referred to the Higher Council for Education who discussed it and signified their approval in November 1971.

The Plan was built around three fundamental objectives:

— to raise the average educational level of the population, especially in the least favoured areas, to achieve their nationwide integration and to ensure for all citizens better conditions of life and thus contribute to the socio-economic development of the country;

28. *Planeamiento des desarrollo educativo, vol.III: programación,* San José, Ministry of Public Education, 1971.
29. See above, Part I, Chapter 3, section 3.2.
30. See above, Part I, Chapter 3, section 3.3.2.

— to modernize the educational system so that it would meet the socio-economic needs of the country and encourage the process of development;
— to maintain within its present limits the share of the education budget in the national budget, without prejudice to the qualitative and quantitative improvement of education.

These three objectives were divided into several goals, the most interesting of which concerned changes in institutional structures, qualitative changes in curricular content, quantitative expansion and changes in the geographical distribution of resources, a teacher-training and retraining programme and, lastly, an administrative reform directly affecting the structure and functions of the Ministry of Education.

As regards the structures, the aim of the new system proposed by the Plan was to eliminate the *de facto* division between the primary school (which was often terminal, for the children of the rural areas who did not continue schooling beyond it) and the secondary school, mainly urban, giving access to higher education. Both the Fundamental Law of 1957 and the reform of middle-level education in 1964-65 had tended to make the first three years of secondary education a first cycle divorced from the second cycle and regarded as the final stage completing primary education. But this intention had not been effective. In reality there was a middle-level education of six years, divided into two cycles of three years each, which was still the sole means of access to higher education. The Minister felt that this dichotomy between primary and secondary education had led to 'a deep sense of disquiet in the country'[31] and recalled that in the Statement of Intentions in the Fundamental Law mention had already been made of consequences of the increased numbers in middle-level schooling, which 'had given rise to social, psychological and cultural phenomena which had not existed thirty or forty years previously'.[32] And yet this Law, which had been implemented only in part, had proposed as a solution the setting up of a common cycle of nine years (six years of primary and three years of the first cycle of secondary).

The Minister considered that 'this was a temporarily good solution, though incomplete, but that its realization would have to wait for seven years and that when it was achieved, other phenomena would make the problems even more acute'.[33] 'Perhaps', the Minister continued, 'it was feared that the democratic feelings of the people of Costa Rica would be offended by frank references to the differences in social class which, in reality, characterized the clientèles of each of the cycles'.[34] This is why the Minister, critical of the measures taken hitherto, proposed a new system of basic general educa-

31. Costa Rica, Ministerio de Educación Pública, *Proyecto de ley general de educación* San José, El Ministerio, 1973. Chapter IV(v), p.44, para.129.
32. Ibid, p.44, para 131.
33. *Ibid.,* p.44, para 132.
34. *Ibid.,* p.45, para 133.

tion (*Educación General Basica*) which should form what he called 'the heart of the new structure'.[35] This general education comprised nine years of schooling (the former primary schooling and the former first cycle of secondary) divided into three cycles each of three years. To meet the aspirations of society, these nine years should be available to the children coming forward in the course of the next thirty years as 'the basic minimum of culture for all Costa Ricans'.[36] It was already forecast that, in 1980, 70 per cent of the children of the relevant age-group would be enrolled at some level of this education. This was the reason why this amount of schooling was declared compulsory (Article 23 of the proposed Law).

This Article alone involved an amendment to Article 78 of the Constitution (which ordained only six years of compulsory eduction), and was approved by Parliament on 17 May 1973. Once this structural change had become a matter of Law, Parliament proceeded to discuss the objectives of the Plan. These, however, were important matters, concerning curricula (in essence, it was proposed to modify cognitive transmission by a capacity to develop the potential of the child and change the rôle of the teacher), the geographical and quantitative distribution of the infrastructure of schools, the teacher-training and retraining programmes (viewed as a continuous process of teacher-training) and the reform of the administration, which implied a certain amount of decentralization and the elimination of structures based on subjects (inspectorates of letters, sciences, mathematics, etc.).

2.3. *The Plan is rejected*
In taking a closer look at the strategy that the Minister intended to follow in order to achieve his aims, we must consider the nature of the eight stages involved:

1. To strengthen and regularize the formal education system, in order to increase access to the first cycle of middle-level education (which henceforth was to become part of general basic education).
2. To emphasize the qualtiative aspect of education, i.e., its spirit, its content, its methods, its evaluation techniques, in order to ensure throughout the system a higher level of retention within the various streams and thus increase the number of graduates at a lower cost.
3. To improve the critical stage — the third cycle of basic general education — by introducing the inductive method based on the pupil's active experience.
4. To extend education in the rural areas through a better distribution of access to schooling and better adaptation to local needs of the rural education offered to both children and adults.
5. To transform and modernize school administration, by eliminating 'routine' activities and formalist testing.

35. *Ibid.,* para 143.
36. *Ibid.*

6. To establish links with the official and private bodies involved in the social and economic life of the country, so as to encourage continuous adaptation of education in relation to the real needs of society.
7. To create a technical body (Institute for Educational Research and Development) to assist the Ministry of Education.
8. Finally, to overcome the weakness resulting from the appointment of teachers and headmasters inadequate in both numbers and competence to interpret and carry out the Plan.

Analysis of this eightfold strategy shows that each stage would demand from the teachers a considerable effort of adaptation and change, sometimes sudden, as compared with the way in which they had hitherto been called upon to carry out their duties and responsibilities. In the various documents, in fact, particularly in the Declarations of Intent both of the Plan and the Law, the Minister sets out very clearly and firmly the demands which he proposes to make on the teachers and on the staff of the Ministry as a whole. For example, in the Declaration of Intent for the Plan (para. 24.2): 'The traditionalist training of the majority of the teaching staff has taken place on the basis of outmoded ideas (for example, with over-emphasized subject specialization for the first cycle of secondary education) and by old-fashioned methods (active and creative methods are perhaps taught, but only by calling upon the master classes)'.[37]

Moreover, the Minister did not want to lose any time in implementing the Plan approved by the Higher Council of Education in November 1971. He laid down a programme with a very tight timetable. This proposed that the application of the Plan should start with the new school year (the beginning of 1972). During this year the rules governing promotion from one class to the next would have to be changed in favour of a system of automatic promotion within each of the three cycles of the nine-year basic general education, so that they should be fully operative by the end of the year.

This implied that the appointment of teachers should be reviewed for each cycle, providing retraining and preparing them for the new curricula and for the new system of evaluation and marking of pupils, which was in future to be carried out with the direct participation of the parents in a continuous 'follow-up' of the pupil.

The Minister proposed to take up in 1973 the second cycle of secondary, which was to become three-year 'diversified education', and also the reform of the Ministry. In 1972 he had drawn up a draft law embodying the essentials of the Plan, and a proposed amendment to the Constitution to exend compulsory education to nine years. He intended to present these texts to Parliament in 1973. The amendment was approved as expected in May 1973; the draft law was to be submitted in July.

37. *Memoria 1971 Plan nacional,* op.cit., Part I, Exposición de motivos, para 2.4.(ii), pp.131-132.

This accelerated timetable placed a double burden on the teachers: coping with a new system of teaching for which they had not been trained and doing so in an extremely short time. This haste met with growing resistance, not only from the unions themselves but also from public opinion, which the unions well knew how to manipulate.

The two principal unions (ANDE and APSE) asserted that the Minister had scarcely invited them to take part at all in the drawing-up of the Plan. While it was true that he had 'consulted' them about texts *already* prepared, the unions considered that this work by Ministry teams, assisted by a few international advisers, had been carried out without their knowledge. They believed that changes in the system were certainly needed, but in a direction more in line with their day-to-day concerns than in the overall manner that the Minister intended.

It is true that the teachers encountered considerable administrative difficulties when it was a question of the payment of salaries, promotion, transfer or appointment. They also felt that the retraining programme had been badly organized for them, and that generally speaking the complex ambitions contained in the Plan should have been the object of a programme of gradual information, training and retraining in order to enable them to envisage their eventual implementation. In other words, not only the complexity of the plan and the speed with which it had to be implemented, but also the fact that they had made no real contribution at the outset to the formulation of the proposals it contained, ensured that the unions would be more and more strongly opposed to it. This was clear in 1972, when they employed the considerable means at their disposal to prevent the Plan being put into action, and even clearer a year later, when they fought to prevent the proposed law from being examined in Parliament.

In the hope of regaining the teachers' support, the Minister relinquished the control and direction of the teacher-training colleges and entrusted to the Faculty of Education of the new State University (*Universidad Nacional*) at Héredia, on the outskirts of the capital, the task of training primary-school teachers. This final effort discouraged many of the Minister's collaborators and advisers (who could not see how the changes proposed by the Plan in the rôle and functions of teachers could be implemented once the Minister was no longer in control), and did little to reduce the teachers' resistance.

From the Minister's point of view it was essential to react to this opposition. There would have to be a confrontation with the unions. Accordingly, in October 1973, three months after presenting his draft law to Parliament and a few weeks before the elections, he summoned a 'seminar-workshop' for revising the Plan, to which the unions were invited together with the Ministry officials concerned and several important national and international personalities. A single representative from a single union attended — as an observer! At the seminar it quickly became apparent that the greatest hazard for the Plan, and therefore for the proposed law, was the opposition of the teaching profession, which showed 'evidence of mentalities and attitudes that it would be difficult to expunge'.[38]

New problems arose each day. The teachers, deeply commited to a curriculum of 'subjects', repeated over and over again lessons based on activities conceived as solutions to set problems. The majority of them believed that teaching should be historical rather than inductive. They saw their rôle as agents of knowledge-transmission, not as catalysts to bring about an active rôle on the part of their pupils. As for evaulation, it seemed to the teachers that it was particularly difficult and complicated to bring in the families and the pupils in any value judgement concerning the performance of these same pupils.

There was clearly no shortage of disputes to block the implementation of the Plan. Accordingly, in November 1973, shortly after the seminar-workshop, the unions called a strike, which became one of unlimited duration before the presidential election in December.

The '*Liberación*' party, in power, and campaigning on behalf of its candidate, had no wish to come up against the opposition of the unions, who represented a sizeable force. The political support which the Minister had counted on receiving from the President and from his own Party was therefore lacking. And so the proposed Law, which since its presentation in Parliament in July had received only a first reading before the Education Committee, was never debated by the full legislature.

The election brought to the Presidency the *Liberación* party's candidate, who was however from a wing of the party opposed to that of the defeated President, Figueres. The Minister's successor, confronted with a strike which was still going on after the election, had to make every effort to pacify the teachers before all else. Among the new arrangements made by the new Minister, the principal measure were clearly intended to end the quarrel with the unions and regain the support of the teachers: houses for rural teachers, school libraries, family allowances, a network of tele-education and correspondence courses principally benefiting teachers seeking new diplomas to assist their professional advancement, etc. As for the Plan, even though the new Minister, in his speeches, praised its merits, it was *de facto* left on the shelf.

Thus, three years after exceptional national efforts supported by considerable international assistance had been deployed in a movement which the Minister hoped would make history, changes in the classrooms were few and far between. Mention of the 'Plan' now evoked no more than cynical smiles or regretful sighs.

38. U. Gàmez S. and C.E. Olivera, op.cit.

Section 3. The field, the system and the game

Having selected the Educational Development Plan as the object of our study, we now have to decide on our angle of attack. Three possibilities seem open: first, the social structures — which would mean analysising the tensions — one might even say struggle — between the two classes which characterize the division of work in Costa Rica. Alternatively, we might try to understand the organisational relationships between the structures, organisms or groupings identified principally by the defence of their interests and the growth of their influence in a field given or gradually settled and conquered. Or we might devote our attention to recognising the nature and dynamics of the systems of action and their actors.

The main purpose of this work is not to analyse the historical current which has fashioned the social tensions in Costa Rica, even though in the preceding pages and in the final section of this chapter the attempt is made to understand certain of the underlying causes of the confrontations studied. The purpose is rather to arrive at an understanding of the situation of the decision-maker at a given moment in the life of the social structures of the country.

In Costa Rica during the period concerned (1970-74), this aspect of national life was of extreme importance. The wage-earners, including the agricultural workers, enjoyed on the whole relatively high levels of earnings compared with those in other countries of the region. The spead of income-levels was being reduced. The resources derived from the export of coffee, with world prices mainly favourable, allowed an appreciable redistribution of incomes through social security measures, family allowances and a relatively equitable taxation policy.

The *Liberación* party, regarded as progressive, came to power with the clear intention of further enlarging the democratic basis and, in particular, access to education.

The teachers' unions, for their part, carried on their struggle not in the name of the principle of class rights but rather in the name of the rights of caste privileges. [39] This is why we choose to follow, for our analysis, the third possibility mentioned above: situating the decision-maker in his organisational relations and in the game of the system of action, without too much reference to the relatively stable social climate in Costa Rica.

This examination of the strategy employed by the decision-maker (the Minister of Education) will be carried out on two distinct levels: firstly of the formal or political field and then in the narrower but more complex context of the system of action, where the game itself and the conflicts it involves take place.

This formal field — where, for example, the power of the political party at the head of the State is exercised, *vis-à-vis* the other powers — will deter-

39. Crozier and Friedberg, op.cit.

mine a great part of the decision-maker's actions. It will be simultaneously the starting-point and the sound-box for the failure of previous actions and therefore for influencing subsequent ones.

Within this field there are many subsystems of 'social action'. We shall single out the one which concerns us and is of particular interest in view of its influence on the disposition of the field of which it is part.

We could continue to use the terms 'System' (educational policies) and 'Subsystem' defined by the actors and the games necessary for formulating the Educational Development Plan. However, we have preferred to reflect the strategy underlying this subsystem by calling it the 'system of action'.

Instead of regarding the totality of the relations between the totality of the games as constituting a single system of action, we have preferred to distinguish the two levels. Moreover, this reflects the decision-making process itself when the Executive takes the initiative of proposing a new law. In practice, once the proposal of a member of the Executive is approved by the whole of that branch of Government, it is not submitted to the Legislature until the latter has to ratify the proposal by giving it the form of law. Admittedly, Parliament can intervene at any time if there is a political stake to justify it. But generally speaking there are three stages:

i)   the political decision of the Executive;
ii) the preparation of a measure by the Executive;
iii) the examination by Parliament.

It is the second stage that concerns us here: the 'moment' when the member of the Executive who has taken the initiative of proposing a law (in this case, the decision-maker of our story, the Minister of Education) has to formulate, negotiate, prepare or impose the measure which will subsequently be placed before Parliament.

The political decision and its consequences, at the Executive level, have practically nothing to do with the day-to-day working-out of that decision. This decision takes place within the political field, whereas the decision we are analysing is more the result of the ability of the member of the Executive to exercise a judgement — which will be confirmed or refuted by the event — concerning his strategy.

As a first step, then, we must define the formal field.

3.1. *The formal field*
This is the level on which a consensus will emerge, or be approved, which will give 'the green light' to the decision-maker. In essence, it consists of four centres:

— the Head of State and his political staff;
— the Minister and his associates;
— the headquarters of the *Liberación* party;
— the Higher Council for Education.

3.1.1. *Movement and background*

A brief review of the record of activity and characteristic functions of the field should help us to determine its nature.

3.1.1.1. *First stage: the Reform*

As far as the first three centres are concerned (the Head of State, the Minister, and the Party headquarters), it is difficult to determine either an order of dependence of a timetable of the decision, since it is precisely the convergence of all three which determines the strictly political area of the field.

In fact, from the start of the presidental campaign which preceded the electoral victory of the *Liberación* party, these three centres made up one complete entity. The unchallenged leader of the Party, J. Figueres, had at his side his former Minister of Education (in the government which he headed from 1954 to 1958).

In a perspective both liberal (politically speaking) and populist, the *Liberación* party could reckon on the support of the organized groups — such as the teachers' unions — and could offer nothing less than 'more' education 'for all'. No trade union could oppose such a programme.

Throughout the campaign the 'once and future' Minister, in constant consultation and contact with his political leader, recalled the measures taken in the educational sphere in 1948 and between 1954 and 1958 to justify the necessity of re-starting the reform movement that the country needed:

> To Don José Figueres and me has fallen the task of justifying and inaugurating a new vision of education in 1948, of planning and enriching it in 1953-58 and now, strengthened by our victories, of putting the finishing touches during the period 1970-74, by giving it a structure that conforms with the new universal trends in education through a coherent scheme of action such as is outlined in the first 'National Plan for Educational Development.[40]

The Party headquarters, directed by the future President and in which the Minister played a leading — quasi-historical — rôle as his 'companion in arms', was naturally solidly behind the promises made during the campaign by the Minister, who enjoyed the complete confidence of his leader.

After the election the Minister, in keeping with his wish to 'put the finishing touches' to the work that had already commenced, tackled the fourth, less political but more formal centre, namely the Higher Council for Education. This body, whose functions are laid down by the Constitution itself, is outside the authority of the Head of State or of the Minister. In the State as constituted the Council is responsible, under Article 81 of the Constitution, for 'the general direction of formal education'.

Without its support the Minister would not be able to continue 'the work undertaken in 1948' and advance towards the historic reform he hoped to

40. Costa Rica, Ministerio de Educación Pública, *Proyecto de ley general de educación,* San José, El Ministerio, July 1973, p.4.

achieve. Accordingly, barely four months after entering upon his duties as Minister, he submitted to the Council his 'Integral Plan for Educational Reform', which contained all the essentials of his proposals during the election campaign. One week later the Council, having studied this work, gave him the expected 'green light', declaring that it 'approves the initiative taken by the Minister of Public Education in connection with an Integral Reform of National Education'.[41]

Schematically, it may be said that there is conformity with the Minister's intentions and ambitions on the part of the three other elements who with him make up the field. The situation in 1970, at the outset of the decision the Minister will make, can be represented graphically as:

Ch
P   M = (R)
C

$\updownarrow$ = Reciprocal encouragement

$=$ = Unreserved support

The Head of State (H), and Party Headquarters (P) and the Higher Council (C) all support the initiative of the Minister (M) to inaugurate a process of educational reform (R). The decision has its basis in a homogeneous field.

3.1.1.2. *Second Stage: the Plan*

The initiative of the Minister in proposing a plan and organising a national debate on its content was explicitly followed by the President. The Head of State attended the National Educational Seminar in October 1971 and declared:

> Today we embark upon a new educational life-style . . . We have travelled a long path before reaching this Plan . . . Let us explain clearly what we hope to achieve, and let this explanation be available to all fathers of families, even the poorest. If we are able to succeed in our effort, it will be a triumph: if we are not, we shall have failed . . . This Plan must be analysed from a non-partisan point of view, and not in the name of party political aims. May the result of these discussions lay the foundations that will enable us to fulfil the cultural ambitions of the people of Costa Rica.[42]

Re-reading the President's declaration with the wisdom of hindsight, we may note the appearance of two concerns of a political nature:

— the Plan is still an abstract idea, and no one can state clearly just what is in it. Might it not be too ambitious, liable to disappoint an electorate accustomed to the bold reforms of the President but worried about the future of its schools?

41. Costa Rica Consejo Superior de Educación: 'Acta' of session No.61, 15 May 1970.
42. National Seminar on Education, Final Act, 25-30 October 1971, Ministry of Public Education, San José, p.30.

—political discussion of this text has already begun, and it should be stopped immediately, otherwise the antagnoism of the unions might lead to serious risks for the President, who must not lose the control of his Party.

In fact, it is precisely these two far-off clouds that are presaged by the mutterings of the unions, and of which the President is not unaware, which will draw nearer and finish by darkening the horizon — in posterity — of the Minister.

At this stage the Party headquarters, sharing the concern shown by the unions, relies upon the President to express the uneasiness felt. In exchange for this warning, he continues to support the Minister.

In the Higher Council of Education some resistance began to make its appearance on the part of certain important personalities in the world of education, a former Minister (of the opposition party) and of the union representative, an official of the Ministry. The Minister was able to win over and convince the latter. With some hesitation, the Council approved the Plan in November 1971.

So, just at the moment in 1972 when the Minister had to embark simultaneously on the application of the Plan and on the formulation of the necessary legal instruments, his support started to waver. The situation of the field might be illustrated by the following diagram:

Ch
P   M = Pl.
C

→ = One-way pressure

――― = Support with some hesitation

----- = Support without hesitation

The Head of State (H) and the Party headquarters (P) support the action of the Minister (M) in favour of the Plan (Pl) even though they forsee the nature of possible future difficulties, while the Council (C), echoing the reservations expressed (particularly by the unions) gives its agreement only after hesitation. The positions within the field begin to change.

3.1.1.3. *Third stage: the Law*

In this stage the field undergoes a redistribution of forces due essentially to the game which takes place in the System of Action (which will be examined later), concerned with the combined teachers' unions being the disturbing element.

The overt opposition of the unions and the doubts expressed by public opinion about both the merits of the Plan and the expediency of a law caused hesitation in the Party headquarters which, in the pre-election climate, 'dropped' the Minister by refusing to allow Parliament to debate the proposed law. The Head of State could not appeal to party discipline; alone he could only offer his personal support to his companion. And many members of the Council no longer hesitated to voice openly their objections to the insistent demand of the Minister to turn the Plan into a law which some considered to be both superfluous and provocative.

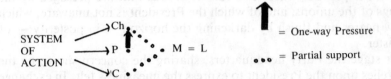

The product of the vectors making up the System of Action — which did not enter the field during the previous stages — becomes a leading factor of direct influence on the Head of State (H), the Party (P) and the Council (C). The Party reduces the President's support for his Minister (M), who without the assistance of the Party or the unanimous agreement of the Council remains practically the only person in favour of the passing of a Law (L) establishing the Plan.

3.1.2. *The nature of the field*

The particular feature of this field is that it represents the frame surrounding the *entire* action of the Minister.

We have already noticed[43] the methodolgial difficulty of trying to deal *simultaneously* with a political phenomenon and a game from inside a whole. It is only by defining the field as *encompassing* the system which will be studied below that we can assess the *product* of power emanating from it and the relative weights of the vectors influencing it.

The two characteristics of this field are its power of decision and its sensitivity to information. It is normal that its power should be decisive, since we have defined it this way, but what makes it specific and — thereby — illustrates its quality as a 'sound-box' is its capacity to hear — and listen to — the 'noises' which will, in the outcome, change the direction of its choices and the power structure of its component parts.

The Head of State, despite his personal authority, cannot ignore the warning shot fired across his bows by the Party which, on the eve of the election, cannot allow one of its members — even one of the most respected — to polarize the opposition of the most powerful professional union in the country.

This opposition is not directed against an ideal, a principle, or even a political interest of this same Party. It is directed against a document (the Plan) which has been drawn up outside this pressure group, and the content of which considerably displeases the group. The tactics (submitting the Plan, once drawn up, to the unions) might have been successful (as in other situa-

43. See above, Introduction.

tions) and on this possibility the Party has no strong views. But the strategy (a 'new' education) does not *a priori* gain the support of the Party, whose ideology of a middle class and social justice in a relatively mobile society does not necessarily include a total 'Reform' of education. After all, is not education the instrument for measuring the capacity to 'get on' socially?

But here is where the opposition of the unions, already important in itself, is intensified beyond all possibility of negotiation by the Minister's determination to crown his project by a law which would enshrine everything that they are opposed to. This hostility is a signal that the Party cannot ignore. The Party therefore separates itself from the Minister, taking the President with it and sounding the knell of the Minister's hopes.

In the originally homogeneous field a split has appeared, which will separate the decision-making actor from the sources of his authority. Thus 'devitalized', he disappears from the field — which itself remains, since his successor, supported by new actors, will find himself in the same 'combination' of influences, to which he will react differently from the decision-maker we have been studying. He will maintain the homogeneity of the field and separate himself from the vital sources of his authority, legitimacy and — consequently — credibility.

The concept of 'field' has enabled us to define the limits of the *synthetic nature* of the game of power politics, which has known how to simplify while still taking account of the greater number of independent variables which characterize and give life to the system. It has played its part as a filter of the Executive's decision by preventing any discussion in the Legislature, which would certainly have been bad for the party in power, but was also not politically justifiable from the standpoint of both the country's cultural past and its current vision of the rôle of education. Let us see now how the 'signal' was transmitted to the formal field.

3.2. *The system of action*
The orginator of the signal is this system which 'co-ordinates the actions of its participants' while at the same time preserving its structure to simplify, we can identify it as the subsystem of formulating and carrying out the Plan. It is this system of action which will witness the progress of the 'relatively stable' but oringally autonomous games, those of the Minister and his team (national and international advisers), of almost all the teachers' unions, and of a mixed group of 'actors-audience' of education (the central administration of the Ministry, students' and parents' associations, etc.).

In parallel with our examination of the dynamics of the field, we shall follow the dynamics of the concrete system of action in order to grasp its deeper nature. But first, we must draw a short portrait of the actors who will appear on the scene.

3.2.1. *The actors*

1) *The Minister,* whose age would seem to exclude the possibility of his occupying the post a fourth time in his career, is a former primary-school master, headmaster, an excellent teacher, and — founder of the principal union (ANDE). Convinced that the length of compulsory schooling should be increased, he sought from national and international 'experts' the universal justification of the renewal of education to support his arguments. Time was catching up with him; he wished to put the finishing touches to work commenced a quarter of a century earlier and thus find a place, with Mauro Fernandez, in the Pantheon of this country with an exceptional educational tradition. He is sure of himself. His decision to force the legislature to examine *and* approve his proposed law will measure up to his ambitions.

2) *His team,* consisting of two mutually-supporting elements:

i) The national technicians, Ministry officials individually selected by the Minister from among the active members or supporters of the *Liberación* party and, on the whole, competent in their field. Their specialized training (all had originally been teachers) had often taken place abroad, mostly in international organizations, some of them having already served as international 'experts' in other countries.

ii) The international technicians, expressly invited by the Minister, specialists in key areas of the Plan: economics, sociology, pedagogy, school building, Public Service, etc. Some had worked for the International Commission for Educational Development or had been particularly influenced by its general concept of an 'Educational City'. They shared with the national technicians a common vision centred on the two principles of educational democratization and innovation. This is the vision that was to be adopted by the Plan and defended by the Minister against the opposition of the unions.

3) *The unions,* four in number: ANDE (the National Association of Educators), APSE (the Association of Secondary-school Teachers), the 'College' (of graduates and professors of letters, philosophy, science and the arts) and the SEC (Union of Costa Rican Educators).[44] Only this last union, recently founded and relatively marginal in its small membership, was not systematically opposed to the Minister's projects. The first three, especially ANDE and APSE, representing the great majority of primary and secondary teachers, were fortunate in having an efficient structure covering the whole country. Their fundamental aim was to defend the interests of their members within an already privileged corporation that dominated the social scene: that of officials of the State. The leaders of ANDE and APSE, supported by the members (some of whom, while devoting themselves — *de facto* — full-time to their union activities) were working in the heart of the Ministry

44. See above, Part I, Chapter 3, section 3.3.2.

itself, and nothing was discussed without the unions being informed of it within minutes. When working hours, salaries or social benefits were discussed the leaders had the facts at their finger-tips. On the other hand, discussions on the content, methods, structures and spirit of education, on the idea of collective learning, on the co-responsibility of the community, were based only on very conventional arguments, in which the dialectic taught in 19th-century teacher training schools triumphed over a more modern dialectic, and in which the tradition of a 'bureaucratic militarism' tended to substitute itself for the innovating spirit of popular participation. The union negotiators, strongly supported by the rank and file (who generally obeyed orders), were past masters at arguing in a circle and played like a virtuoso on the organs of public opinion (full-page insertions in newspapers, public speeches and meetings, etc.). The large financial resources of the unions enabled them to make use of a wide range of the modern techniques common to any experienced pressure group.

4) Among the *actors-audience* making up the concrete system of action the following should be mentioned:

i) The adminstrative officials of the Ministry of Education opposed to the Reform, to the Plan and to the law. This group, more numerous than the Minister's 'team' and his sympathizers inside the Ministry, was composed of persons either affiliated to or favouring the opposition party ('Conservatives') or one of its numerous factions, or members of one or more unions, or simply officials who saw in the slightest move towards reform or modernization a threat to the established order which, they considered, existed for their benefit. Among these there were many who were opposed to particular items in the Plan which were directed — very exactly — against their own posts. The prospect of a central administration structured by 'objectives' (in which sections based upon 'subjects' would no longer have any place) was met by a closing of the ranks, as was to be expected, organised by the Inspectors of these subjects.

ii) Although it might be expected that the group most concerned with education would be the users of the public services — the pupils and students — they were in fact of very slight importance in the movement for reform.

— The associations of secondary-school students, which played a useful rôle at the level of the schools themselves, had neither the experience nor the means to undertake any useful activity on a national scale. Their support for the Plan at the National Seminar thus had no sequel when the confrontation between the Minister and the unions took place.
— Primary-school pupils, mostly too young, saw their interests defended by the Parents' Associations. These were practically non-existent outside the towns. But both the urban ones and the few rural ones were principally concerned with financing out-of-school activities (sports, music, leisure, etc.). In any case the most numerous and most

117

active members of these associations were, in the majority, teachers as well as parents of pupils. In other words, their rôle was by and large the same as that of the unions.

3.2.2. *The scenario*
STAGE 1: THE REFORM

Assisted by a few national technicans (who, during the pre-electoral period, had collaborated with him in drawing up the educational section of the *Liberación* party's political platform) the Minister prepares a proposal for reform centred mainly on increasing the duration of compulsory schooling. With the Council's endorsement, he selects a definitive team headed by the man who, nominated at first as Head of the Directorate of Planning in the Ministry, will subsequently become vice-Minister. For the great majority of the administrative officials, however, even if they cannot but be pleased by the increased duration of schooling (consolidation of the system, therefore of their authority), the intentions of the Minister and his team of 'modernisers' (or 'economists' — the words are synonymous in the minds of some ex-teacher administrators) are suspect. The proposals (the details of which they are ignorant, since these have been drawn up by a small group) are already regarded as a threat directed against them. They begin to express doubts regarding the competence of the team — and of its leader.

The unions keep a close watch, but do not as yet oppose the Minister's intentions. In fact, the extension of the duration of schooling can, *a priori*,

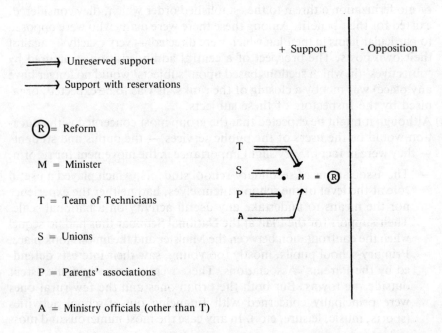

+ Support   - Opposition

⟹ Unreserved support

⟶ Support with reservations

Ⓡ = Reform

M = Minister

T = Team of Technicians

S = Unions

P = Parents' associations

A = Ministry officials (other than T)

only bring advantages for the teachers, since any increase in the number of pupils must entrain a proportionate increase in the number of teachers and the opportunity of offering to negotiate — who knows what? — a reduction in working hours, an increase in salaries, or social benefits.

The students do not react on a national scale. As for the parents' associations, they can see only advantages for the interests of both their children and the teachers.

Schematically, it can be said that the actors in the system are in an expectant mood: some regard the Minister's initiative with enthusiasm (his team), some with good will (unions and associations of teachers and students) and some with anxiety (officials opposed to the team).

The diagram of the first stage can be presented as follows: (see preceeding page)

STAGE 2: THE EDUCATIONAL DEVELOPMENT PLAN
The team of technicans is reinforced by international experts, suspected by the unions of importing reformist ideas from abroad (especially from Peru, where an educational reform is in progress). The unions move over to opposition, together with many Ministry officials, followed gradually by the parents' associations. Only the students remain attached to the idea of a remodelling of the educational system (the *rapporteur-général* of the National Seminar is a 15-year-old student). The Minister's isolation is increased, as shown in the following diagram:

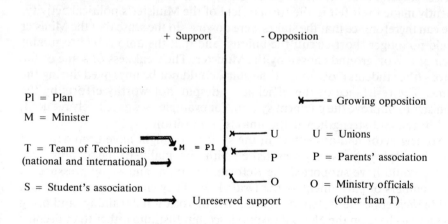

STAGE 3: THE DRAFT LAW
The technicians try to dissuade the Minister from taking this step. 'The Plan can well be put into operation without this legal sanction. To insist on it will

119

be useless provocation', they say. But in vain: the Minister insists, and comes up full tilt against the unions, the parents' associations, and the majority of the Ministry officials. In this struggle the students carry scarcely any weight and the technicians are no longer of use. The Minister is on his own, as this third diagram shows:

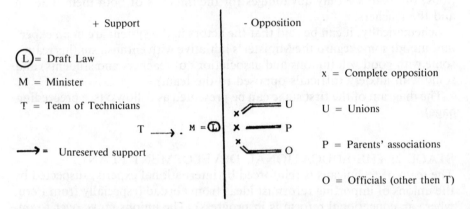

The concrete system of action within which this confrontation and this break have taken place, is carried by the weight of the forces present in an opposite direction to that hoped for by the Minister. As we have seen above, it is this that has displaced the entire field and upset the Minister's strategy.

These successive stages in the life of the concrete system of action have shown the modifications to the game caused by the actors — who have nevertheless stayed inside the structure of the system, even though this has subsequently made itself felt in the formal field of the Minister's political activity. We can therefore see that the stakes were down — in the sense that the Minister could no longer short-circuit the unions, and that the unions had to mount their attack on ground chosen by the Minister. The weakness of some of the actors (the students), obvious at the start, could not be improved during the game. The resistance of the officials — despite noteworthy efforts by the Minister to improve the payment system, for example — was scarcely reduced, and in the end strengthened the unions' opposition.

No new actor had any effect in the system. It might have been expected that the employers, usually dissatisfied with 'the quality of the schools' product', would have supported the Reform, the Plan, and — by pressure on the members of parliament — the Draft Law. They chose instead to remain inside *their* concrete system of action, that of vocational training, and bring pressure to bear on the National Apprenticeship Institute rather than become involved in the structure of a game over which, historically, they had no powers of control.

In the event, the employers considered themselves in this system as playing the 'social rôle' of parents, and thus transferred its potential for intervention to the teachers. A similar phenomenon accurred at the other end of the scale — among the workers. Their unions might have felt that the social status, the income, the productivity and the privileges of the teachers were out of proportion compared with their own situation. It might be thought, too, that the appeal in favour of a democratisation of education and of a more open attitude towards modern technology would at least have been listened to by the leaders of the industrial and agricultural workers' union. However, these workers and their unions, abandoning the 'class struggle', took no part in the concrete system of action other than as parents fighting for the future professional and social advancement of their children. And the guarantors of the successful achieving of this ambition could, in their view, be no other than the teachers themselves.

We have here, then, a system which firmly maintains its structure and its rules of the game. Any one of its actors who does not accept the rule that 'regulatory mechanisms' must be sought only *inside* the system thus becomes particularly vulnerable.

It may well be said that if the Minister believed at the start that he could convince the unions, he should then, as the opposition that he incited in them mounted, have sought support on the level of the formal field (President, Party headquarters, members of parliament) and from public opinion (prominent people, employers, workers' unions). As we have seen, that would not have been successful. Had the Minister exhausted the possibilities of the games inside the system, or had he not known that it could be opened to other participants?

The answer to such questions should enable us to draw a first boundary to the Minister's zone of indetermination.

Section 4. Indetermination and determination

The foregoing account has been strictly one of 'events' and has described the fluctuations of alliance, taken chronologically. Without attempting to discover and analyse the 'deep-seated' causes (which, as we have already suggested, would hardly apply to the surface of the events studied), let us now seek for some more general ideas which might apply well beyond the borders of Costa Rica.

It might have been of interest to try and justify, in the light of a State policy, the (relatively unilateral) attempt of the Minister to impose a Plan which was subsequently to be enshrined in a Law. While it is true that there was no contradiction betwen the policy of a new team favouring, for example, decentralization and industrial diversification, on the one hand, and the Educational Plan on the other, there was for all that no political directive for it.

The origin of the Minister's wishes must rather be sought, then, in the long saga of Costa Rican education. The Educational Plan must be seen in the context of the Minister's ambition to be the originator of a reform which would be the latest link in the chain that had commenced with the independence of the country. The myth of education in Costa Rica is a reality rooted in the long series of laws and measures marking the course of its 150 years of existence. When Figueres came to power for the third time, there was no chance that his associate in charge of the Ministry of Education would let slip an opportunity to improve — and even add to — a monument already erected, already respected.

For this purpose, principles to which no one could take exception were invoked. For example, 'The adaptation of education to the demands of modern society'. Furthermore, such aspirations were current coin in international circles where 'lifelong education' was being preached. It must be remembered that the period of the Educational Plan (1970-74) coincided with the publication by Unesco of the report *Learning to be,* under the chairmanship of Edgar Faure,[45] which highlighted the universal principles of a democratic, lifelong and essentially humanist education.

The general principles were an echo of Don Mauro, the positivist, but they came a century and a half later. Was it possible that these aspirations reflected a real wish on the part of the population as a whole? Did not the Plan change these principles into terms that in themselves ran the risk of distorting the educational and cultural 'mission' of the country? In fact, the new rôle assigned to a reformed education (inductive and pragmatic method, active rôle of the pupil, participation by the community, use of modern technology, close links with the productive sectors, etc.) was regarded by many not as a means for producing bourgeois citizens for the town and the tertiary sector, but as a way of building a society of 'manual workers', technicans, or rural workers implicitly condemned to remain just that.

The existing 'educational project' was not, in fact, rejected by public opinion, and even less by the unions. The 'New Project', on the contrary, was the work of a small team meeting *its own criteria*. The 'Diagnosis' thus had very few links with the proposals in the Plan. It did not describe the 'dysfunctions' which justify the 'Objectives' and the 'Programming'. Its reference to human resource requirements is static and arithmetical, using figures quantifying the relationships between employment and years of study, and does not take account of structural changes, as the study on Costa Rica by a team directed by G. Rama[46] mentioned earlier, tries to do.

In fact, the 'New Project' is based on a hypothesis built on universal ideals rather than on the national 'Diagnosis'. The Minister had borrowed from international organizations certain key ideas, and entrusted their definition

45. E. Faure *et al.,* op.cit.
46. Op.Cit., UNDP/CEPAL/Unesco, *Education and society.*

and elaboration to international advisers and to 'internationalised' national advisers. He accepted them and incorporated them in the Plan in order to enhance the value of 'his' project: nine years of compulsory schooling.[47] In so doing he neglected to put the 'international' ideas through a filter of realism, which might have spaced out the stages, arranged for negotiation with a wider sample of interlocutors, and brought to light problems — and solutions to them — likely to be of more direct interest to the teachers' unions. At an even deeper level, this filter of realism might have reminded the Minister and his advisers of the real nature of the society which was eventually to be transformed by the Plan.

But Costa Rican society (whose educational system, according to the words of the Plan, did not meet its needs) is in fact characterized by the growing importance of the tertiary sector, i.e. that of services, which is frequently fed by a bourgeois educational system producing managers of a type to cope with an urban society, essentially divorced from the centres of production.

Between 1963 and 1973 the number of persons with moderate and higher incomes had increased by 15 per cent, while the percentages of the economically active population with a level of secondary and/or higher education corresponding to these occupations had increased three times as quickly. This unequal expansion of employment opportunities and education would seem to indicate that there was at this time a tendency to train a larger number of persons than society could absorb in non-manual tasks. It should also be noted that secondary and higher education was attracting a growing number of students from the urban lower-income groups.

In other words, each year there was a higher proportion of persons who, even if they ended up performing tasks which did not fulfil the hopes raised by the formal education they had received, were attracted by the activities of the tertiary sector.

There was, then, in the minds of Costa Ricans a model of society which did not imply such profound changes as those forecast in the Reform Plan. In fact, the middle classes (on the whole, the most representative section of Costa Rican society) found in the type of education apparently based on the criteria of urban life the emancipating instrument which seemed the most effective means of escape from the rural milieu. The tertiary sector in the towns was a more attractive alternative than either the traditional agricultural sector or the industrial sector. These were relatively poorly developed and

47. The international team, while not rejecting the principle of nine years' compulsory schooling, did not regard this as a priority goal, in view of the need to make six-year schooling general in the first place, above all in rural areas, and of the importance of seeking alternative to the 'vertical' one-way type of education leading to the university. To many international 'experts', making nine years' schooling obligatory seemed to be a case of 'putting the cart before the horse'. In spite of these reactions, it is nevertheless clear that the proposal fulfilled a national ambition and, in this sense, was 'realistic'.

123

neither offered advantages, in income or status, comparable in the rural mind to those offered by the town, the administration and the private-sector services.

In analysing the causes of the Minister's failure, it is already clear the the principal cause lies in a vision of education which did not correspond with that held implicitly by the population. But the teachers were the principal beneficiaries — and, therefore, defenders — of the educational system as an instrument of social advancement. It was only natural that their unions should echo the concern felt by those for whom a condemnation of the education system would destroy this vision of the society to which they aspired.

A second cause of failure is not historic and ideological but strategic. In a highly democratic country such as Costa Rica — where the process of decision is shared by representatives of the people and of pressure groups such as the professional associations — a unilateral decision which does not include any negotiation (with one of the better-organised groups such as the teachers) amounted to a rejection of the traditional system of inter-organizational relations proper to Costa Rica. In such a democracy, recourse to a strategy of rupture is unthinkable.[48] It is completely at odds with the social fabric and political tradition of the country.

In fact, the Minister, in insisting on a debate on the whole system of education and so refusing to single out certain concrete points which might perhaps have been negotiated with the teachers (a directly interested party where any change in the system was concerned), cut out any possibility of a dialogue with them. The very idea of an overall reform, affecting the whole system at all levels and the machinery as a whole, included the teaching staff and the administrative staff. This strategy, decided upon unilaterally by the Minister on taking office, and which seemed to be rooted in the great reform of Mauro Fernandez some 130 years earlier, was unthinkable in the Costa Rica of 1970. To imagine that decisions could be taken other than by means of this 'game' is to close one's eyes to the way in which decisions are made daily in Costa Rica.

The rejection of a strategy of point-by-point negotiation with the unions, and the marked preference for overall reform,[49] decided upon in the privacy

48. Crozier and Friedberg, taking as an illustration the reform of hospital medical teaching in France in 1959, which was practically imposed by force, point out that there was a 'breaking-off' stategy in the decision making 'to the extent that, unconsciously at least, it aimed above all at shattering by a sudden stroke some of the basic mechanisms of the former system without caring much about the consequences, in particular about the subsequent application of the reform it was introducing. The reasoning underlying this strategy assumed that the system was incapable of assisting its own development, that if the interests concerned were consulted they would prevent the reform, and finally that the political system was too much in the hands of the establishment and that any public debate, as a result, would tend to give advantage to the latter'. Op. cit.

49. Even though between the first stage (Reform) and the second (Development Plan) the Minister seems to have given up the idea of change in which the Plan would be

of his own office, made the Minister vulnerable to the very strong reaction in not only union circles but also political. While he suffered the attacks of the teaching world and the malevolent neutrality of the political world, he had no support from other alliances on which he might have counted.

In fact, believing that he could win a victory on his own, which would then be entirely to his credit, he underestimated the support that he might have gained from 'new' allies who might have changed the system, and therefore did not seek the support — possible, though not certain — of the employers' organizations or the workers' unions. Staying inside 'his' system of action, he preferred to assist in the founding of a new University, whose representative would support him in the Higher Council of Education. He also believed that this University's responsibility for the training of teachers would bring about, if not the support, at least the abstention of the teachers' unions. Here he made an error of judgement.

Does this mean that our analysis of the selected 'event' should be restricted to the behaviour of a single man, his personality, his preferences, his choices? Can we ignore historical determinism, the consequences of social conflict and currents of public opinion? Asking the question in this form shows the process we are studying to be much more complex, and cannot — and should not — be limited to the will of one man.

Three vectors determine his behaviour to a great extent. They are more powerful than the will of a single man in the position of decision-maker, who only has this authority for a period limited to four years:

a) *The current 'traditional project of society'*
— the marked preference by parents and public opinion (for whom the unions were fluent spokesmen) for a traditional education, guarantor of the 'project of society' dear to the middle classes;
b) *The current 'reformist tendency'*
— the aspiration towards a continuity, made up of cultural tradition and the myth of education, spaced out by Reforms — milestones marking the 'great moments' in the history of education — reflecting a national reality;
c) *the current 'international principles'*
— the universal idealistic tendency towards 'democratisation of education'.[50]

The Minister is, therefore, carried by these currents and, like a sailor who knows his destination but is pulled by several forces, he tries to steer his ship

the first step, the remained faithful to the vocabulary of 'Reform' characteristic of the history of education in his country.
50. This expression must by no means be understood as equivalent to 'offering the same thing to everybody'. It refers to the decentralization of decision-making regarding the *nature* of the supply, and regarding the production and consumption of the resulting demand (see below, Part II, Chapter 2, section 4.3., footnote).

by making use of the force of each current while keeping his rudder in the direction he intends to go.

Of the three currents indicated, our decision-maker will try to make the most of the reformist tradition, for this will lead him to his goal. This goal, according to the evidence, is to enter history by the passage of a law bearing his name. We must not forget his promises to 'put the finishing touches' to the work begun 20 years earlier, his reference to all the heroes of the country's education who have preceded 'his' work. Finally, how else can we explain his determination to impose 'his' Plan on Parliament when its approval by the Higher Council of Education assumed that the necessary *and* sufficient conditions for starting the process of change had already been fulfilled?

In the sequential process of the decision relating to the draft law he found a few areas open to his activity in which his free will could intervene, always guided by his own choice. We shall call these 'areas of indecision'. On his ability to navigate across each one, without running into counter-currents, will depend the success of the undertaking.

We have selected the three decisions which seem to reveal most clearly the apparently free exercise of will: calling upon international organizations, refusal to invite direct and constant participation by the unions, and insistence upon a formal legal sanction.

4.1. *Internationalization of the goal*

One of the first acts of the Minister on his appointment was to request — and obtain — an exceptional degree of support not only fróm Unesco, but also from OAS and numerous bilateral sources, in particular the Federal Republic of Germany. He wanted this order to 'avoid the mistakes and profit from the satisfactory experience of other countries'.[51] The importance, both in numbers and in the variety of competences, of the Unesco mission which was to become identified with the drawing-up of the Plan was a fact unique in itself.[52] There is no doubt whatever that the Minister, in all good faith, hoped to surround himself with the 'best' advice so as to ensure the greatest possible chance of success with regard to the *quality* of the undertaking.

The Minister had read the 'Faure Report'. He was acquainted with the writings of Ivan Illich on the deschooling of society and sincerely felt that these theories, adapted to the situation in his country, could offer it a new horizon. His natural boldness led him to minimise the risks of such an undertaking, in the confidence that he could overcome any doubts about the wisdom of such innovations.

51. Op. cit., *Plan nacional — preentación a los Sres Miembros del Consejo Superior de Educación*, p. (i).
52. On two previous occasions, in 1951 and 1956, Unesco had played an important part in the preparation of educational reforms, but never on the scale of that international organization's participation by the mission of 1971-72.

However the wish to meet international standards in the concept of the social rôle of education came up against two serious difficulties. On the one hand, the number of competent national officials speaking the same language as the international 'experts' was very limited, most of them belonging to the Minister's 'team'. For this reason, though they could join in the discussions on an equal footing, they were neither numerous enough numerically, nor sufficiently high in the hierarchy to make their views prevail over the entire company. The 'demultiplier' effect of the advisers, therefore, remained in the end fairly limited. On the other hand, the number, seniority and experience of the foreign personalities made impossible total resistance by the nationals, who translated into local terms the general principles advanced by the experts. This translation was essential, not only to provide a realistic version of certain rather insubstantial concepts, but also to define in a concrete manner the exact steps between a universal goal and its realisation 'in the field'.

If we weigh these difficulties in relation to the three currents, we shall see that they come up against, above all, the 'project of society' current. In fact, the imperfect application by nationals of criteria imported from outside and recommended by non-national personalities could not fail to lead to opposition from the defenders of the established national order. It was on these grounds that the decision-maker's opponents criticized his objectives by rejecting the methods used (recourse to foreigners, influence of countries with a different ideology, incomprehensible language and rhetoric, etc.)

On the other hand, the taking-over of this area by the decision-maker in the chosen direction strengthens the 'reformist tendency' current, since just as in the past (when in the 1920s, 30s and 50s the country was seeking a new direction with the assistance of pedagogical and university experts from the exterior) recourse is being had to whatever is found to be most advanced and enlightened in educational matters so as to bring about a successful new reform. There is no incompatibility between the wish to do 'more and better' and the appeal to non-nationals to do it. What Decroly or the Chilean teachers proposed 30 and 40 years earlier enabled Costa Rica to have an educational system which was envied throughout Latin America, with the exception of the three countries in the extreme south. So, the decision-maker said to himself in 1973, why not make Costa Rica the show-room of what the international organizations recommend?

Lastly, it is obvious that the 'international principles' current could not but be strengthened by a determination so exactly matched to its nature.

So the decision-maker makes a choice in the area open to him which runs parallel to his aspirations: an international 'opening' conforming both with the reformist tradition and, naturally, with the 'international principles' even though this may be incompatible with the 'project of society' current.

This occupying of the area of indecision is the result of his subjective choice. We may well imagine that another decision-maker — his successor, perhaps

127

— will avoid battling against the 'project of society' current by refusing the assistance or presence of this same international organization. Here, then, we have a situation in which a personal choice can change the balance of forces, at least temporarily.

The decision-maker, consciously or unconsciously, estimates what he thinks he can gain and — sequentially — agrees to pay the price. Here, in the name of history and of the international reputation of his country, he runs the risk of being opposed to the existing image of the national society. He is not the creator of the currents, admittedly; but he hopes to take advantage of them. Now let us see the nature of the game in the second area of indecision.

4.2. *The edging-out of the unions*

As a founder-member of the teachers' union ANDE[53] and a former Minister of Education (twice), skilled at getting the better of the teachers' unions, the decision-maker was well aware of their basically conservative attitude towards any profound changes in the rôle of the teacher in the community. At the same time, he did not omit to keep them informed of his intentions, either through their representative on the Higher Council of Education or by direct contact with the leaders of the major unions.

In the Great National Consultation which culminated in the 'National Seminar on Education' he took care to invite the teachers' unions to take part in drawing up the Plan in the various working committees — on the same footing as the various Departments of the Ministry, headmasters, the University, the National Apprenticeship Institute, numerous international organizations, etc. The Minister did not fail to present the Plan at the congresses of the two major unions (APSE and ANDE), so that the teachers could be kept informed.

However, as a result of the fact that right from the beginning of the work of the committees, the unions criticized the spirit of the Plan and attacked most of the proposed measures, the decision-maker estimated that a direct dialogue with them could only lead to the gradual disappearance of all the proposed innovations. He therefore preferred to 'play the fish' by not giving them any privileged place in the preparatory work. Treated in the same way as the other participants mentioned above, the unions were offended — in their own view, they were the only interlocutors capable of conceiving and formulating a revision of the educational system.

The Minister therefore deliberately kept them at a distance, negotiating personally for their support with their representative in the Higher Council of Education and then trying to 'by-pass' them through the regional and national seminars.

In estimating the significance of the Minister's determination in relation to the three currents described above, we find that the gradual but firm

53. See above, Part I, Chapter 3, section 3.3.2.

elimination of the unions as privileged interlocutors, co-authors or even principal authors of an innovative plan was not entirely in contradiction with the historical path of the reforms undertaken in the 19th century (when the unions did not exist) or those which marked the first half of the 20th century, when the unions had very little power or were still working out their constitutions. In this area of indecision, the decision-maker, by choosing to act personally, was simply following the line of the great decision-makers whom he quoted as examples. His determination, therefore, is in line with the 'reformist tendency' current.

It seems unlikely that the 'international principles' current had any influence in either direction. Admittedly, the international organizations recommend 'participatory planning', but they do not put forward a table of precedence for those participating in the decision which would give the unions a favoured position. All the same, the personal feelings of the international technicians, seeing the systematically negative attitude of the unions towards any reform not conceived and carried out by themselves, cannot be ignored. It would certainly be an exaggeration to claim that these non-national officials regretted the absence of the trade unionists — as such — in the groups drawing up the Plan, but it would be equally false to conclude from this that the elimination of the unions from the decision-making process was in accordance with criteria laid down by the international community.

There remains the third current: 'traditional prospect of society'. There is scarcely any question that here also the decision-maker deliberately chose to go against the image — an image not admitting any improvement — that the unions were defending. By eliminating them from the dialogue, because he suspected them of being opposed to any deep-seated reform, and by reducing them to the level of mere participants *inter alia* in a national process, he opted for a more dynamic image of Costa Rican society then the one that the unions were defending.

In penetrating into the area, he scarcely let himself be carried along by the current of which the unions were making use. His choice did not have the assistance of a reforming current sufficiently strong to offset the movement started and developed by them. Whether or not he had selected this area in full consciousness of its consequences, it is a fact that the negative attitude of the unions had forced him to follow sequentially a path whose ending was, as we know, was not the one on which he had counted.

4.3 *A law at any price*

Although the Plan now had legal existence, and some of its proposals were beginning to be implemented, the Minister did not consider this enough. To conform with the reformist tradition, a reform, if it is to gain an unquestioned place in the national educational history, must be embodied in a law. This seemed so obvious to the decision-maker that even in the second year of the implementation of the Plan, when the curricula for the reformed education still had not been prepared, he set in motion the drafting of the law and its submission to Parliament. At the same time, he commenced his campaign among the members of his own party with the aim of winning over the Members of Parliament.

All this shows the decision-maker to have been strongly influenced by the custom of marking each new step in progress of education by a law. He himself had been responsible for steering through Parliament the Basic Law on Education in 1957, when he was Minister for the second time. It was in his view unthinkable that the most definitive work that he had undertaken should not go down to posterity in the form of law which his Cabinet colleagues and the members of his party in Parliament could not fail to endorse.

This deliberate choice was not only compatible with the 'reformist tendency' current but also seemed to the Minister, caught up in the confrontation with the unions, to be the only answer to their obstruction.

But, as we know, the Members of Parliament preferred the 'traditional project of society' current, which the unions defended and which, of course, was incompatible with the decision-maker's determination.

If the Plan contained principles and measures that would change the face of society as the members of Parliament conceived of it, how could these Members stand up against the unions, who had succeeded in imposing themselves on public opinion as the only people competent to deal with educational matters? The decision-maker's choice was a paradox: he wanted to be faithful to the reformist current, but at the same time he hoped to obtain the support of those who preferred the *status quo*.

His other support, the 'international principles' current, was of little help to him at this stage. Naturally, there was no international decision justifying an intransigent appeal to a law but, in addition, the international team was also opposed to it as a matter of principle. If the Plan was a 'step in the continuous process of change', why embalm it in a law which would in due course entrain yet another in order to continue the process?

The decision-maker's choice of this area of indecision as a battlefield was as much a product of the wish to satisfy his own preference as a tactical necessity for overcoming union opposition. It could be argued that this game was the product of the preceding game, that of carrying out his operation without the overbearing participation of the unions.

In the light of this analysis, and by comparing the three selected areas with the three currents to assess their compatibility, we arrive at the following diagram. (see opposite above)

This diagram shows that the decision-maker has chosen, in the areas open to him, a direction clearly oriented towards the reformist tendency and has shown clear opposition to the image of the 'traditional project of society'.

Can we conclude, therefore, that the decision-maker's criterion was simply incompatible with the prevailing conservative tendency of the Costa Rican middle class? This would be an over-simplification, since if we examine the

Currents	Areas		
	Internationalisation of the goal	Edging out of the unions	A law at any price
1 Traditional project of society (TPS)	−	−	−
2 Reformist tendency (RT)	+	+	+
3 International principles (IP)	−	$0^{(+)}$	$0^{(-)}$

− Incompatible   + Compatible   0 Neutral   ( ) Advisers' tendency

way in which he acted in a fourth area of indecision, that of the Constitutional Amendment for the nine years of compulsory schooling, we shall see that while satisfying his own private criterion of rationality, the Minister was carried along by all three of the currents identified above.

In so doing, he succeeded in 'playing' all three forces and not opposing any:
— Respect for the cultural tradition and the myth of education ('reformist tendency' current): Costa Rica becoming one of the first Latin-American countries to offer nine years of compulsory free schooling.
— The image of the project of society as transmitted by public opinion and the unions ('traditional project of society' current): the increased schooling means both a greater possibility of absorption of the 'educated' in the urban middle class and a still greater influence on the part of the teachers.
— Application of an international trend ('international principles' current): extension of schooling in the 'Educational City', where other forms of learning will continue the process.

This can be shown in the following way:

Currents	Area
	Constitutional Amendment
1. TPS	+
2. RT	+
3. IP	+

Let us try to draw some conclusions. Are there in fact areas in which the decision-maker can direct, or is not he himself directed? Of the three currents that influence education in the country, the Minister himself seems to

131

be directed completely by one and partly by another. The reformist tendency has apparently carried him along all through the areas we have analysed, and so have the international principles whenever they were applicable. The decision-maker seems to have been sent off course by the current which bears the society — somewhat conservative, urban, tertiary — of a Costa Rica which, 100 years after Mauro, no longer wants to run any risks.

The structuring of the middle class, so clearly illustrated by the teachers' trade-union organization, becomes a factor for maintaining the results already gained rather than one for conquering new values. The decision-maker seems to have insisted on defending his convictions, without taking much notice of the hesitations of the unions and political class regarding innovations in the country's education.

That this should have happened at the price of what will be considered *a posteriori* as tactical mistakes or errors of judgement matters little. The decision-maker, in 'secret session' with his advisers, was pursuing a dream. His authority and will were not enough, on their own, to make it a reality. The 'determiner' has become the 'determinee'.

And yet. . have we not the right to enquire whether this battle really was waged in vain? Certainly, ten years later, in the Universities and in the Ministry itself traces of this great national debate can be found. Can it be held that education in the country and the controversy that continues to surround it have not, after all, gained something from the seeds that were sown? Are there so many examples, throughout the world, of reforms as far-reaching as this one being effectively carried through?

CHAPTER II
Guatemala

Section 1. Description of a micro-structure

1.1. *The social context*

Guatemala, former seat of the Captaincy-general of Central America during the Spanish colonial period, was in 1974 the most populous country of the region, with six million inhabitants in an area of 110,000 sq. km. The structure of society is characterized by two factors: (i) it is predominantly rural (65 per cent of the population live in collectivities of less than 2,000 inhabitants) and (ii) the population is divided by a combination of criteria (race, ethnic group, language) into two separate categories: Indians (at least 50 per cent of the population) and non-Indians or *ladinos*.

Unlike Costa Rica, Guatemala was colonized very rapidly and forcibly. The result was a régime of *latifundios,* large properties concentrated mainly in the low-lying fertile plains and in the hands of a few large landowners specializing in exportable produce (coffee, cotton, bananas, meat).

The system depends on the existence of a manpower reserve. This consists of 56 per cent of the economically active population, employed (on average) for 120 days a year and receiving, on this basis, an average yearly income of about $.80 per rural inhabitant.[1] The rest of the year these seasonal workers live by subsistence cultivation on land that is becoming more and more scarce.

This social organization gives an incomes pyramid which is sharply pointed, with a very wide base, and with little permeability between the two principal layers. A Guatemalan sociologist and two collaborators have constructed a table which shows the ethnic and economic segmentation in 1964 (Table 5).

In the book which this Table is taken, its authors describe the socio-political situation in Guatemala more than 20 years ago, as shown in the Table, as a 'taking-over of the means of production that results in a monopoly', on

---

1. This should be compared with the average income per inhabitant in urban areas, namely $745 — nearly ten times as much.

the one hand, and an 'antagonism between *ladinos* and Indians amounting
to a class relationship' on the other.

TABLE 5. Guatemala: social structure, 1964, by numbers and percentages

Ladinos (non-Indians)			*Indios* (Indians)		
	Number	%		Number	%
Middle class, international, professional	4,000				
Middle class, agro-export	15,000	0.3	Middle class	500	0.06
Middle class, services	150,000	3.3			
Lower middle class	700,000	15.7	Lower middle class	200,000	4.5
Proletariat, industrial and agricultural	700,000	15.7	Proletariat, agricultural[1]	200,000	4.5
Semi-proletariat	600,000	13.5	Semi-proletariat[2]	1,300,000	29.0
			Mozo Colono[3]	300,000	6.7
Sous-proletariat			Lumpenproletariat	300,000	6.7

1. Seasonal workers with some guarantee of regular employment.
2. Owners of *munifundios,* obliged to do seasonal work as harvesters.
3. Agricultural workers without *munifundias* and without the slightest guarantee of
   employment — inevitably swell the ranks of the 'lumpen'.

Source: S. Guzmàn-Bökler, J.L. Herbert and J. Guan R., *Las clases sociales y la lucha
de Clases en Guatemala,* Revista Alcro, 1971.

Table 6 shows the distribution of income from agrarian property in 1970.

TABLE 6. Guatemala: distribution of population and revenue from agrarian holdings,
1970 (percentages).

Category	Population	Revenue
Wage-earners without land or owning a maximum of 4 hectares	83.3	34.8
From 4 to 35 hectares	14.1	21.8
More than 35 hectares	2.6	43.4

Source: *Datos e indicadores para el área educación y desarrollo rural: Guatemala,* op.
cit., p.78, Table 7.05.

The public sector has only limited means, as the State Budget represents barely 10 per cent of the GNP — virtually half the corresponding proportion in Costa Rica. The result is a public service which is weak both in numbers and qualifications compared with the private sector, which in practice dominates the economic and political scene. This scene is characterized by an authoritarian climate maintained by a very small number of centres of real power.

The period we are studying (1974-78) cannot be described as one of continuous armed confrontation between the forces of order and the clandestine forces opposed to the régime and its structures. All the same, these were certainly years of bloodshed: 820 people were assassinated in 1976 and 890 in 1977, nearly all for political reasons.[2]

1.2. *Types of education*

In a context such as we have described there was no tradition of schooling and no pressure groups working for the generalization of education. The educational system is mainly urban, a direct descendant of Spanish colonization, which from the beginning of the 18th century to the middle of the 19th founded, first, the San Carlos University and then various centres of religious instruction in the larger towns.

Both in content and structures the school system was designed for the sons of créole and propertied families. It was affected by certain European influences, English and German in particular, when colonists of these nationalities came to replace the Spaniards. Next North American type colleges and universities were established, as the opening of the Panama Canal and, later, investment linked to the exploitation and export of tropical fruit drew Guatemala into the United States' sphere of influence. These various foreign contributions, however, did not affect the actual objective of schooling.

Despite declarations in the various Constitutions and Laws on Education, primary schooling can in no way be described as compulsory, universal or free. The reality can best be shown by some statistics.

The literacy level of the population had been rising gradually during the previous twenty years, reaching some 46 per cent in 1973. But this average figure conceals considerable disparities.[3] For example, the rural average is

2. *El grafico,* 18 December 1977, p.5, Guatemala. According to Amnesty International (*Le Monde,* 17 December 1979), 20,000 persons 'have been victims of the army, the security forces and the 'death squadrons' between 1966 and 1976'.
3. See the three following studies on this subject:
   a) A. Gutiérrez-Renon and W. Moreno-Sineiro, *Alfabetización, dessarrollo y participación,* Unesco, Guatemala, May 1977, published on the occasion of the Seminar on legislative policy for literacy and the execution of a national programme for the five-year period 1978-82 (3-6 May 1979, Giudad de Guatemala).
   b) A. Gutiérrez-Renon, *La desigualdad de opportunidades educativas de la ninez Guatemalteca,* Unesco, Guatemala, April 1977, published on the occasion of the Seminar for the Institutions for Child Protection.

27 per cent, while that of the towns is 82 per cent. In the rural world, 15 per cent of the Indian population are literate (men: 25 per cent, women: 5 per cent) and 43 per cent of the non-Indian population (whereas in the towns 88 per cent of non-Indian men are literate).

This situation is accounted for by figures of school attendance. In 1974 only 48 per cent of children aged 7 to 12 years were enrolled. Once again, behind this national aggregate there exist two very different worlds: 56 per cent of urban children are in school, 25 per cent of rural children, and 15 per cent of Indian children.

The lack of rural schools and teachers on the one hand, and the language gap between teachers and Indian children on the other, account for both the low enrolment figures and the high rates of drop-out and repetition. Less than 40 per cent of rural children entering the first year complete the cycle of six years. Among Indian children enrolled in the first year of primary education, 80 per cent drop out of the system before the sixth year.

At the secondary level enrolment is very slow, covering only 10 per cent of the 14-19 age-group. But this figure hides a simple truth: 28 per cent of non-Indian urban youth attend colleges (mainly private), compared with 0.92 per cent of rural youth. The corresponding figures for the Indian population are 4.6 per cent in the towns, and 0.19 per cent in the countryside.

Higher education, in 1974, was divided according to its cost. The State University (San Carlos) teaches the 'expensive' subjects (medicine, science, engineering) and has 80 per cent of higher-education enrolment, while the subjects that do not involve expenditure on infrastructure or high running costs (law, letters, social sciences, company management, etc.) are taught in four private universities who share the remaining 20 per cent of students.

As for the enrolment rate in higher education, while it is very small overall for the age-group (4.6 per cent in 1974), given the great number of students who are working and who, generally speaking, are older than the official age, it covers mainly the output of urban private colleges. The 'filtering' rôle of private secondary education is obvious: education at this level is not subsidised, but it guarantees entry to a free and subsidised university. So the well-off families 'invest' in secondary education in order to reap the benefit of an 'expensive' education which is in fact free, since it is subsidized in part by the taxes paid by those who can send their sons to fee-paying secondary schools.[4]

c) S. Lourié, *Inequalities in education in rural Guatemala,* Paris, October 1978, published on the occasion of the Seminar organized by the IIEP on educational inequalities, Paris, October 1979.

4. See the comments by S. Lourié on the contribution by C. Munoz Izquierdo y A. Hernandez Medina, 'Financiamiento de la educación privada em América Latina' In M. Brodersohn y M.E. Sanjuro (eds.), *Financianmiento de la educación en América Latina,* Mexico, Fondo de Cultura Económica, Banco Interaméricano de Desarrollo, 1978, pp.321-331. This work, based on the official data of five countries (Colombia,

This trend appears very clearly when we examine the relative amount of public funds available for each level of education. While only a fraction of the children of primary-school age in fact receive the education guaranteed by the Constitution, and the very large majority of those who complete their secondary education are admitted to a higher education, the Government, which in 1972 devoted 60 per cent of its educational budget to primary education and 13 per cent to higher, announced five years later a cut of 10 per cent in the resources allocated to primary education and an increase of 50 per cent in those for higher education.

To conclude this brief survey of the implementation of educational policy in Guatemala during the 1970s, let us assess the political disposition by means of that infallible indicator, the allocation of public funds (Table 7).

TABLE 7. Proportion of the State budget devoted to the Ministry of Education

Year	Percentage	Year	Percentage
1970	16.2	1976	11.7
1973	14.9	1977	9.6
1974	14.2	1978	9.6
1975	13.5	1979	8.9

Source: Official figures from the Directorate of the Budget (USIPE), Ministry of Education and Culture, quoted in 'Insuficiencia del presupeusto de Ministerio de Educación, para 1979', submitted by the secretary of the Higher Council for Economic Planning to the Minister of Education, 1979.

We have already seen that in relation to its GNP Guatemala spends less on education than its neighbours or — with the exception of Haiti — than any other Latin-American country. In relation to public funds alone, the figures show a gradual but continuous reduction.

1.3. *Juxtaposition of context and types*
This series of figures leaves us with the impression that the Government is not making very much effort to mobilize additional resources in order to compensate for the shortcomings of the educational system. On the contrary, it seems to prefer a further reduction in the slender resources available.

The lack of a system that would be a true reflection of the educational needs felt by the people, on the one hand, and the small number of teachers,[5] as well as their lack of union organization and their feeble

Guatemala, Mexico, Peru, Venezuela) clearly demonstrates this 'filtering' function. See, in this connection, the works of J.P. Jallade, in particular *Public expenditure on education and income distribution in Colombia,* Washington D.C., World Bank, 1974. (World Bank occasional staff paper No. 18).
5. 0.2 per cent of the total population; in Costa Rica the proportion is 3 per cent.

political power on the other, are clearly different from the situation in Costa Rica. This explains why no particular pressure is brought to bear on the Government that could possibly act as a counterweight to a system which has as its outcome the maintenance of a rural manpower in an under-educated condition. In other words, the maintaining of this reserve of manpower, untrained and with no professional structure, is made possible only by not educating it.

There is thus practically no complete rural education, and the chief means of entry into university education lies in urban, private secondary education.

Section 2. The immediate antecedents

2.1 *Trends*

In contrast with the case of Costa Rica, where the analysis was based on a brief survey of the past history and the educational tradition, the examination of the selected 'event' in Guatemala will not try to find a historical foundation. Quite simply: education as an instrument of the people has scarcely any antecedents. With the exception of the period from 1945 to 1949,[1] when a civilian, Juan José Arevalo, was in power, and directly afterwards under the government of Colonel J. Arbenz-Guzman (1950-54), we can identify scarcely any real attempts to base education on the deeply-rooted wishes of the peoples live in Guatemala.

Although the main objective of these two governments was to initiate and consolidate a process of agrarian reform Arevalo, an educationist and philosopher, was concerned even before taking up the reins of government with 'the two orphans, education and agriculture'. The greater part of his efforts was concentrated on the second of these 'orphans'. Arbenz made the effort to create a myth of 'peoples' education', by generalising primary education (especially in the rural areas), creating numerous rural teacher-training schools, developing the use of the various vernaculars as the means of expression in the high plains, homeland of most of the Indian population, and by making compulsory a legal disposition ordering the creation of schools in all agricultural or industrial enterprises with more than 100 employees.[2]

1. It was in 1944 that General Ubico, a dictator whose authoritarianism is not denied by any section of the Guatemalan population today, was defeated in elections generally recognized as 'free'.
2. This was laid down by Article 103 of the 'Organic Law on National Education', which was in force until 1979. The 'Law on National Education' which replaced it in 1979 repeated this requirement word for word in its new Article 85. According to this Article, every private enterprise that recruits seasonal workers is bound to provide education for children accompanying their parents, in schools functioning on the property of the enterprise concerned. Unfortunately, while there is an obligation to send the children to existing schools, there is no equal obligation for the proprietors of such enterprises to provide such schools. It does not appear that these two obligations have been particularly strongly insisted upon since 1954.

But the 'counter-revolution' which put an end to Arbenz' experiment also did away with the changes he had started to introduce, and set a more conservative mark on the educational system for the twenty-five years after the ten years of Arevalo and Arbenz. There were, it is true, certain humanist Ministers who from time to time toyed with the idea of a relatively more open system of education, but on the whole the governments that followed one another after 1954 preferred, by and large, an educational policy that can best be described as somewhat cautious. To combat the deficiencies in schooling and the widespread illiteracy, only mobilization on a national scale could have generated and channelled the necessary human and material resources for improving the situation. This did not happen, as the budget figures in Table 7 above make clear.

Except for these two 'moments' in an educational history which started with the 'discovery of a continent by Europeans (but which goes back for centuries before that, with the traditional teaching of the Mayas and earlier civilizations), no historical trend in education can be traced which was not a continuation of the traditional European education designed by and for the foreign colonizing class to begin with, and then for the créoles.[3] The historical current is therefore the one which gave rise to the 'project of society' limited to the micro-structure described above.

The event which we intend to describe in detail will be related solely to the government immediately preceding it. In fact, whatever moment we may choose (outside the period 1945-54), we shall find the same social structures which set their mark on the educational system all through the period 1954-74.

We will commence our story with a rapid glance at the educational policy of the Government headed by Colonel Arana Osorio, who from 1970 to 1974, with an iron hand admired by all devotees of order, completed the repression of the insurgent movement that had developed since 1963.

2.2. *Yet another plan*

Colonel Arana's Minister of Education, halfway through his period of office, drew up a report of the activities he had carried out and set out the objectives to be reached in the form in which they were included in a 'National Educational Plan' for the period 1972-79.

As far as the past was concerned, the Minister noted in his Plan that for the period 1969-72 the proposed goals had not been reached and that certain educational projects had not been realized. 'To sum up, it is evident that the purpose for which the Plan (1969-72) was drawn up has not been fulfilled at all, and that population growth and the services offered to this population had followed a completely natural trend'.[4]

3. See the impassioned and exhaustive work by Severo Martinez Pelaez, *La Patria del Criollo,* San José, 4a ED., Editorial Universitaria Centroamericana, 1976.
4. Guatemala, Ministerio de Educación, Oficina de Planeamiento Integral de la Educación (OPIE), *Plan Nacional de Educación para la República de Guatemala, 1972-1978,* Guatemala, 1973, p. 5.

In the light of this experience, the 1972-79 Plan proposed to make up for past errors, and — without any change in the 'natural' trend — the Minister, recalling what education ought to be 'in the future', proposed to reach a 'complete coverage of primary education', to make the first cycle of middle-level education compulsory, to give clear priority to adult education, to make use of 'new concepts and techniques for out-of-school education', to introduce 'a polyvalent middle-level education in which there would be a wide range of specializations', to improve teaching by making use of 'basic contents' (*sic*), 'to plan the development of human resources before the development of economic resources', to regard education not only as a government responsibility but also as a process involving 'the entire society', and, lastly, 'to give a stimulus to lifelong education'.[5]

The new Plan laid down numerical targets for the extension of the rural primary-education network, the total enrolment of which should progress from 31.7 per cent of the 7-12 age-group to 33.3 per cent in three years and to 36.9 per cent in eight years. To reach this goal it would be necessary to make good the 'deficit' of rural teachers (only 18.5 per cent of the demand was satisfied in 1972) by aiming at filling 41.6 of the demand in 1980.

Using the same calculations, the Plan proposed additional enrolments in the teacher-training colleges, secondary education, the literacy programmes etc.

What was the outcome of all these ambitions? In addition to the 'natural' growth of the system, the years 1970-74 saw three new programmes under way. The first aimed at the extentsion and improvement of primary education (PEMEP), and the second, Basic Rural Education (EBR), was intended for the adult population. The third programme was concerned with middle-level education (PEMEM). The first two were financed by bilateral aid from the United States (USAID), while resources for the third were provided by the World Bank. All these were limited both in size and in impact, the first two being essentially of an experimental nature, even though PEMEP did set a new fashion in its two Rural Teacher-training Colleges, one of which (in the High Plains area) was intended for young Indians of both sexes. The third took the form of new building with modern equipment — but without suitably trained teachers. The training school for middle-level teachers (EFPEM) was, in fact, under the University, and jurisdictional quarrels with the Ministry meant recruitment of its graduates by the Ministry was non-existent or at best doubtful.[6]

5. Ibid., pp.x-xi.
6. In this respect, it is interesting to note that the Dean of Faculty of Letters, responsible for EFPEM, and the Director of EFPEM, were to become Minister and Vice-Minister respectively in the following Administration. This did nothing to reduce tension between the Ministry and the University, as the new Minister had been defeated as a candidate in the elections for the Rectorate of the University, and his relations with his ex-opponent in no way fostered the use that the Minsitry might have made of EFPEM graduates, victims of two successive antagonisms.

Six month before handing over to his successor, the Minister reduced to more realistic proportions the tasks which he considered to be the responsibility of his Department: reducing the rates of drop-out and repetition, improving the training of teachers, and making the Ministry itself more efficient. We are a long way from the exhaustive list drawn up barely eighteen months earlier. This is not surprising, since that list was the outcome of wishful thinking, general and generous, which was inconsistent with the Government's budgetary decisions. In hard fact, the 'natural' inclination was still continued — a few schools were scattered grudgingly about the countryside, and most of these offered only an incomplete education — on average two years.

Section 3. A film in two parts

3.1. *The plot and the scenario*
At the same time (the beginning of 1974), six months before the take-over of power by the team that would be elected in the following spring, the Secretary-general of the Higher Council for Economic Planning (the Minister of Planning) announced his intention of preparing, for the first time, a sectoral plan for education.

The Secretary-general, although basically a 'technician' with economic training, already enjoyed a solid reputation in Latin America. He considered that the education sector had been neglected in previous Plans and it was time to regard it as a whole, closely linked with the economic and social realities of the country. It no long suffced to patch together a collection of abstract projections, worked out in the privacy of the Planning Office of the Ministry of Education alone. He wanted a document that would break clean away from the traditional repetition of the same old rhetoric and give particular importance to a programme aimed at overcoming the effects of the scarcity of rural schooling. In his view, the marginalization of the Indian population was not only incompatible with the social obligations of the State but also acted as a brake on the development of a more diversified, more productive and better integrated market.

He entrusted an official of his Secretariat with the task of setting up teams of specialists from the Ministry of Education and various public and semi-public bodies. Two or three international officials were invited by the Secretary-general to take part. In the inspiration and approach of the Secretary-general we can recognize the same ambition and dynamism that were characteristic of the Costa Rican Minister.

Already, then, before the 'elections' of April 1974 and immediately after, but before the new Government took over, these teams were at work on a plan. This Plan had two main features: (i) a more equitable allocation of resources for a generalised rural primary education of at least four years and a search for means of avoiding wastage, and (ii) a programme for out-of-school education in line with local conditions and designed to absorb the non-enrolled children and illiterate adults of the rural areas — starting with the High Plains.

This attempt was the first of its kind in Guatemala, in the sense that since 1954 there had been no such clear definition of the precise goal to be reached, nor any such setting-up of interministerial teams, collaborating to work out its modalities. They based these on an inventory of all out-of-school educational acitivities, public and private, to form part of a proposal for an education intended for the entire population. The 1975-79 Plan was a realistic first step, since it almost corresponded with the term of office of the Government elected in 1974 and was based on the Secretary-general's forecast that there would be an appreciable increase in the proportion of the Budget devoted to education, of which at least 10 per cent would be devoted to out-of-school programme alone.

This document, an integral part of the multisectoral Plan, was completed in time for the Secretary-general of the Higher Council for Economic Planning to present it formally to the outgoing Minister of Education some weeks before the handing-over of power to the new Government. And as soon as the new Minister was appointed, his predecessor handed over to him the draft Sectoral Plan for Education.

Between these two formal acts of handing-over, a dramatic event took place: the Secretary-general who, it was rumoured, would become the new Minister of the Economy (but who most wanted to remain in his office to ensure the appropriate 'follow-up' of the Plan he had prepared) was the victim of an attempted assassination. This attempt nevertheless produced the result probably desired by its perpetrators (never certainly identified) the victim, miraculously spared, left the country.

Before this event, however, the Secretary-general had decided to strengthen the team dealing with Human Resources (Education, Health, Social Welfare and Housing) so that the sectoral Plans could be finalized — especially for Education. He laid particular stress on this in the recommendations he left for his successor.

The new Minister gave the responsibility for these sectors to an engineer, previously the Executive Secretary of the Association of Private Universities in Central America. This official, politically very discreet, was dynamic and well received by external aid agencies. He set up a group (as numerous as it was inexperienced), financed almost entirely from out-of-budget sources. This team, assisted by one or two international 'experts', took over the draft Plan for the Education Sector, added a chapter on Science and Technology and one on restructuring the entire Education sector including the Ministry itself. This document, ready in November 1974, was to become the 'National Plan for Education, Science and Culture, 1975-1979'.[1]

1.Published subsequently under this title by the Ministry of Education, Official Publishers 'José de Pineda Ibarra', Guatemala, 1975.

Between June and November 1974 the Minister was acquainting himself with the working of his Ministry; in September 1974 he was faced with a teachers' strike — a very rare event and the only one in the four years that he held the Education portfolio.[2]

During this period of adaptation the Minister had to face not only the tension caused by the strike but also the inertia of the administrative machinery, whose structure seemed to offer a challenge to his authority.[3] Unlike his opposite number in Costa Rica, he himself had not known during the election campaign that he would be chosen as Minister. In consequence, he had not been called upon to define a 'platform' for education which could provide him with a framework for action at the time of his taking up of his duties. His reactions during his first weeks in the ministerial office were essentially empirical. He found that the senior permanent officials of the Ministry were playing a corporativist kind of game, and that the Planning Office, which could have been useful to him as a Private Office, was leaderless since its chief had been elected to Parliament.[4] He therefore surrounded himself with trustworthy persons with a University background.

At this moment that there comes into play one of those random factors that influence the shape of final decisions: the Director of Human Resources for the Plan is a close relation and intimate friend of the Minister. Too much occupied with daily problems, the Minister himself has no time to prepare a policy that could be considered as his contribution to defining the educational future of the country. He has admittedly inherited the 1972-79 Plan from his predecessor, but this document is not his own work and he has no wish to follow the path laid down for him by another.

When his relative presents him with the Plan drawn up on the initiative of the Executive Secretariat for Economic Planning and revised by his team, the Minister does not appreciate the link between this document and the draft Plan bequeathed to him by his predecessor, which he has not had time to read, so very forbidding is its appearance.[5] He listens attentively to the ex-

2. He settled this problem in an original way, by asking the Journalists' Union (whose members had at first been on the side of the teachers) to arbitrate between himself and the strikers. The Association of Guatemalan Journalists (APG) were faced with the demands of teachers who had been dismissed for protesting against the transfer of two of their number. After a long period of negotiation between the teachers and the journalists, during which the Minister took no part but was kept informed, a compromise was agreed and adopted by both sides: the Minister re-engaged the dismissed teachers, and the entire profession undertook not to resort to strike action during the Minister's tenure of office.
3. See above, Part I, Chapter 3.
4. This former Ministry official was later to become Chairman of the Education Committee in the Congress of the Republic, and was able to give occasional support to the Minister.
5. Mimeographed on thick paper this lengthy document, full of tables and diagrams, weighed one kilogram. It was duly placed on a shelf in the library, where it stayed for a long time, apparently, before joining other records in the waste-paper basket.

planations given by the reviser, and studies the document itself in detail. He finds that it meets with his approval, and decides to adopt it as his own — in agreement, of course, with the General Secretariat for Economic Planning.

Thus, in spite of his relative isolation from the rest of the administrative machinery, he succeeds through his frequent and direct contacts with his personal friend, in winning over to his side *de facto* the Human Resources team for the Plan, which plays the part of his 'think tank' and provides him with the 'platform' he needs.

In this way, less than six months after taking office he is equipped to inform the Cabinet of his Plan and arrange for information lectures at the Institute of Vocational Training, meeting-place for representatives of the private sector, the University, foreign and international aid sources etc., in order to make known his intentions.

On 12 February 1975 the President of the Republic signed the decree setting up the Out-of-school Programme and creating the Governing Board for Out-of-school Education, as recommended by the Plan. On 28 Feburary, during his monthly press conference, the President, surrounded by his Ministers, presented the complete Plan to the public in the name of his Government.

He commenced by giving the figures of illiteracy and of school enrolment, emphasizing that '70 out of every 100 children are deprived of any possibility of education'. He recalled his declarations during the electoral campaign to create an education 'for life and for work'. 'This', he said, 'is precisely the aim of the Plan'.

He emphasized that traditionally, education had been dependent on foreign theories and solutions, but that — at last — his Government's Plan for education scrapped out-of-date models and offered 'a new perspective with suitable Guatemalan solutions for education'. He then quoted the Plan's aim to have 80,000 children in school in 1979 and set up educational activities for those who had not been able to benefit from schooling. 'We shall reach some 600,000 Guatemalans by the end of the five-year period, ands thus reduce illiteracy to 30 per cent of the population'.[6]

At the same press conference the Minister indicated, after the President's declaration, that the Plan was intended principally for the rural areas, 'for the countryside, for our peasants and workers, for it is in these areas that we find our chief problems, our chief needs, and our chief obligation', and he emphasized the importance of the out-of-school programme, which he described as 'innovative'. He reminded his audience that in 1979, 80,000 children would be in school.

In the full assurance of a policy and a programme endorsed by the highest authorities of the State, the Minister entrusted the reponsibility for the out-of-school Programme to the Directorate of Human Resources of the

6. The newspaper *El Gráfico* (Guatemala), 1 March 1975, p. 4.

Secretariat-general of the National Council for Economic Planning (CNPE), presuming that the Governing Board would appoint the necessary personnel.

In the meantime, the Minister turned his attention to his own Ministry with the aim of implementing that chapter of the Plan which dealt with its restructuring. His first priority was to provide himself with a more useful system for decision-making than the one he found on his arrival. The Plan had proposed the creation of a Secretariat-general with five branches: Infrastructure, Teaching Content and Curricula, Information and Statistics, Budget, Organization and Methods. The Minister set up a working group to define the legal and administrative bases of this new body, whose existence would depend on the legal arrangements to be approved by Parliament, probably as part of a Law on Education. However, Members of Parliament are in no hurry; whereas the Minister cannot start on changes, even minor ones, that he hopes to effect in the content and structures of the educational system as long as he is without 'his' instrument, the Secretariat-general.

The year 1975 passed in meetings and negotiations for matters concerning the Out-of-School Programme and preparing the text of a law authorising the setting-up of the Secretariat-general.

Despite the President's press conference, the Executive as a whole gave scarcely any priority to the Ministry of Education; the 1975 Budget, it will be recalled, amounted to no more than 13.5 per cent of the total State Budget. In 1976 it dropped to 11.7 per cent. The oil crisis, the clearing and exploiting of the *Faja transversal* (a belt of fertile land on the edge of the northern jungle), the defence of cotton prices, difficulties caused by increased urban traffic, some unrest among civil servants demanding a rise in salaries, military requirements — all these matters required the attention and resources of the authorities.

At the end of 1975 the Minister regretted the delay caused to the implementation of the Plan, which was due to commence in January 1976. He explained the situation by blaming the Legislature: 'certain activities will not be possible on the dates foreseen, since they require the legal foundation which they will receive in the new Law on Education, regarding which the Minister has submitted observations and suggestions to the Congress. To the extent that the honourable Congress has delayed the adoption of this Law, it is only to be expected that certain restructuring measures cannot be started until a later date than that originally foreseen'.[7] He could not hope for a decision in Parliament before March 1976 at the earliest.

On 22 Feburary 1976 the country was shaken by an earthquake which resulted in over 20,000 dead, 100,000 injured and 200,000 homeless. While this event necessitated a faster timetable of activities in connection with the Out-of-school Programme, as we shall see later, it obviously delayed still further Parliament's examination of the Law on Education.

7.The newspaper *La Tarde* of 24 December 1976 (Guatemala), p. 6, gives a full report of the press conference.

This Law was not finally adopted until 1 December 1976. The whole of the following year was devoted to drawing up the Decree of application. During the years 1976 and 1977 the Ministers, while awaiting these measures, were dealing with strikes and demonstrations by secondary-school students, caused mainly by their demand for the dismissal of certain teachers and heads of colleges on the one hand, and for the provision in the schools of furniture and equipment considered essential (especially after the destruction caused by the earthquake) on the other. In this connection the Minister signed an agreement with the World Bank with the aim of obtaining a second loan to finance the building and equipping of secondary schools.

During this period the Minister was not neglectful of the teachers, and created for them an Institute of Social Prevision (pensions fund and supplementary benefits).

In April 1978 elections were held, and in June the Minister handed over his department to his successor.

The Minister of Foreign Affairs, the Minister of Labour and he himself had been the only three to have remained at the head of their Ministries throughout the life of the Government that had appointed them. Their seven colleagues had all been replaced during the period. The Minister had been able to put out the fires before they could gain too great a hold.

This rapid, jerky and impressionistic film of the four years of the Minister's mandate has prepared the ground for an analysis of two of the three decisions which he himself[8] regarded as the most important during his tenure of office: the Out-of-school Education Programme, and the creation of a Secretariat-general. By retracing the steps that led to these two new activities we may perhaps be able to identify the area of indecision of the Minister, the nature of his strategy, and the effect of his decisions in the context of the micro-structure which was his field of action.

3.2. *The out-of-school education programme*

We have seen that a Governing Board (Junta) for out-of-school education had been set up in February 1975 by the President of the Republic. This Board, with the Minister as Chairman, consisted of representatives of all the public bodies responsible for out-of-school educational activities, and had two principal tasks. The first was to co-ordinate in a sectoral perspective on all of these activities (carried out by Ministries such as Agriculture or Health and bodies such as the Institute for Vocational Training, the Programme for Community Development, etc.); the second was to be concerned with the initia-

8. During an extensive discussion with the author on 11 May 1980 the former Minister referred to his three 'principal' decisions. The third, which is not dealt with in the present work, concerns the initiative taken by the Minister in August 1975 to set up the Central-American Educational Co-operation, a loose structure enabling the six Ministers of Education of Central America to hold periodic meetings and, through a permanent secretariat, work towards close co-ordination in certain priority fields.

tion and orientation of the new 'module' programme of out-of-school education to which the President and the Minister had referred during the February 1975 press conference.

This 'modular' programme had formed part of the Plan in a long-term perspective, the proposal being that between 1975 and 2000 the entire population without schooling, regardless of age, should have the benefit of the programme throughout the national territory. The activities proposed for the first five-year period should reach 600,000 people, particularly in the High Plains area where the inhabitants are mainly Indians.

Given the importance that the Minister attached to the new programme,[9] he was naturally anxious that his Ministry should be responsible for it. At the same time, he realized that the inertia of the Ministry would frustrate the development of an innovating activity which, by definition, needed to have a significant degree of autonomy. In addition, the Plan had proposed the creation of an authority relatively independent of bureaucratic constraints. These two trends were likely to be contradictory. Undoubtedly they would become one of the principal concerns of the 'Junta'.

The Minister had appointed his Vice-Minister as delegate to the Governing Board. In her view, the solution to the problem of the education of the illiterate population and the non-school population rested principally with the schools. As a result, she could hardly asset herself as co-ordinator of out-of-school educational and training activities when dealing with the representatives of other bodies. The oppressive bureaucratic procedures of the Ministry and the financial difficulties resulting from a very limited budget[10] delayed the appointment of an Executive Secretary for the Programme. In turn, this made it necessary for the Human Resources team of the Secretariat-general of the Plan to attend to the preparatory work for the

9.'When I was informed of the school enrolment figures I realized that there would never be sufficient resources to offer six years' primary schooling to all the children of my country. Something had to be done, regardless, without embarking on never-ending educational reforms. Out-of-school education was the solution. As well as offering a genuine opportunity to a large number, it would need the support and participation of other Ministries, thus reducing the burden falling on me without minimizing the leading rôle that would be played by my Ministry. This could become the star programme in social affairs; education would be the guiding and co-ordinating sector of of change at village level. Excellent social prospects would be opened up. The programme could become a powerful political instrument. At the same time, there was a risk: the programme might become a sort of Sorcerer's Apprentice . ..' (interview of 11 May 1980). To obtain the necessary support of the President, the Minister pointed out to him the importance of this programme as a complementary activity to the co-operativist movement, which the President had said he supported. By this means the Minister obtained the commitment of the Cabinet and of the President.

10.The Minister was seeking external financing. The fall in the world price of coffee and the first major petroleum crisis caused a spectacular reduction in the resources which had been envisaged by the former Secretary-general of the Plan.

Programme, work consisting for the most part in studies and field surveys which were considered to be too theoretical by certain critics.

The preponderance of the Ministry and the complicated delays in the introduction of the 'module' gave the Junta hardly any opportunity to exercise its function of co-ordinator of the entire out-of-school subsector.[11]

The February 1976 earthquake obliged the programme to take practical action in three villages particularly affected by the catastrophe. In May, the head of the secretariat was appointed at long last. Little in his previous career can have predisposed him for his new functions: he was a graduate of the Military College (*Escuela Politécnica*), a Public Works Engineer, an architect. Nevertheless, he enjoyed the Minister's personal confidence.

Between the summers of 1976 and 1977, the programme reached 124 communities — some 8,000 people — and was beginning to build up its structure.[12]

Institutional difficulties were not lacking: a 'school' tendency, competition with other programmes directly under the Ministry of Education, poor co-ordination with other public bodies, excessive formality and gradual bureaucratisation, etc. At a deeper level, villagers found noticeable difficulty in defining their 'educational needs'.

In 1981 the 'module' reached some 30,000 people. The Executive Secretary was a very good teacher, fully aware of the rôle that this programme could eventually play. In spite of the changes of government, the spirit and the methods of this programme remained the same. Although the Government had also started up a literacy campaign based on the schools, a significant number of men, women and children remained faithful to the 'module' programme, feeling that its empirical approach had more to offer them.

3.3. *The sectoral unit for research and planning*

In accordance with the Plan for which he had made himself responsible, the Minister was determined to create an instrument that would give him a better knowledge of the work of the central administration and, therefore, enable him to control and orientate the officials and teachers who composed it.

In June 1975, four months after the public announcement of his objectives, he submitted a draft Law to the Congress. In December he was forced to realize that the Legislature had not yet approved the text, and that the introduction of a number of measures was being held up.

In anticipation of the adoption of this Law, the working group that had been set up to define the modalities of the future Secretariat-general became

11. The Education Plan covered three subsectors of the Education 'Sector': in-school education, out-of-school education, and science and technology.
12. Three technical departments formed the backbone of the central programme administration in the capital; 6 departmental and 19 zonal co-ordinators were appointed by the Secretary of the programme, and 220 monitors, villagers responsible for local encouragement, were chosen by the rural collectivities themselves.

a Mixed Commission (Ministry of Education, Secretariat-general of the Plan, Directorate of the Budget, Directorate of the Public Service) with the task of drafting the Regulations for implementing the Law, specifying the new functions of the interministerial bodies of the Education Sector and the Ministry, and defining the rôle of the unit originally conceived of as a Secretariat-general, but which was now to be called the Sectoral Unit for Educational Research and Planning (USIPE). In May 1976 the Commission agreed the functions of the USIPE and the levels of recruitment (and therefore of remuneration) of the specialists who would compose it.

In the Congress the debate on the Budget was slowly proceeding. By the beginning of November 1976, only 10 of the articles of the new Law (out of 74) had been adopted. The Minister therefore made strong representations to the Chairman of the Congress, who prevailed upon the Members to speed up the debate on the Draft Law, which was finally passed on 1 December. This Law was not itself the authority for setting up the USIPE, but it made possible this setting-up by nullifying previous texts.

In the draft Decree prepared in May 1976 by the Mixed Commission, two articles define the nature and functions of this structure. In the first (which will become Article 7) it is laid down that the USIPE is 'responsible for studies, for the planning and for the organization of various programmes of the Sector, and is responsible directly to the Minister's Office'. In the second (Article 8) the USIPE is given the responsibilities drafting, and of controlling the implementation of, the Plan for Education, Science and Culture, and of co-ordination with the Secretariat-general of the National Council for Economic Planning.

The regulations for the Law on National Education, in theform of a Decree of Application (*Acuerdo Gobernativo*) was not finally signed by the President of the Republic until 7 November 1977.

In the interval between the passing of the Law and the signing of the Decree of Application, the Minister was able to nominate the Director and Assistant Director of the USIPE, four Heads of Division to be the basic 'framework' of the organization), and the staff taken over from other units suppressed or changed by the decree and for whom integration into the USIPE had been planned. The slowness of the administrative process prevented the appointment of the remaining personnel.

It seems likely that one of the reasons for these considerable delays was the lack of discussion in the Mixed Commission. In fact, as long as the Commission could not define the criteria for staff recruitment, neither the Directorate of the Budget nor that of the Public Service, both of which were represented in the Commission, could ratify the proposals put forward to it by the Minister for staff appointments, which often reflected preferences based on criteria more personal than professional. It was not until January 1978 that the full technical staff, composed for the most part of teachers, was in fact in readiness, just at the time when the Administration was entering that period of almost lethargic caution normal in pre-election periods and which is the prelude to the arrival of a new Minister and his team.

An experienced observer who had followed the whole affair very closely has stated: 'Given the nature of the organization of the Ministry and its lack of high-level staff, particularly in professional fields other than teaching, it may be said that the lateness of the reorganization of the Ministry and the delay in starting up the USIPE were an important cause of the feeble capacity shown by the Minister of Education to make any significant progress in implementing the National Plan for Education, Science and Culture, 1975-79'.[13]

Section 4. The areas and the decision-maker's game

The useful distinction between the formal field of the political system and the system of action by which the Minister operated within his administration enables us to trace the double path of our decision-maker. In contrast to the situation in Costa Rica, any analysis of the education game in Guatemala must start by an appreciation of the phenomenon of the struggle between the two classes that occupy the contemporary socio-cultural area. There will therefore be frequent references in the succeeding pages to 'social and ethnic class' or a 'propertied and dominant category', or to the strength of the 'established powers'. In fact, education in Guatemala is still the outcome of a structure built up by the history of the 19th century and hardly changed since. Hence any study of this area must start with the forces that have shaped and preserved it.

4.1. *The field of the political system*
Here we shall find two movements which are complementary but which function at different rhythms resulting from the extremely individual political context of Guatemala.

4.1.1. *In the Executive*
The decision-maker had a clear objective: to make 'his' Plan a Government instrument, with the support of the President and the Cabinet and in, particular, to obtain unqualified support for a programme of out-of-school education. The first stage consisted in his receiving the 'raw material' from the Council for Economic Planning who in turn, in the second stage, gave their full support to the adoption of this document during Cabinet discussions.

13. A. Gutierrez Renon, *Informe de fin de misión: Proyecto de Apoyo al Plan de Desarrollo Educativo de Guatemala,* Guatemala, Unesco, 1978. (Proyecto PNUD/UNESCO GUA/75/002, GUA/76/014, GUA/77/008)

During this second stage the decision-maker found a willing listener in the President, to whom he submitted the Plan as the instrument for fulfilling the President's intention of successfully introducing a co-operativist policy in the rural milieu.

In a third stage, once the Plan had been endorsed by the President and the Cabinet, the decision-maker sought to gain the collaboration of two bodies without whom the Plan would remain a dead letter: the Directorates of the Budget and the Public Service. The first obstacle now appeared: the Ministry machinery resisted this call for open communication by a world vowed to secrecy: the world of the 'teacher-bureaucrats.[1] It seems that the Minister was not able — or did not want — to overcome this resistance too abruptly. He let precious months go by before the resistance of the two Directorates gave way — they demanded a show-down with the machinery, but this never took place.

We can already see a considerable difference between this situation and that of Costa Rica, where the President had encouraged, right from the start, and then supported the voluntarist and 'engaged' initiative of the Minister.

4.1.2. *With the Congress*

All through the period there were skirmishes with a Congress jealous for its formal prerogatives — the only realm in which it could exercise any kind of power. In fact, the legislative body, composed of Members representing the 'official' parties, had in reality very few opportunities to use its powers of political initiative. As far as the major options were concerned the ruling party, or the coalition on which it is dependent, represents the interests of a certain class which has a direct influence on the activities of the State through the intermediary of the elected Government. The quasi-automatic support of the Congress is assured from the moment that the majority of the Members belong to the same party or to the coalition — to which they owe their election.

When it is a matter of questions which do not affect the direct interests of the class which controls the party and, through the party, the Government, the task of law-making is willingly left in the hands of the Congress. Guatemala has, in fact, inherited from the days of the Spanish colonialism a legalism which today has reached proportions verging upon blockage.[2]

In other words, when a question is presented for debate in the Congress, it can be taken for granted either that its solution is not a matter of great urgency, or that it is not of high political importance, or, finally, that it is a matter which is of absolutely no general interest but concerns the functioning of the legislature or the position of the Members as such.[3]

1. See Part I, Chapter 3, section 3.
2. A law governing the operational budget forbids any Minister to authorise the transfer of funds from any budgetary item, including one covering his own subsidiary units, without a Government decree signed by the President and the entire Cabinet.
3. Thus the parliamentary sessions of 1976 and 1977 discussed in the most elaborate detail

It may be deduced from this that if the Congress took so long to pass the Law on Education, which was simply a legal device to enable the Minister, by means of the Decree of Application, to make the changes that he wanted in his Ministry, it was because this Law, in the opinion of the ruling party, had only a secondary degree of interest.

In spite of the Minister's speeches in the Congressional Committee on Education, this Committee referred the text back with amendments from the Legislature which had nothing to do with the original objectives of the Law as submitted by the Minister. The text was then sent back to the Committee for 'cleaning'. In accordance with the rules, three readings in full session were necessary before final approval of the text. Above all, it was essential for the Minister to play the game of appearing and speaking to the Members, and to 'negotiate' the examination of the draft while closing — or pretending to close — his eyes to the bargaining among the Members over the use to be made of the special funds allocated for the appointment of teachers. Let us recall the situation in Costa Rica, where the Legislature enjoyed real power and where, by refusing to permit a debate on the draft law, they condemned it without a hearing.

4.1.3. *The confluence of apparent indifferences*
From our examination of these two movements it appears that on the whole, while the Executive has not hampered the Minister's initiative, it has not manifested a directing attitude or a dynamic support which would have enabled the Minister to accelerate the process. In the case of the legislative power, the delays have meant that the Minister is far from achieving the objectives he had set himself. It should be noted that, unlike the Costa Rican situation, there have been no 'stages' clearly differentiating the attitudes of the field. Admittedly, the President's press conference in which he denouced the shortcomings of the past and pointed out the merits of his Government's Plan for a better future might be considered as a first stage, followed by his indifference or benevolent but silent neutrality as the second.

The control of national life is in the hands of the agro-exporting class (and the 'service middle class' dependent on it), the military, and the established church.[4] These three organise a consensus among themselves in which each reaps the benefits that justify such an alliance. It follows that if there is *no* consensus between these three centres there is little hope that any measure whatsoever will be given concrete expression.

When the President announced that he was firmly on the side of the Minister and his Educational Plan, his speech — for public information — was coloured by a certain political liberalism. When he took an interest in the development of the co-operative movement his speeches were, once again, apparently

the way in which Members would use the credits which had been allotted to them direct
for the payment of the teachers appointed by them.
4.R.N., Adams, op. cit.

in favour of change in the rural milieu and in the structure of the agricultural sector. In the same way, when — at last — the Legislature approved the Law on Education, certain of the Articles of this Law expressed the aims of education in terms that showed a notable willingness to make changes.[5] But these speeches and texts do not necessarily reflect a consensus of the forces conditioning contemporary society; rather, they reflect wishful thinking and good intentions. These intentions are, all the same, approved by the 'consensus', who from the viewpoint of the particular interests of the ruling classes find in them nothing that needs to be re-worded.

In such a field, the word and the action follow skilfully patterned paths; though they sometimes cross, they never join in a single united movement in the same direction. For the decision-maker, the field is neither hostile nor favourable towards him. He rejects, all the same, any measure opposed to the implicit consensus.

Thus, for example, to demand of the President that he intervene with the Legislature to speed up the debate on the draft law, or that he sign the Decree of Application that has been sitting on his desk for the past year, would be tantamount to assuming the validity of one or both of the following hypotheses:

1. There is a consensus of the 'three' powers in favour of an Educational Plan, of a programme for out-of-school education, and of a law to bring them into being.
2. The decision-maker is prepared to meet with a refusal which could have negative consequences for his project and his personal position.

Let us look at the implications of these two hypotheses in detail:

Hypothesis 1
i) The Plan
The idea of a plan drawn up by public servants to specify collective behaviour in advance is incompatible with the consensus. Indeed, neither the private lay sector of education, which supports and defends the agro-exporting class, nor the private religious sector, which is protected by the same class and the church, is particularly interested in the public sector's attempt to 'direct' the orientation of education in the medium term. Since empiricism had hitherto guaranteed the maintenance of the *status quo,* it is somewhat disquieting to see the 'technocrats' attempting to take over a sector which is still faithful to its reproductive rôle. The Army, for its part, had no objection to a Plan which would at least have the merit of proposing activities that would be visible and controllable. Its support, however, did not go so far as opposition to its two allies. There was thus no feeling of enthusiasm for a Plan.

5.*Article 14:* (c) encourage critical analysis . . ; (d) encourage commuity progress; (e) strengthen the spirit of human solidarity . . .; (h) bring about the defence, the knowledge and the respect of human rights . . .; (j) strengthen democracy, liberty and social justice.

ii) The out-of-school programme

The private sector, though not yet fully informed of the content and ambitions of the programme, had already made known its reservations. Admittedly, it could not openly oppose an embryo programme which had not yet been given a trial, and it could not but be pleased that an education which was, after all, 'second-class' should be provided for the little Indians. A few isolated voices could none the less, be heard[6] questioning the need for thrusting on 'people who do not want them and are quite happy as they are', educational programmes which they would not know what to do with. In any case, activities of this kind, they said, could be organized more efficiently by private bodies. The church regarded the programme with interest but would prefer the religious organizations to be in charge of it. The Army was not against it. Here again, there was no consensus in favour of the project.

iii) A Law on education

A legal text could not in any case impose too precise principles or measures which might, in some cases, be opposed to the specific interests of the 'three powers' which made up the consensus. It was necessary, then, to see that this text did not contradict any of the positions upheld by the consensus. Provided it consisted of generalities and declarations of a universal nature, a law might be admissible. *A priori,* the consensus had no wish for new dispositions in the legislative field. The text would therefore have to be found acceptable or — at worst — harmless in the eyes of each of the 'three powers'.[7]

For none of the measures taken by the Minister, then, was there a common will reflected by the 'consensus', which should be seen as the expression of the majority equivalent to the principal 'pressure group' in the country and, as such, capable of supporting the Minister in his dealings with the President.

Hypothesis 2

The sensitive tolerance of the power exercised by the agro-exporting class, when faced with decisions affecting the *status quo,* gave rise to a situation of unstable equilibrium. In this situation the decision-maker probably felt that any attempt on his part to force the President's hand would be particularly unwelcome, for two reasons. First, such insistence would have become known

6. Especially the representatives of CACIF (Federation of Employers' organizations, consisting of the Chambers of Commerce, of Agriculture and of Industry) sitting on the Governing Board of ICAP (Institute for Vocational Training).

7. The first Preamble to the Law does not fail to describe education as having for its goal 'the integral development of the personality, physical and spiritual well-being . . .the civic advancement of the population, the arousing of patriotism and respect for human rights . . .' The second lays down, among other things, that 'education is the most efficient means of capitalizing on the richness of a nation, and therefore the economic resources invested for its development are transformed into immeasurable profits of all kinds for the country; etc.'.

by those who did not want the Minister's inclinations for change to develop into actions. The 'powers' had become used to a situation in which the *activities* of the Executive did not become *actions* without their *carte blanche*. To violate this accepted code was the surest way of seeing a ministerial mandate come to a rapid and abrupt end; and the resignation of the Minister would almost certainly be followed by the interment of his favourite projects. Secondly, to emphasize the urgency of certain decisions was equivalent to inviting suspicion. Many questions would be asked, seeking to uncover the presumed hidden motives of the Minister for forcing the hand of Member of Congress or the Executive. In the political context surrounding every move of the Minister, it was more than likely that some would wonder what profit (material or political) the decision-maker would gain from the implementation of an out-of-school programme or from a new machinery in his own Ministry.

In either case, the personal situation of the Minister would become extremely precarious. In fact, it is likely that any insistence on his part would have been interpreted either as wishing to impose a new order without passing through the normal decision channels, or as defending a private interest not specifically negotiated and therefore suspect. The price of such inclinations could only be his exclusion from the decision circuit.

From examining these two branches of the alternative we see that the decision-maker — whether to succeed in his designs or for political survival — could use only very slight and very rare pressure while waiting for the Legislature and the Head of the Executive to choose their moment to intervene so as to enable him, in due course, to take action.

4.1.4. *The search for support*
In such a heavily mined field the Minister could advance only with the greatest caution making sure that each step that he intended to take was known in advance, thus freeing him from all suspicion. For this purpose he needed to be able to count on a network of acquaintances who, once informed, would inform others (who might not otherwise always understand the reasons for his behaviour).

Thus did the Minister systematically establish links so he could periodically keep the President (with whom he had a private meeting each week, in addition to the regular Cabinet meetings) fully informed of his intentions and actions.

Furthermore, he knew he could count on the support and understanding of the Secretary-general for the Plan, who hoped to see a better structure given to a Ministry which in the past had only rarely given proof of any finanical or administrative strictness. The rôle of modern 'manager' which this high-ranking official played allowed him to support the Minister's initiatives as conducive to greater efficienty of the State machinery.

Finally, the Education Committee of the Congress was kept informed of the decision-maker's projects and knew that certain of its own preferences would receive a favourable hearing from the Minister.[8] This Committee acted as a go-between with the Chairman of the Congress — politically friendly with the Minister, but for this very reason not anxious to identify himself too closely with the views of the decision-maker — regarding the Minister's wish to see the Law finally approved.

In thus building up a restricted network the decision-maker was in a perfect position to keep a watch on the activity of the Legislature and on the President's decisions. This vigilance would be rewarded: it gave him the opportunity to intervene at the few rare favourable moments. We have already seen that the decision-maker's game in his political field was characterized by caution; now, we can add vigilance.

4.2. *The decision-maker's private office*
His cautious nature and his distrust of the administrative machinery led the decision-maker to surround himself with persons of his own choice who would not be likely to misinterpret his intentions. The drawback to this *in camera* procedure is obvious: it would reinforce the climate of suspicion of the Minister already prevailing within the Ministry and among the teachers. Knowing this less than a year after his appointment he dismissed his vice-Minister, who — though a faithful friend from University days — was liable to compromise his relations with the high-ranking officials of the Ministry, whom his immediate collaborator had usually ranged against him. Furthermore, the vice-Minister did not enjoy the full confidence of the political superstructures, so undermined the Minister's own credibility.

The Minister replaced him by a teacher, formerly the Headmistress of a private school and — more recently — Secretary-general of the Faculty of which the Minister had been Dean. She succeeded in re-establishing an appearance of administrative cohesion. The Minister delegated all the day-to-day administrative matters to her, keeping for himself the control of the game in the political field and the preparation of certain decisions which he was resolved to take during the course of his mandate.

The three other actors with whom he intended to go forward were:

---

8 While the out-of-school activity was being developed the Chairman of this Committee (formerly the Director of OPIE, see note 3, page 171) suggested the organization of a public meeting on the expediency of starting a literacy campaign of the traditional type, taking the Brazilian movement (MOBRAL) as a model. Though this was contrary to his own intentions the Minister was careful not to discourage the Member, who organized a seminar entitled Seminario sobre Política Legislativa en Alfabetización y Ejecución de un Programa Nacional para el Quinquenio 1978/82, Ciudad Guatemala, 3-6 de Mayo de 1977. Certainly the holding of this Seminar ensured that the Minister could count upon the gratitude of the Member . . .

The Secretary-general of the Ministry, future Director of the USIPE, a personal friend and University fellow-student;
The Executive Secretary of the Council for Out-of-school Education, a personal friend;
The Director of the Department of Human Resources in the Secretariat of the Plan, a close relative and personal friend.

It seems very clear, therefore, that the closed system in which the decision-maker worked was characterized by the network of extremely personal alliances woven between himself and those he had selected[9] in order to entrust to them the task of either thinking out his actions or of realising them. It should be noted that, naturally enough, he pursued his game well outside the Ministry machinery, since his other plan was to take it over.

He avoided widening his decision system at any time by incorporating in it any consultation whatsoever with the teachers or students. We have seen that in the power hierarchy the trade union organization — teachers or students — has scarcely any place in Guatemala. So he sought neither to inform them nor to provoke them, not wishing to have them either as allies or as enemies.

The two 'loopholes' he had chosen (USIPE and Out-of-school) were precisely of a nature not to *arouse* the interest of these two potential forces. But this is exactly the nature of the political field too: the absence of interests or motivations which the decision-maker had carefully not aroused. The decision system where texts were prepared, tactics and manoeuvres discussed and actions worked out which would consolidate the choices, could well remain restricted, to the same extent as the two possible openings retained by the Minister could be developed without have recourse to anyone else. The decision-maker could pursue his game through a personal network of confidence that he himself had created with persons coming from outside the Ministry. There was no group of national and foreign technicians working in full view inside the Ministry, such as we saw in Costa Rica.

This work, relatively concealed and necessarily slow, permitted the gradual drawing-up of the texts (Law and Decree of Application) in an atmosphere where the negotiation went on entirely *outside* the concrete system of action. This system was of use only for preparing the decisions and — in a second very brief phase at the end of the Minister's mandate — for their execution. It was never the place for negotiating; this priviliged place, as we have seen, is found at the level of the political field.

In complete contrast to Costa Rica, the system of action is a closed world, limited to intimate friends. There is no appeal to pressure groups or to public opinion. The Guatemalan microcosm is, obviously, the explanation of this

9. We cannot avoid mentioning the part played by certain international advisers, though without regarding it as important other than at the conceptual level. They certainly played a part in the formulation of the concepts and the texts that subsequently gave rise to the USIPE and the Out-of-School Programme.

difference; but, perhaps paradoxically, it enables the decision-maker to set in motion new methods which carry in themselves the potential for change.

4.3. *Openings and delays*

Let us recall the characteristics of the Guatemalan microcosm. Since the Spanish colonisation there are two populations (Indian and *ladina*), mainly but not exclusively following the town/countryside separation. By and large, the school system reproduces and maintains this structure. The weakness of the public sector, which is designed to serve the ruling interests, considerably reduces the initiative that the bureaucratic machinery might otherwise show. Closed in upon itself, it tends to become a source of employment rather than a reforming current for education.

This situation is dramatically different from the popular current, the democratic aspiration and the national myth of education which are the mark of public life in Costa Rica, where pressure groups, unions and the legislature share with the Executive the national responsibilities. All the same, this situation creates possibilities of change — but at the price of considerable delays. And it is difficult to say to what extent these delays cancel out the expected advantages.

i) *The openings*

The opportunities for change occur in the gaps which the routines of bureaucratic behaviour leave open. The absence of pressure in favour of a complete democratisation of education[10] enables the scholastic institutions corresponding to the aspirations of the dominant class — essentially urban in their way of life — to continue unchanged. At the same time the administration, since it is powerless, remains in a sort of political twilight. Since it is not feared, its day to day activities are not watched. Provided that it does not bring about a clash with the interests of the dominant class, it can manoeuvre discreetly inside the areas which are considered harmless and, consequently, as its own preserve. An administrative initiative taken under such conditions does not encounter any oppostion of a political nature.

Of the two openings chosen by the Minister, it is clear that the first — the creation of the USIPE — cannot give rise to any fears or suspicions. Improving the functioning of a Ministry notorious for its laxity, its delays, and its budgetary and administrative incompetence cannot but be recognized as a salutary measure by the currents which run through the political field. And in so far as the decision-maker's system of action is deliberately restrained

---

10. The 'democratisation of education' implies a qualitative change (an education chosen and defined by those who hope to profit by it, and in conditions which correspond to their conditions and to their vision of their future) and a structural change (forms and methods effectively available to the greatest number). See ''Major Programme II: Education for all'', in Unesco, *Second Medium-Term Plan 1984-1989,* Paris, Unesco, 1983 (4XC/4 Approved), pp.67-85.

in order to prevent any reaction by the machinery (which might feel itself threatened), all opposition is minimized.

As regards the other opening — the out-of-school education programme, in which the principal innovation was to be the 'module' — this would certainly be unlikely to worry the Establishment. The dominant class were convinced that the sole instrument — of which they could envisage only the maintenance — for social reproduction was the school education on three 'floors' reserved for their sons and daughters. In their eyes, therefore, the module of out-of-school education could be nothing more than an 'education on the cheap' for the Indians — children and adults. They estimated that the eventual consequences of a programme of this nature could always be brought under control before they reached the critical mass beyond which qualitative 'jumps' might ensue. In the meantime, they could only be pleased with an activity which was addressed to only a minority of the population of the High Plains but which demonstrated to the eyes of the world that Guatemala was inaugurating an original type of learning with a mass vocation. The President, too, could sing the praises of this programme. Need we add that the feeble capacity of the Minister as principal executive agent was reassuring for those who might fear that the launching of the module would happen too rapidly?

In such conditions the Minister could venture into an area of indecision and fill it with these two operations, having taken beforehand every precaution not to provoke a sudden — and definitive — reaction.

ii) The delays

Delays take place at three different levels: the Executive, the Legislature, and the Ministry machinery. These delays are at one and the same time mechanisms of inertia and mechanisms of defence.

We have already seen that the delays which occurred in the examination of texts by the Legislature or in the signing of texts by the Executive were due less to a resistance — or even opposition — than to an indifference which could be explained by the absence of pressure from the power consensus.

Admittedly, on the side of the Members of the Congress, there was the permanent negotiation, balancing the advantages which they sought from the Minister against the examination and approval of projects that he awaited.

In the two cases we are considering there was the tragedy of the earthquake of 1976, which relegated to a very low order of priority the regularisation of the solutions proposed by the Minister.

It is only at the Ministry machinery level that we can speak of delays as partly deliberate, due to the fact that many of the Ministry officials took an unfavourable view of the recruitment into the USIPE of professionally qualified persons who were not teachers and whose salaries would be considerably higher than their own. In so far as negotiations about the status of future members of the USIPE depended on the willingness of the educational administration to hold discussions with the Budget Office and the Directorate of Public Service, delays in this connection were not inconsiderable.

On one side, then, potential openings — but the possible results would not be attained until after the Minister's term of office expired. On the other side, delays — through inertia or resistance — occurring during this same four-year period. Would they not cancel each other out?

The relative weights of these two vectors will be precisely reflected in the judgement of the Minister. He alone who will integrate his actions in the continuity of his predecessors — the fruits of whose 'investments' he has gathered — and of his successors, for whom he will have been able to have only invested, without being able to gather anything.

It is in this perspective that we must try to understand the decision-maker's action. He is not in a hurry, and does not wish either to force decisions or to abandon them. He has become the slow helmsman who steers, without undue zeal but not without a touch of conviction, two operations deliberately chosen in his 'area of indecision'.

He has relied on the legality of the Plan, the political text of which has been endorsed by the President. He has chosen his openings carefully, avoiding objectives concerned with school education which could not have failed to provoke reactions both from public opinion and from the teachers. Such reactions were to be avoided at all costs: he had no wish to cause fires which he would find it difficult to put out.

Thus by negotiating with the Congress, by waiting for the President's decision, and by wearing down the resistance of his own administration, he has succeeded in not hindering the realisation of the two chosen operations. His strategy has been that of negotiation. All though his term of office he knew that a strategy of breakdown would be fatal for him. More than any of the other Ministers, his aims were circumscribed by his ability to remain Minister until the end of his mandate.

While pursuing this strategy he has constantly borne in mind the nature of the Guatemalan microcosm. Not only do the proposed actions not imply a new model of society; they are in no way inconsistent with the existing structures.

What he has initiated is still in embryo, both as regards the USIPE and the out-of-school education. Both these operations present possibilities of seeing future areas of indecision open up. There is no way of telling whether they might not have been more effectively carried out by a more aggressive, creative or dynamic Minister. Is it possible to calculate what measure of politico-administrative aggressiveness could be safely prescribed, without provoking a breakdown in the Guatemalan microcosm?

Section 5. Undetermined determination

Carried by the currents that flow through the Guatemalan microcosm, the Minister has attempted to profit from this motive energy to open two breaches in the traditional defensive wall that protects the educational system and, by means of the structures of this system, the institutions and customs of the dominant forces in contemporary society.

He has done this in his own way, with prudence, vigilance and circumspection — some might even say, too much so. Does this mean that his influence on the progress of education has been minimal? It is obvious that several years after the end of the decison-maker's mandate, the events studied still do not constitute a coherent historic event. For that, a distance of twenty or thirty years is needed. We shall therefore restrict our examination of the choices to the ability of the decision-maker to 'open breaches'. For this purpose, it is of interest to see which currents have influenced him. In other words, how has he made up his mind in his chosen areas. It is useful to come back to the reference-grid we used for Costa Rica, where we identifed three basic currents:

— traditional project of society;
— reformist tendency;
— international principles

These have general validity, and can be applied in Guatemala in the same way as in Costa Rica.

Once more, following the chronological order of three decisions, we will attempt to measure the influences determining the choices that appear to have been made arbitrarily. We have selected three acts that can be directly imputed to the decision-maker and were not the result of any hierarchical directive or outside influence (political party, advisers, 'private office', etc.). There are:

— The decision to use the Plan which had been prepared before his appointment by the Secretary-general for Ecnomic Planning with the participation of international advisers;
— The decision to introduce the out-of-school programme in the areas devastated by the 1976 earthquake;
— The decision not to convoke the Mixed Commission in 1977.

5.1. *Using the Plan*

On arriving in his new office, the Minister finds two documents: a plan prepared by his predecessor, and a draft plan drawn up by the officials of his Ministry with the collaboration of international advisers. He rejects them, judging the first to be of doubtful competence[1] and the second of suspect

1. He did not consider that the Office for Integral Educational Planning (OPIE), which

origin.[2] Not until a random phenomenon intervenes — the arrival of a close relative in the Secretariat of the Plan — is the Minister informed that there is a new version of the second document. He makes it his own, and then renders it public once it has received the approval of the Head of State.

This arbitrary decision, guided by instinct and profiting from a unique opportunity — is this not the prerogative of the 'political man' as conceived of by Max Weber?[3]

We think that if the decision-maker lets the 'facts act upon him', it is that he also feels the force of the currents that flow through the microcosm in which he acts. But what are they? In choosing a Plan for Education, Science and Technology, is he going against the *'Traditional Project of Society'* current? If in its analysis of the educational situation the Plan criticises earlier shortcomings and proposes a reorganization, it does so *inside* the existing system, not rejecting either the principle of three-level schooling or the rôle of the private sector or that of the University.

Even the existence of the Plan, though its principles may not be to the liking of the traditional class, is not a challenge to administrative custom: it is, after all, the fifth plan in fifteen years!

In deciding in favour of a Plan the Minister is being faithful to the custom of his predecessors and is merely adding an extra sentence to the traditional speeches.

In so far as a *'reformist tendency'* can make itself heard, especially in the Secretariat of the Plan and among certain teachers or Ministry officials who had taken part in drawing up the first draft, it will not go unanswered. In fact, the avowed intention of the Plan to balance up rural primary education in relation to urban schools, on the one hand, and the proposal for the creation of a 'module for out-of-school education' on the other, were a response to the reformist current, concealed but still present in society.

Lastly, the contribution of the international advisers, a faithful reflection of the *international principles* current, had found an audience in the national authors of the Plan, who found in it their inspiration for the sections dealing with the expansion and renovation of rural primary education and the establishing of out-of-school education.

---

had produced the first document, possessed sufficient judgement and analytical capacity. One of his aims in setting up USIPE was, in fact, to abolish OPIE.

2. More than a year passed between his appointment to the Ministry and the establishment of mutual confidence with the international advisers.

3. Weber speaks of the 'coup-d'oeil' (lit. 'good judgement') of the politician, and explains this as follows: 'It means that he must possess the faculty of letting the facts work on him in a state of withdrawal and inner spiritual calm, and thus know how to 'keep at a distance' men and matters. A lack of detachment as such is out of the deadly sins of the politician.' Max Weber, *Le savant et le politique,* Paris, Plon, 1959, p.177.

This decision (the acceptance of a 'present), while apparently easy, was obviously more complex and subtle , since by acting in this way the Minister made a wide range of activities possible and at the same time established the legality of his proceedings. He also ensured that he would have the support of the international bodies and their possible sources of financing.

5.2. *The module gets under way*
The year 1975 had been devoted to 'studies of the environment', very protracted, in order to define the first objective of the module for out-of-school education. The presence of the vice-Minister of Education as Chairman of the Governing Board for Out-of-school Education, was reassuring to the 'traditional tendency' because of the modesty of her ambitions and her relatively school-oriented conception of the programme. The twelve months which followed the presidential decision to implement a massive programme throughout the country saw scarcely any concrete actions for the benefit of the rural Indian population of the High Plains. This lethargic beginning caused not the least anxiety among the partisans of the traditional current.

The earthquake of February 1976 gave the Minister an opportunity to bring out the module from the files and put it in contact with reality. He insisted that the technicians abandon their theoretical studies and come to grips with reality in several of the villages destroyed by the earthquake. The programme thus took its first steps, and — in conformity with the reformist current, and helped by the international advisers, impatiently pawing the ground — the first villagers defined their educational needs and organized themselves to bring to life this hitherto utopian vision.

At the same time, the decision-maker was careful not to appear too rash in respect of changing the ways of the traditional educational system. In fact, his Secretary-general drew up an Emergency Plan for the primary schools in order to mobilise pupils and teachers around a school programme centred on the reconstruction of the country, which would take advantage of the unused hours of the day (more than a third of the normal school hours) because several schools were having to share the same building following the destruction of numerous establishments, resulting in a reduction in the hours of attendance. But despite his appeals to the Directorate-general of Education, to the Primary Inspectorate, and to numbers of teachers, the Minister had to accept the evidence: the teachers, delighted at having several unexpected hours free, had little wish to throw themselves into extra-mural activities with their pupils. To insist would have risked provoking the mass of teachers, in the already troubled period that the country was passing through. The Minister let himself be carried along by the traditional current of the educational system, and abstained from making waves.

Here again, we see that he had taken over an area of indecision by bringing the out-of-school module out of the bureaucratic groove in which it was stuck, without repudiating any of the three currents that shaped his microcosm.

5.3. *Repudiation of the Mixed Commission*

It will be recalled that in order to bring about the creation of the USIPE the decision-maker had agreed to open his Ministry to a Commission consisting of his own representatives and those of the Secretariat for Economic Planning, the Directorate of the Public Service and the Office of the Budget. Budget. The aim of the combined work to be carried out by this team was twofold: first, to prepare the texts which would subsequently be incorporated in the Decree of Application (*Acuerdo Gobernativo*) of the Law on Education and which would establish the USIPE; secondly, to ensure that the competences of the candidates finally selected for the USIPE corresponded to the job descriptions for the posts, which had been worked out and described in minute detail.

However, once the first part of the work was completed, the Minister made no move towards convoking the Commission to finish its task. He hoped in this way to avoid a conflict with the Ministry machinery and with the traditional tendency, who might not be very enthusiastic about the idea of recruiting for the key positions in the control of the administration, not only teachers (who, for the first time, would benefit from high salaries) but also non-teachers: economists, engineers, sociologists, architects, etc., all paid at rates considerably higher than those current in the Ministry. Also, the Minister did not want any rumours of possible dissension among his staff to endanger his own tenure. His judgement or instinct brought him closer to the traditionalist current.

Does this mean that the decision in this area would bring him into conflict with the reformist tendency and the international principles? There are two possible answers. If the protagonists of these two currents judged that the weeks and months lost, without any meeting of the Commission and without the USIPE being started up, were crucial for the future of education, they could only regard the Minister's action as negative.

On the other hand, if the important thing was to inaugurate the USIPE with a minimum of fuss and instal in it specialists of the level and quality intended, it would be more difficult to regard the Minister's decision as contrary to the reformist current and to the application of international principles that demanded planning, modern techniques of management and monitoring, close liaison between planning and the working-out of new curricula, etc.

It may well be claimed that the delays did away with any chances that the Minister himself might have had to benefit from the rôle of the USIPE. It is clearly more hypothetical to assert that the USIPE, whose birth had been so long delayed, would not render useful service to the Minister's successors.

It is therefore difficult to conclude that even in this decision the decision-maker had not been influenced — consciously or not — by the capacity of the three currents before he entered this area of indecision. All the same, the final conclusion is that this third decision was not made in accordance with the three currents.

5.4. *Diagram of the choices*

By presenting the relationships between the three areas chosen for decision and the three 'bearing currents', as we have already done in the case of Costa Rica, we obtain the following diagram:

Currents \ Areas	Using the Plan	The 'module' gets under way	Repudiation of the Mixed Commission
1. Traditional tendency	+	0	+
2. Reformist tendency	+	+	−
3. International principles	+	+	0 $^{(-)}$

+ compatible   − incompatible   0 neutral
( ) tendency of international advisers

With all the reservations that this necessarily simplifying diagram implies, it appears from this summary that the decision-maker's entry into each of the areas of indecision has been met with only a minimum of opposition from the vector currents.

In complete agreement with the vectors of his microcosm, and in line with his own standards, neutral by nature ('stay where you are'), he has nevertheless imposed his will in previously unoccupied areas. Admittedly, this expression of will underwent some erosion — caused by the delays which by their very nature cancelled out the intended effects. For example, the Minister wanted to have avaiable — for himself, not for his successors — an instrument for the control of the machinery (the USIPE). He did *not* succeed in this, sinced in actual fact the USIPE began to function just when the decision-maker who had wanted and created it was about to leave his post. But the USIPE still exists and, in view of the legal formalities that attended its creation, it is unlikely that it could be easily abolished.

Out-of-school education is a fact in the national field of education. The module, though still limited in extent, is a reality. Men and women today are being trained for tasks which, formerly, were not even in the vocabulary of participatory mass-education. Only in several years' time will it be possible to judge whether the intentions of this exceptional programme have been respected.

165

The man who presided over the slow, painful and sometimes despaired-of birth of these two harbingers of the future did so in a stratified and supervised (some would say closed) microcosm, with a conservative attitude of defending its acquired structures and advantages. At first sight, all the indications are that the action that an actor may take in a political field or decisional system such as that of Guatemala is necessarily pre-determined. Nevertheless, it appears that within this determinism there are areas which are *not* determined, inside some of which our decision-maker was able to insinuate himself.

PART THREE

CHANGE AND ITS ACTORS

CHAPTER I
Two different events

In presenting the two situations, we have already drawn attention to their different contexts. Now that we are better acquainted with the events and the actors, it will be useful to take a closer look at the differences, in order to decide whether they preclude any attempt at generalizing, or whether they might guide us towards formulating, with the help of other more profound and diversified analyses, some general hypothesis. If these apparent differences in fact form part of a wider order, they might provide confirmation of its general direction.

For a better grasp of this order we shall compare the two events described in Part Two according to the three parameters already identified. First, we will observe the characteristics of the areas of indecision from the standpoint of the two actors; next, by examining the strategies, we shall try to measure the vector which affects the decision-maker in his system. Finally, we shall compare the 'criteria of satisfaction'[1] which will enable us to distinguish the subjective vectors of those whom chance — or fate — has placed upon the stage that we are studying.

These three preliminary tests will bring us back to the nature of the microstructures inside which the education phenomenon has been studied.

---

1. See the model proposed more than twenty years ago by Herbert Simon in the work published in collaboration with James G. March, op.cit. Man, says Simon, is incapable of following an absolutely rational model, in the first place because he cannot be aware of all the possible choices and secondly because he reasons sequentially and not synoptically. Therefore the decision-maker does not look for the optimum — the best solution, absolutely speaking — which is in many cases beyond his reach. But he looks for a 'rational' solution. This will be the solution that meets *his own criteria* of rationality. Man is an animal with a tendency not towards the optimum but towards *satisfaction*. M. Crozier and E. Friedberg (op.cit., p.227) summarize Simon's thinking in the following terms: 'To understand the choice of a decision, it is of no use to try and imagine the best rational solution and then try to understand the obstacles that prevented the decision-maker from discovering it or applying it. Instead, one must define the options that presented themselves to him sequentially, because of the structural nature of the field concerned, and analyse the criteria he used, consciously or unconsciously, to accept or refuse these options.'

This, in turn, can lead to consideration of the relative plasticity or rigidity of the phenomenon in relation to the specific changes that have been introduced and which we must not confuse with those of a general nature which can affect the whole of society.

Section 1. **The areas of indecision**

We will try to identify these by placing them in the natural paradigm (time and space) and in the paradigm constructed by human thought (reason and structures).

1.1. *Time and space*
In Costa Rica the decision-maker was carried along by an historical notion, which allowed him to regard himself as the conscious heir of a tradition of reforms — and successes — that have left their mark on the almost 'insular' condition of Costa Rica in the Central-American context.

Throughout the 19th century and the first three-quarters of the 20th the instruments of Costa Rica's democratic society were being gradually hammered out; and one of the most noteworthy was education. However, then — as in the event we have described — the decision-maker acts in his area of indecision, the notion of time which guides him is short term, defined by the duration of his mandate. The event runs its course rapidly and ends in breakdown, since in the first year of the Plan it was necessary to take action, and the whole event had to culminate, barely three years later, in a Law.

In Guatemala the time was short *before* the decision. The Story of Education had not made any run-up before jumping. It might almost be said that in the absence of any antecedents for the decision we are studying, time 'started' with, and for, the decision-maker. Influenced, in his hopes of success, by knowing the consequences of intemperate haste, he accepted — or at the very least, did not attempt to oppose — the slow passage of time, a little as though, since this was a new creation, its period of gestation should not be curtailed.

In one case, the passing of time was rushed: in the other, respected. In the first case, a rhythm existed *before the decision,* and had to be recognised and respected. In the second, a first attempt was being made to work out a process that would establish new rules, still to be discovered. In Costa Rica, therefore, education existed, and its development had to follow the rhythm of the social entity of which it was a part. In Guatemala education, and the changes hoped for in it, are somewhat *sui generis* and appear to be easier to manipulate — prudently and discreetly — without disturbing the social fabric whose vitality, though limited, hardly depends on its educational system.

Turning now to the 'space' of the event, we see that the Costa Rican decision-maker wanted this to be as wide and far-reaching as the entire school — and out-of-school — system. The actors who would be affected by the decision could be found in the entire universe of public education at all its levels.

This occupation of so large an area not passing unnoticed, the event became one of increasing impact, and one to which those who would be affected by its consequences could not remain indifferent. In contrast, the space of the area of decision of the Guatemalan decision-maker was small, limited to a small number of actors in the system of action and an equally small number in the game that would be the outcome of the two decisions studied. The event, cautiously organised in fear of inciting reactions, did not attract a great deal of attention. But the reason why both the space and the attention were small was the marginal place occupied by education in the national scene.

It is possible that if the Costa Rican decision-maker had chosen decisions similar to those of his Guatemalan colleague and had conducted his game with subtlety and discretion, he would have found it impossible to make any headway. The close involvement of education, its symbolic rôle and of its actors in the social vitality of Costa Rica rendered very risky any attempt to get by unperceived, as the Minister of Guatemala might successfully manage in a very different microcosm. In Costa Rica it was possible only to act openly or be condemned from the start to failure.

Do we then have to give a double interpretation to the notions of time and space? On the one hand, those of which the decision-makers are conscious and which they believe they can control and, on the other, those which determine their actions in the context they are trying to bring about without their knowledge.? In Costa Rica time is long (because of the importance of the historical current) and space is short (the neighbours have to put up with the noise) and the decision-maker believes in acting in a minimum of time while covering a maximum of space. On the contrary, in Guatemala the time is short (since it is necessary to take advantage of any opportunity that arises for beginning an action) and space is large, since few people are concerned with what is happening as long as the decision-maker stays well outside the political game played by the Major Decision-makers. As a counterbalance, he plays his own game of long time (not rushing anything) and short space (his opening).

From this we can draw a first conclusion: the 'structured' microcosms in which education is intimately interwoven in the social fabric, as the example of Costa Rica suggests, have in reality very long times (necessary for negotiating) and very short spaces (entry points or narrow openings), which do not lend themselves to reforms on a grade scale (*a fortiori*, if it is assumed that they can be carried out in a limited period).

In microcosms which have not yet built up modern social structures in which education has its place, the times are short. The span of four years, which is very brief when it is a question of beginning to build, sufficed for intervening and leaving a lasting impression. The space is large, but it is mined. The number of openings is practically unlimited. The main thing is to be able to choose them without being overcome.

1.2. *Reason and structure*

By attacking the ideal of education in Costa Rica, the decision-maker was obliged to challenge the legal and institutional foundations of the system. Not satisfied with upsetting the teachers in their *modus operandi*, he could do no less than revise the machinery and rules of the game.

The Law became, for him, an objective: for the teachers, a symbol. The Reform of the entire Administration was, for him, a condition: for them, a threat.

The event took place in a regulated and structured area. It directly affected the machinery and the guarantees which ensured for the actors of the national educational system the certainty of being able to integrate themselves perfectly among the meshes of the 'Great Social Net' which belonged to them.

His opposite number in Guatemala saw in the Law only a concession to avoid treading on one of the many mines which infested the area he was proposing to occupy. Similarly, the modest control unit for the administrative machinery he wished to create did not threaten the entire bureaucratic structure, even if it antagonized certain of its members. However, even if that were so, those ousted from the Ministry had very little to do with the 'Great Social Net' of the country. As minority civil servants their complaints awoke scarcely any echo in the 'agro-exporting/military/religious' organization that controlled national life.

Once again, at the level of Laws and Institutions we continue to be aware of phenomena similar to those already suggested. The more a microstructure is law-bound and institutionalized, the more difficult it appears to introduce into it a new event without its being felt as a danger to the entire structure.

Conversely, the more the Law is symbolic and the institutions fictitious, the less risk there is in introducing an event, provided that it does not tear any of the meshes of the 'Net' which, though they may have nothing to do with education, might be considered essential by the big national fishermen.

Section 2. **The games**

The analysis of behaviours inside organizations often takes as its starting-point the concept of social 'rôles'. This concept gives rise to the problem of the constraints resulting from the unsuitability for his rôle of the actor being studied. This problem is criticized as univocal by Crozier and Friedberg, who replace it by the 'concept of the game'.[2] They centre the analysis not on fixed concepts (structure, rôle, person) but rather 'on the mechanisms of integration of these phenomena themselves'. Thus the game becomes a

2. M. Crozier and E. Friedberg, op.cit.

'concrete mechanism, thanks to which men structure their relationships of power and regulate them while leaving them — and themselves — their liberty. The game is the instrument which men have constructed to regulate their co-operation. It is the essential instrument of organized action.'[3]

This concept integrates — without reconciling — the 'two contradictory orientations, that of the egotistic strategy of the actor and that of the final coherence of the system. The one applies to the behaviour of the actors in the game, and the other to the results of the game. Only the game in its quality of socially integrating mechanism succeeds in going beyond them.'[4]

In examining the areas of indecision of the two decision- makers of Costa Rica and Guatemala we have tried to determine the possible area of intervention for their determination inside the systems they sought to transform. Faced henceforth with this 'finalised coherence' of the system, how will they act to ensure that the choices they have made may have some chance of transforming themselves into *new* structures which in turn will give rise to *new* problems and eventually to the search, by others, for *new* choices?

Crozier and Friedberg identify two types of strategy, 'breakdown' and negotiation. The decision-maker will choose the method most in conformity with the 'bets' he intends to make, bearing in mind the areas in which he hopes to intervene and the proper nature of his motivation (criteria of satisfaction) which we shall see in the next section. Let us try to apply this definition to the two events of our study.

2.1. *Breakdown strategy*

This consists, in essence, in trying to improve by force of authority a new system, without allowing any intervention by the representatives of the previous system. In the end, it is assumed that — no matter what sort of dialogue might be started up with them — they will oppose any reform which does not tend to strengthen their own power.

It cannot be denied that, from the moment that he decided that an integral reform must be imposed on the entire school system, the Minister in Costa Rica wanted a breakdown with the unions. It was in the heart of his own private system, far from the unions' representatives, that he intended to draw up the design of the reform and then the texts that would form the framework of the Plan for Educational Development. He consulted the unions only after setting up a national campaign which would enable him to develop alliances direct with certain teachers, with students, with parents, with rural notables, etc.

This breakdown strategy relied upon tactics of isolation — and even intimidation — of unionised teachers.

The Minister hoped to find support among the rank and file that would weaken the union leaders; meanwhile, he counted on the Head of State and

3. Ibid., p.97.
4. Ibid., p.204.

his friends in the Liberación party to stand up against the foreseeable reactions of the teachers on a national scale.

This was nothing less than a turning movement, having as its object the breaking of the links between the unions on the one side, the teachers' establishment on another, and the political superstructure on the third. The decision-maker reckoned that this isolation was the only means of imposing a massive reorganisation of the machinery and the customs of education.

The Minister deliberately by-passed the objections, criticisms and protests of the unions by having his draft Plan approved by the Higher Council for Education, including the unions' representative, who duly rallied to his side. Estimating that the unions would be pleased with his action, he transferred control of the Teacher-training Colleges to the National University (practically created for this purpose). But we have already seen that even if certain teachers could only be pleased with such a measure which allowed primary teachers, who would not be university graduates, to enter a level of the Public Service better paid than their previous level. However they showed no sign of wishing to use their influence to change the reaction of the unions as a whole.

Despite the protests and strikes of the teachers, the decision-maker remained imperturbably attached to his strategy, and caused the final breakdown by submitting the draft Law to Parliament.

We have seen that the success of this strategy, which ran counter to the negotiation process proper to the system of pressure groups which characterized the democratic way of life in Costa Rica, was not long-lived.

In Guatemala, such a strategy could be used by the Minister only against the Legislature or the Head of State. In that context, this would have been suicidal. But even if a dialogue with the unions had been possible, we saw that there too he would probably not have used a strategy of breakdown. We have seen that he tried to negotiate with the teachers, even through intermediaries. His experience in the realms of university, politics and administration had been valuable, enabling him to make a better choice.

The choice of a strategy of breakdown led the Costa Rican decision-maker into a course which made him lose sight of the nature, organisation and weight of the forces that opposed his initiative. He disregarded the historical development of a movement whose origins were known to him but which had since become one of the most resistant and decisive constituent elements of the structure of a modern society whose functioning he no longer controlled. Here, the experience which should have strengthened his ability to choose — and therefore to decide — was disadvantageous to him.

2.2. *Strategy of negotiation*

Even though it would take more time than was compatible with the duration of the Guatemalan Minister's mandate, he nevertheless chose this strategy. Obliged to accept the very slow evolution of customs and the need to give every measure a legal dimension, and above all conscious of the consequence on the political scene of any sudden movement or — what amounts to the same thing — a sudden acceleration of the rhythm of decision — he could not but choose a strategy of negotiation.

The situation is paradoxical. In a microstructure where the 'democratic dialogue' with the grass-roots or with the pressure groups — including the unions — has not yet become customary, why negotiate? In fact, for a strong régime, strong measures and — why not — a strategy of breakdown. But this would fail to take into account the equilibrium imposed by the forces inside the Great Social Net, where the education sector and its Minister do not appear as preponderant elements. Merely to maintain a presence and en-sure survival, it was already necessary to negotiate (we have seen that the Education budget had fallen in relative terms nearly 30 per cent during the mandate of the decision-maker, who, even if he did not lack arguments, had perhaps not raised his voice sufficiently to be heard).

A fortiori, if he wished to innovate, even on a modest scale, he could not himself copy the strategy used by authority to impose policies in sectors con-siderably more powerful than Education. In other words, if the strategy of breakdown was generally applied by other Ministers, and even by certain groups with strong representation in the inner circles of the State machinery, the education Minister could only negotiate, so feeble were his means and his alliances at the heart of the great system.

In Costa Rica, a strategy of negotiation between Minister and unions from the start of the decision-maker's mandate would have permitted a debate to be opened on subjects of real interest, aiming at results in the short term for the teachers. Such a strategy might possibly have resulted in all the ac-tors winning 'something', instead of a situation in which each side's gains represent the other side's losses. If all changes are a collective process of learn-ing and exchange, where the game allows each side to draw some advantage, then — in a context in which negotiation, not to say bargaining, is the norm as it is in all democracies, and in Costa Rica in particular — negotiation was an imperative.

Admittedly, some think that in the educational field the teachers' unions will never negotiate over their acquired rights: working hours, work routines, wages, leave, retirement, etc., and that as a result a reform as ambitious and liberal as that envisaged by the Minister could never become the subject of a dialogue with the teachers.

To this it might be replied that a dialogue could be based on an agenda detailing a list of the measures to be taken; the dates on which these measures would come into force could be negotiated in exchange for concessions in favour of improving certain of the teachers' working conditions and tending to their professional and social betterment. It was not necessary, perhaps, to insist upon *everything* being brought into force *at one and the same time*.

Lastly, a *real* negotiation on the future of education ought to include a number of other direct participants, such as the industrial or agricultural workers' unions, the professional organizations, associative groups, regional collectives, employers' associations, etc. If education is the business of everybody, the first step in a negotiation with the teachers' unions should perhaps consist in demonstrating that they do not necessarily hold a monopoly in the matter. In the case of differences between the Minister and the unions, the possibility of having recourse *systematically* to arbitration might be envisaged: arbitration by a body on which the various actors mentioned above would be represented, but from which the teachers would be excluded even though they might also be members of the other groups represented.

Behind the choice of these two strategies lies the personal equation of the man who chooses them, and it is this that the third aspect of the decision will attempt to define.

Section 3. **The criteria of satisfaction**

Let us recall H. Simon's[5] definition of man: 'an animal seeking satisfaction', and not the so-called optimisation. But this satisfaction must meet certain criteria, standards reflecting those of the milieu in whose name he acts. These 'standards' which an individual uses are the outcome of a cultural apprenticeship, i.e., a socialisation reinforced by the 'sanctions of the environment'.[6] The sum total of the socialisation and the memory of the sanctions is nothing other than *experience*, and this is not measured exclusively by the yardstick of time.

It is this experience which determines the 'criterion of satisfaction' of the decision-maker. However, as the choices of the decision-makers we are studying can be evaluated only in terms of their political survival, it is as politicians, and not as men of the administrative machinery (concrete system of action), that we need to study them. For this purpose we have chosen, for its suitability, a systematisation inspired by the thinking of Max Weber in his treatise on *The trade and the vocation of the policician*. It will therefore be this experience, compounded of chance, necessity and the instinct that results from it, that will make the man we are studying a personage motivated either by the Weberian ethic of *conviction*, or by that of *responsibility*. However, if 'all activity oriented according to the ethic may be subordinated to two maxims totally different and ineluctably opposed',[7] the two ethics

5. See above, footnote on p.170.
6. M. Crozier and E. Friedberg, op.cit. Interestingly, these authors consider that the transformation of these standards is due to multiple contributions drawn from individual and collective experiences, but that education is a key factor since it 'plays an increasing part in the development of standards of diffusing the process of knowledge, but also the modes of apprehension of the real and the intellectual paradigms that underlie them and result from them.'
7. M. Weber, op.cit.

co-exist in each man. It is in this perspective that we shall try to identify the strongest influence under which the criteria of satisfaction of the two decision-makers can be determined.

3.1 *Ethic of conviction*

The partisan of this ethic, according to Weber, 'cannot put up with the ethic irrationality of the world'.[8] He will be swayed by an ideal born of his culture and his experience, as was the decision-maker in Costa Rica who heard only, it would appear, the reformist voice of his country in educational matters.

We have seen that the decision-maker has been able in certain cases, to make the effort of uniting the vectors that carry him. In most of those we have studied, however, he has chosen his vector by virtue of his criterion of satisfaction, which itself is made up of two elements: history, and the passage of time. We have already seen the influence of the latter;[9] the weight of history remains to be determined.

In the name of history, it is his *conviction* that carries him: education can influence, or at least anticipate, socio-political changes. Education is conceived by him as a 'good' to which the State has a duty to ensure that *all the children* of the country have effective access. He takes in his arms the body of 'the entire system' and lays it at the feet of 'the sovereign people' so that they may draw from it 'strength, justice and wisdom'. This conviction, grown into an obsession, becomes a real allegory of the public, free and compulsory school. In addressing the Higher Council for Education and the Parliament, he finds a humanist and impassioned language.

May we then unhesitatingly place the decision-maker in the Weberian category of men of conviction? Apart from the subjectivity of Max Weber's analysis, his own definition indicates for us more a *tendency* than a 'belonging'. In fact, Weber tells us that 'when the consequences of an action done from pure conviction are unfavourable, the partisan of this ethic will not blame the agent but the world, human stupidity, or even the will of God who created men in this way.'[10] In the case we are exploring, while the decision-maker has not put the blame on God, he has all the same thrown the responsibility for his failure on to a determined group (the teachers' unions), which shows that he possessed, in spite of everything, a certain sense of the responsibilities. . . of others. It is nevertheless true that his refusal to admit the possibility of failure in seeking his criterion of satisfaction places him in the category of those in whom conviction is stronger than calculation.

Admittedly, the pressure of time and his impatient desire to leave a historic impression on the education of his country explain his haste, his deafness to all alternatives. While he has made himself the spokesman of the socialisation of the national microcosm, by wishing education to play an innovating,

8. M. Weber, op.cit.
9. See Section 1.1.1. of this chapter.
10. M. Weber, op.cit.

177

breaking-new-ground rôle, he has not shown sufficient awareness of the sanctions to which this same society will submit him. It is this deficiency, this lack of sensibility, that places him — in spite of everything — in the category of those whose criterion of satisfaction is marked more by conviction than by responsibility.

On the other hand, is the ethic of the Guatemalan decision-maker so little marked by conviction? We have seen that if prudence and circumspection characterize him, he is not without a certain measure of normative volition, especially as regards the programme for out-of-school education. His conviction, all the same, is not overflowing, or even very elaborate. It is retrained. It does not rule his actions and his choices. Rather, his criterion of satisfaction is the reflection both of his own socialisation (in a microcosm where any change in favour of a form of progress for the rural and indigenous population can be perceived as a threat) and of his lucid knowledge of the sanctions that await him if he should fail to observe the general rule laid down by the dominant social forces.

He will not praise, either extravagantly or too often, the merits of the out-of-school modules, and he will not take over, directly or indirectly, the running of the Governing Board of the programme. In this way he will not run counter to the very slow rhythm of the social organization of which he is part, since he is fully aware of the sanctions it can impose. This deep respect for socialisation *and* sanctions scarcely suggests that his criterion of satisfaction has been affected by what might have been a conviction.

3.2. *Ethic of responsibility*
'The partisan of this ethic will take account of the failings common to mankind and will judge that he cannot pass over to others the consequences of his own action, for all that he may have been able to foresee them'.[11] This observation applies, with a relative degree of precision, to the Guatemalan decision-maker, who was conscious at each step of not being able to share with anyone the consequences — read 'sanctions' — of his decisions. He was not unaware of the extent to which he 'played on the brink' in his national context. Each phase and each delay reflected his determination to accept the responsibility for his actions.

In the microcosm of Guatemala, this signifies that he sought continually to lessen the risks by clinging closely to the Executive or the Legislature, without abandoning the precautions with which he surrounded his approaches.

This ethic of responsibility was certainly due to a sense of the possible inside the microcosm, but it cannot be denied that it was also due to the same sense regarding anything that affected the decision-maker's own political survival. His initiatives, therefore, were characterized by a sharp perception of limits he could not overstep.

11. M. Weber, op.cit.

It might be thought that there is very little difference between this behaviour and simple opportunism, wrapped up in the necessary amount of demogogy to satisfy the harsh reactions of a public opinion otherwise very undemanding in educational matters. Once again, nuances come into play. Our decision-maker did not accept just any opinion nor recommend any old option at the mercy of changing event so fashions.

He chose a path in which he foresaw long detours, knowing that its destination would be important for a future society. In doing so, as we have already seen, his sense of responsibility did not exclude a certain conviction — not to be confused with a certainty of conviction.

Admittedly, his Costa Rican colleague was, perhaps, swayed by conviction more than the Guatemalan was by responsibility.

In defining these two ethics, Weber warned us: 'this is not to say that the ethic of conviction is the same as the absence of responsibility, or the ethic of responsibility as the absence of conviction. Obviously this cannot be so.'

3.3. *Criteria and ethics*

It is tempting to establish certain lines of relationship between the determinants of 'socialisation' and of 'sanctions' that define the frame of the criteria of satisfaction, on the one hand, and the ethics of conviction and responsibility on the other.

It appears that the decision which *was applied* within the limits of the period studied reflects a criterion on the part of the decision-maker inspired by a socialisation that conforms with the inner image of it made by those who dominate the political scene. In the same way that the unions in Costa Rica are decisive because they represent an important factor of the multiplicity of the representative power, the Executive in Guatemala is the key factor since it is supported by the real sources of power. In Guatemala, therefore, anyone who would wish to add to or change the ingredient 'education' in the microcosm concerned must be conscious of the same quality of socialisation that is transmitted by the Executive and the dominant class. Otherwise, he would show that he was not aware of the sanctions that would ensue, and so would become an agent, not of change, but of a challenge to the established order without the power to ensure its success. For that reason, he would fail.

The notion of an ethic of responsibility — is it the necessary *condition* to ensure that the application of the criterion of satisfaction, for the person carried along by it, will afford a chance of success? Since this situation hardly excludes the existence of conviction on the part of those characterised by the ethic of responsibility, what is this amount of conviction which then becomes the second condition for the 'success' of the decision? It is tempting to conclude with a utopian vision in which the application of the ethic of responsibility by a person who remains motivated by a 'certain' conviction would represent the *necsssary and sufficient* conditions for the survival of a public decision in educational matters.

179

CHAPTER II

Is education changing in Central America? Three elements for a reply

As suggested in the previous chapter, the differences we have noticed between the two decision-makers studied and the parameters conditioning their choices, far from suggesting the impossibility of a comparison, contribute to the fixing of the *boundaries of the decisional order* inside which they are *both* situated. The areas, the strategies and the criteria of the two decision-makers were often found at the extremities. We may therefore proceed as though these latter define the field in which the decision-maker anticipates, feels and acts.

The examination we have carried out in this work is insufficient, both by the number and the nature of the events described, to cover the whole field of the decisional order. By adding the example of other strategies[1] it will nevertheless enable us to suggest certain elements which will help to situate it, if not describe it. Three series of considerations will be the first markers of a path that this work can hardly claim to outline: they concern the *possibility*, the *demands* and the *limits* of change.

Change, says Everert M. Rogers in his study of the interaction between communications and innovations, 'occurs when a new idea's use or rejection has an effect. Social change is therefore an effect of communication'.[2] But if the change is to be effected by the use of rejection of an innovation, communication, for its part, can only take place between those who see — decide upon — the utility or the inopportunity of what is proposed. In this connection, for Crozier and Friedberg, change can only be understood as a process of collective creation by means of which the members of a given collectivity learn together, that is to say, invent and decide upon new methods of playing the social game of co-operation and conflict — in short, a new social praxis — and acquire the corresponding cognitive, relational and organisational capacities. It is a process of collective apprenticeship, leading

1. See above Nicaragua (Part I, Chapter 2, section 2.3.) and below Peru (Part III, Chapter 2, section 1.2.) and Panama (Part III, Chapter 2, section 2.1).
2. E.M. Rogers and F.F. Shoemaker, *Communication of innovations, a cross-cultural approach,* 2nd ed., New York, The Free Press, 1971.

to the institution of new 'constructs of collective action which create and express at the same time a new structuration of the field or fields'.[3]

The criterion of change, according to Rogers, will be the existence of an effect or consequence which, as Crozier reminds us, will be possible only if there is 'collective apprenticeship'.

In the two events studied, how do these criteria apply in the three stages proposed in our approach?

Section 1. **Possibilities of change**

Let us recall two conditions already stated:
The decision confirming or causing a change will depend on the degree of tension of the social 'net' and on the temporal vision of the decision-maker, who will — or will not — agree to inscribe his decision in a continuum.

1.1. *A loose or tight mesh*
The first condition will depend on the nature of the social fabric which facilitates — or inhibits — any change according to the degree of integration of the educational system (as we have identified it in its three dimensions:[4] education as system of values of the microculture, education as function (structures and economic and social modes of functioning) and education as machinery (public service and unions).

When these three dimensions of the educational phenomenon are found to be relatively free from the constraints which the society to which it belongs can impose upon them, it may be deduced that the phenomenon is not considered an essential instrument by the structures and groups that dominate the collectivity. In other words, it can be subjected to modifications, innovation or manipulations without setting up a chain reaction leading, in the most favourable hypothesis, to the *status quo ante.*

Choosing for once examples from outside Central America, let us look at Tanzania after independence and France after 1968. On achieving independence in 1964, Tanzania had barely a third of the relevant age-group of children enrolled in primary schools. By means of a thorough change of structures, inspired less by the methods inherited from British colonisation than by the rural reality of the country, the new government set in train an educational process which not only led to a doubling of the rate and the enrolment in ten years, but also enabled a third of the adult population (96 per cent of them in rural areas) to study subjects of their own choosing.[5] Both the organization of education and its rôle — defined in the spirit of 'self-

3. M. Crozier and E. Friedberg, op.cit.
4. See above, Part I. To simplify matters, these three dimensions will hereafter be referred to by the generic expression 'the educational phenomenon'.
5. Budd, L. Hall, 'The United Republic of Tanzania: a national priority to adult education', *Prospects,* Vol.4, No.4, Winter 1974, pp.512-516.

reliance' which President Nyerere stressed in the Arusha Declaration of 1967
— demonstrated the advent of a radical innovation, on the scale of the entire society.

Granted, this was possible only by means of a complete break with the
European colonial past, and also through the installation of a political régime
inspired by a socialist model, which broke away from the earlier modes of
reproduction. This political militancy was to define the objectives and mobilize
the resources of this New Education.

All the same, and — looked at from the aspect which interests us here
— this is essential, for such a transformation to be possible on such a large
scale it was necessary that this phenomenon, to which were to be given a
vigour and direction hitherto unknown, should not be identified with the
social organisation which would characterise the young State.

But until the Arusha Declaration, education was a phenomenon quantitatively limited, depending on a fixed social order — that of English formalism, foreign to the political movements and the cultural depth of what
was to become a new Nation.

The imported education became 'off-centre' from the moment that the
values and forms of the new society led to the creation of centres of power
different from those which the previous forms of education had introduced
and maintained.

Though it still existed, the earlier education appeared marginal (limited
and exogenous). In contrast, a strong educational current, having its origins
and extensions in the traditionally rural society, had to be built up completely
from scratch. The educational phenomenon was therefore open to offers,
since the old system could be eliminated without destroying a vital organ
of the new society.

In reality, in Tanzania, two situations met head-on, mutually reinforcing
each other: on one side, an old education could be reformed since it was
no longer part of the new Great Social Net; and on the other, this same new
social fabric needed, in order to acquire strength, a new education. Unfortunately for our demonstration, today the impulses for the draconian change
in the educational system — as it was willed fifteen years ago — are felt less
than the desire to regain the security of schooling with an urban ambition.
The social net recently woven has tightened, and it is only at the price of
painful lacerations that it would be possible to get back to the purity of the
original dream of the New Education. Nevertheless, it is a fact that the dar-
ing leap forward to new forms of education was possible only because —
for a limited period — the social structure was loosened and in the market.

In contrast, let us consider the case of France, which in May 1968 experienced considerable convulsions arising from student unrest. Thirteen years
after the tumultuous events and the series of decisions taken by the Government under the influence of the then Minister of Education, the system is
still essentially the same — if not actually strengthened by a professorial class

more concerned, on the whole, with its status and its privileges than with its social responsibilities. Neither the public authorities, guarantors of the values of French society and its methods of production and reproduction, nor the teachers' unions, could permit any loosening of those meshes of the social net which enclose the educational phenomenon.

This is clear from a consideration of the unions' resistance and opposition, as well as other pressure groups (parents' and students' associations, in particular), each time that a Minister, since May 1968, has attempted to bring in a reform which, in reality, affected a single aspect of a single structure of a single level of education. What would have happened if the duration, the curricula, the methods, the relations with the productive sector, of the *entire* system had been made the object of a re-shaping?

Education, whether dispensed by the constitutional bodies which protect it or by the collusion between the *Grandes écoles* and *Grands corps* which characterize it at the higher level, is a phenomenon that cannot be dissociated from the social organisation and the values which it transmits, protects and perpetuates. This intimate relationship renders illusory the ambition to attack any one of the education meshes in the social net without immediately provoking a reaction, at various rhythms, from *the whole* of society.

Coming back to Central America, Nicaragua, which underwent a Sandinist revolution in July 1979 and in the following six months set on foot a literacy crusade,[6] could face this problem directly, thanks to its political militancy — as was the case in Tanzania — but also because the mass of children not in school and illiterate adults did not belong to anyone except to the Revolution. In fact, Somozism had hardly taken any interest at all in this population, marginal because deliberately marginalized, even though it contained the majority of the school-age children.

On the other hand, the Sandinist government is already finding difficulties — that time will not dispel — in coming to grips with the reform of the University or the teacher-training colleges. These are, in fact the home of the structures, the values and the sources of power already firmly embedded in the social fabric which is the heritage (unchangeable in present conditions) of the Government of National Reconstruction.

It therefore seems probable that any decision aiming at change in the realm of education will have that much more chance of being followed by 'effects', in the sense meant by Rogers, if it is born of an unfinished social microstructure, like that found in numerous countries — in a state of internal decolonisation, or issued from a recent or earlier decolonisation — which still have to structure and integate the educational phenomenon in their social net,[7] but where there are already the means of organising 'collective apprenticeship',

6. See above, Part I, Chapter 2, section 3.
7. Admittedly, the 'traditional' school remains the prerogative of numerous nationalisms that reject the rural school, ruralising and segretative.

in the meaning intended by Crozier, which will allow change to inscribe itself in the reality of facts.

1.2. *The seed and the field*
The second condition is connected with the decision-maker's capacity to place his decision in a temporal continuum. By wishing to hurry too much the progress of measures, he disregards the natural rhythm of a process that is not under his control, and his graft will not take. In fact, in educational matters the line of decisions taken by his predecessors represents the fertile ground in which he will sow his own contribution but gather the ripened fruits of an earlier sowing.

This solidarity in time is imposed by the slow evolution of the values of the project of civilization to which the area of the decision-maker belongs, made up of the structures of production, the social stratification and the bureaucratic machineries that it engenders.

Only exceptional events can bring about a new form of social organisation and consequently, relatively rapid change in the scale of values which underlies the social entity of which schooling is a part. Normally, the ethical values — or even the spiritual background — that determine the nature of this same society and — therefore — of the rôle which it entrusts to education — will scarcely change during the period of the decision-maker's mandate. We have seen this in Costa Rica, where the myths connected with the bourgeoisie of the towns were hardly touched by the decision-maker's intention to 'democratise' society by means of an educational reform.

The experience of the Educational Reform in Peru is a convincing demonstration. In 1968 the 'revolutionary' military government of General Velasco seized power and, immediately, decided to give the highest possible priority to the Agrarian Reform and the Educational Reform.

The Commission which was given responsibility for the latter recognised in its Report that 'the frame and aim of all processes of educational reform will develop around two main factors, both of them completely foreign to education: first, the development policy and, second, the political orientation of the State. . . In this perspective, any reform of education in Peru must be a part of the transformations which the Government has set as objectives of the structural changes. It must correspond to the Peruvian model of revolutionary policy'.[8]

The authors concluded, logically enough, that 'the problem of education cannot be resolved by an action carried out in this field alone, but must be envisaged in the context of the overall structures of the country, the defects of which are reflected in the educational system, preventing it from playing a positive rôle at the heart of the said structures'.[9]

8. Quoted in Judithe Bizot, *Educational reform in Peru,* Paris, Unesco Press, 1975, (Experiments and innovations in education 16, International Bureau of Education).
9. Ibid., p.2.

But the principles which inspired the Reform came from the Political Project of the revolution, and comprised: the humanist value of education, the creation of a national culture overthrowing the traditional myths proper to colonised countries, the massive general participation of the population, the establishment of new forms and structures of the educational system, and the bilingual literacy programme necessitated by the spread of Ketchoua and Amara, vernacular languages of the Inca Indians who make up more than half the total population.

These principles were finally included in a General Law on Education, adopted in March 1972 and known as 'Number 19326'. The man who had been the guiding spirit of the Commission and the principal inspirer of both the Report and the Law, Augusto Salazar-Bondy, described this effort as the 'manifestation of a profound volition to transform in its very bases the educational system which the country has known for many years'.[10]

To assess the amplitude of this transformation, it suffices to quote the 'basic ideas' defined by Salazar-Bondy: 'a redefinition of the idea of education and of educational rôles; a redefinition of the ends and the objectives of the work of national education; the introduction of a new system and the application of new forms of organisation of the teaching; the importance given to the participation of the community in education'.[11]

But, after the passage of years, we can see how far this reform, which was to end a few years later in undeniable failure, was from the hypothesis of 'factors totally foreign to education'. In fact, the authors and militants of the reform attempted to go further and faster than did the society that education was intended to serve — by following it and accompanying it, not by overtaking it.

One of the officials responsible for the implementation of the Reform, who subsequently became the National Director of Further Education (*Extension educativa*) summarised this difficulty as being a telescoping of time. Referring to the difference between conception and execution of the Reform '. . .between the period when it was conceived and five years after its application was due to commence, one must recognise an enormous distance between the social model that the Reform aspired to and the concrete social situation modified by the process of change. It should also be noted that the social transformation which had become apparent in the country had not attained the progress and coherence necessary for the materialisation of the propositions put forward both in the General Report of the Commission for Educational Reform and in the General Law on Education'.[12]

10. See A. Salazar Bondy, 'On educational reform in Peru', *Prospects,* Vol.2, No.4, Winter 1972, pp.383-391.
11. Op.cit., p.429.
12. José Rivero *La educación no-formal en la reforma Peruana,* Unesco-CEPAL-UNDP, Project Development and Education in Latin America and the Caribbean, DEALC 117, May 1971.

This 'distance' between the desirable and the possible became accentuated by the rapidity with which those in charge of the Reform insisted that it be implemented. More than any other factor, this was an error of strategy, which is always subject to the temporal dimension. The extent to which the time required for an idea such as the Reform to mature is a fundamental parameter may be illustrated by a quotation from an unpublished analysis of the Reform. 'The teachers remained reserved, if not hostile; the attitude of the administration remained ambiguous in the face of deconcentration and public participation; the University[13] was opposed to the transformation of the first cycle of higher education into a period of vocational training. Against all these there was no organised group capable of defending the Reform and overseeing its implementation. It is tempting to say that the Reform tended to favour the social groups who did not entirely believe in it and had no means of helping it, while the same Reform antagonised well organised groups possessing relatively important powers'.[14] But an undertaking of the wide scope of the educational reform in Peru needed either to be backed by a clear ideology embodied in a major political movement, or else to champ at the bit while measuring out little doses of change that would not be incompatible with a society in a condition of slow transition.

Quite simply, the authors of the Reform had not taken on the real rhythm with which the ideological and political values actually alive in the country had been implanted. As a conclusion (coming back to Central America), the decision-maker will scarcely attain success if he thinks he can outpace the productive structures by defending, for example (as in Costa Rica), technological education — in which education and work were mixed and the learning of technologies was to replace academic memorisation — while the mode of production is based on agriculture for export purposes and the growth of the nonformal and service sectors. Furthermore, if education tends to reproduce urban élitism, it is hardly likely that the same decision-maker will be able to impose a participative and egalitarian system taking its inspiration not from the single criterion of academic selection, but from a multitude of norms and possibilities. In all his initiatives the decision-maker can only follow closely the modes of production or reproduction, often go along with them, and on a few rare occasions outpace them by a hair's breadth — but never precede them in the sense of showing them the way.

Once again, it seems that the residual effect of change will be a function of the decision-maker's capacity to reflect, or to allow to appear, an aspiration for collective apprenticeship. This hardly happened at all in Costa Rica or in Peru, where the Reforms were imposed prematurely in the name of a social model which had not been achieved and had therefore not been

13. By 'University' should be understood the Faculty and, where appropriate, the students, defending their interests and their trade-union or association ideologies.
14. C. Tibi and F. Thorkildsen, 'The Rôle of training in the planning of educational reform in Peru', Paris, IIEP/RP/25/1E, February 1977.

assimilated by the actors who would be responsible for the adoption of a new principle and, above all, for its application.

In such a hypothesis, we must note the particular case represented by the decisions taken in Guatemala. In the actual event studied, although the slow passage of time was respected, can we say that it was used to allow a decision to emerge as the result of a 'process of collective creation'? The answer will depend on the interpretation given to the notion of the neutrality of time. But the delays and compromises enabled the innovations to be retrieved by the inertia of the machinery and the indifference of the collectivity.

At this point we must grasp the sense of the expression 'members of a given collectivity'. The two decisions studied in Guatemala should have been made the subject of a collective apprenticeship, with representatives of the rural population in connection with the module and with all the officials of the central administration — or a wide cross-section of them — in connection with the USIPE. But were they members of private collectivities which, taken together, are responsible for the entire process of decision in Guatemala?

We have tried to approach this process by defining 'system' and 'field'. In both we were able to identify those who, together, should have learned how to deal with a new idea and its institutional consequences, but were prevented from doing so. It cannot be denied that throughout the interchanges between the members of the Executive on the one hand, and between the Executive and the Legislative on the other, there was a sort of collective apprenticeship. But when we identify the actors we see that they do not include those at whom the decision is aimed. The given collectivity is not the one that will be subjected to the *direct effects* of the decision.

It might be concluded from this that the forms of collective — i.e., political — organisation in Costa Rica and Peru *demanded* that collective apprenticeship imply the active participation of the groups affected by the decisions relating to the reforms. In this sense, their resistance — largely caused by the rapid implementation of the reforms insisted on by the decision-makers, who judged that it was impossible or inopportune to allow the necessary time for an effective apprenticeship to take place — prevented the decision from maturing. This gave the death-blow to the decisions, since its application on a national scale made it essential for such groups to form part of the given collectivity.

In Guatemala the structure of the national politico-administrative set-up limits the notion of given collectivity for a private decision. It is in this sense that it is possible to speak of collective apprenticeship limited to those who form the dominant power. The Guatemalan experience is therefore in essence open to criticism, since it is placed in a politico-administrative context whose actors are a small minority whose influence is absolute as regards the survival, success — or death — of any decision which they consider likely to affect them.

187

We may remark in passing that it is possible to speak of a more open or more closed society,[15] depending on whether the composition of the collectivity implied in a collective apprenticeship is limited to those who have uncontested and relatively discretionary power based on their *authority* to take a decision or, on the contrary, based on their *responsibility* regarding the application of the decision and their insistence on *contesting* such an authority and on participating in the process. The latter would define a relatively 'open' structure compared with the former.

Section 2. **Demands of change**

In every society (whether more or less 'open') the tangible effect and collective apprenticeship which characterise the change brought about by a given decision in the realm of education, will be determined by the application of a strategy of negotiation. Whether the change implies the participation of a large number or a handful of actors, the educational phenomenon is too complex and widespread to form the object of a 'diktat' born of a strategy of breakdown. Each intermediate grade upstream of the deciding Minister (Head of State, Legislature, political parties, pressure groups, etc.) or downstream (administrative machinery, teachers, students and pupils) can question, dilute, transform, distort, sterilise or ignore what has been imposed upon it. Too many interests are at stake, as we have seen, for the decision-maker not to negotiate the forms of application of his criterion of satisfaction.

Two questions seem relevant: one concerning the expediency of a negotiation, the other the nature of the participants in that negotiation.

As regards the first, the example of Costa Rica and the reference to Peru confirm the necessity of a strategy of negotiation when the teachers and/or administrative officials have in their hands, in the type of society corresponding to these two microcosms, the relative success or probable failure of a reform. The situation is less clear-cut in the case of Guatemala, where we have seen the decision-maker negotiate with the Head of State and Parliament the conditions and — above all — the forms of the decisions whose acceptance, he felt, he had to ensure.

It appears that the decision process was even more complex in Panama, which, without ever relying on a strategy of negotiation, first set in motion an overall Educational Reform and then, secondly, annulled its effects practically completely.

2.1. *Expediency of a strategy of negotiation: the case of Panama*
In 1970 the revolutionary government, born of a *coup-d'état* in 1968, decreed the setting-up of a Commission for educational reform. By a Constitution

15. For an attempt to apply the concept of 'open' and 'closed' societies to their respective capacities of welcoming or rejecting change, see S. Lourié, 'Education and society: the problems of change', *Prospects,* Vol. 4, No.4, Winter 1974, pp.541-548.

voted in 1972, centred on the recovery of full Panamanian sovereignty over the Canal and the zone around it,[16] the new Government defined education as one of the main axes of its new policy, which also included the intention of reforming the legislation concerning work and the ownership of land.

In its Report the Commission proposed a total reform of education, understood as the entire system of all the levels, cycles and forms of schooling, and the creation of an out-of-school system. The great originality of the proposed reform lay in its articulation with a growing network of 'schools of production' in rural areas, combining learning with agricultural activities.[17] In January 1974 the new Minister, who had been a member of the Constitutional Board, attempted (with a team of reformists, including the vice-Minister and the National Director of Educational Reform and Planning) to set in motion services in line with the concrete objectives of the Reform and based upon the multitude of recommendations (20 volumes) of the Commission. Some months later a trade union of teachers who approved the revolutionary principles of the Reform was created: the Reformist Front of Panamanian Educators (FREP).

At the first meeting of the FREP the Minister, in the presence of General Omar Torrijos, '*Lider maximo*' of the Revolution, declared: 'The Educational Reforms are part of the Constitution, and anyone who opposes them opposes the political Constitution of the country, that is, the Panamanian people themselves who adopted it'.[18] In the same speech, addressing the teachers, he reminded them that 'the teacher must be the best agent of change, the most revoluntary agent of change in our country'.[19]

In 1975 a 'Seminar-workshop' was attended by most of the educators of the country, aiming at defining the quantiative objectives of the Reform, and deciding upon the new curricula and standards of education.

However, in 1976 resistance to the Reform started to become more and more overt. The majority of the representatives of private schooling, the church, the urban parents' associations (half the national population is concentrated in its two large urban centres), and the teachers' unions protested against a reform. . . 'imposed', not negotiated, and 'imported from Peru'. They accused those in charge of the Reform of including in the content of the curricula materials for communist indoctrination, and of wishing to transform teaching into a production activity. The Minister was obliged to distance himself from those of his closest collaborators regarded as too 'reformist'.

16. Article 3 of the Constitution lays down that 'the national territory may never be ceded, transferred or alienated, either temporarily or partially, to another State'.
17. See S. Lourié, 'Panama and Honduras: a promising blend of education and productive work' in *Learning and working,* Paris, Unesco, 1979, (Prospects report), pp.181-202.
18. 'La revolución y la reforma educativa', National Assembly of the Representatives of the 'Corrigimientos' (Parliament), Bulletin No.4, Panama, 1974, p.129.
19. Ibid., p.30.

In 1976 and 1977 negotiations were entered into with the United States regarding revision of the treaties concerning the Panama Canal. The Minister, while retaining his post, was nominated by General Torrijos as one of the principal negotiators.

When the new treaties were concluded and signed in September 1977, the objectives of the Reform had still not been incorporated in a Plan of Action and the principal 'reformed' programmes were being revised and encountering considerable delays in their implementation.

The Minister was elected President of the Republic in September 1978. Shortly after taking on his new responsibilities he had to face one of the longest and most difficult strikes the country's teachers, supported by much public opinion, the quasi-unanimity of the urban population and the unanimity of the representatives of the major economic interests. On 20 November 1979 a Law signed by the Chairman and by the Secretary-general of the National Council of Legislation and countersigned on 7 December by the President of the Republic, laid down in its Article 1 that all the legal dispositions relating to the creation and application of the Educational Reform 'in all its forms and modalities' were annulled.[20]

The dependence on foreign influences and trends — a feature of Panama — and its urban type of society, concentrated in the service sector, are the components of the reproductive action of its educational system — and this dates from before the accession of the revolutionary government of 1968. The new government saw its main task as regaining sovereignty over the Canal. Its tactics were based on a massive popular support arousing the motivation of the rural population, with the exception of certain landowners. Participation by the rural areas had hitherto been nonexistent in the political game and could offer an alternative project of society. An education rooted in the agricultural production schools became one of the means of bringing about this mobilization, through a reform led by the FREP and the 'militants' in the Ministry, supported by the rural milieu.

Once the sovereignty crisis had been settled, the alternative project of society was no longer fashionable. The criticism of the Reform came from groups who felt that the new education threatened their model of society. When the need to bring about a new society became less urgent the criticism had more influence — the more so since the model of a popular rural education based on the production of foodstuffs (in application of an eventual policy of import-substitution) no longer coincided with the urban services-based way of life implied by the new treaties (strengthening the rôle of the tertiary sector and the two key towns of the Canal). The more the negotiations progressed towards a favourable outcome of the agreement concerning the treaty, the less pressure there was in favour of the Reform.

To deal with the criticisms the Minister (first period), supported by the militants of the Ministry, had chosen a strategy of breakdown in order to

20. Gaceta oficial, No.28 968, 13 December 1979.

threaten his opponents by mobilising against them a rural public opinion. It is not unlikely that the possibility of setting up an alternative to the traditional urban educational 'project' was an influence, combined with other arguments of which many had far greater political and economic weight, in favour of concluding the agreement. Naturally, the agreement accelerated the arrival of the second period. To deal with a Reform which had become the target of too many opposing groups, the Minister (second period) still chose a strategy of breakdown, this time by cutting himself off from the militants who had been mobilized to ensure the conditions for the first period.

The departure of the militants, who were only a small minority of the Ministry officials and unionised teachers, paved the way for a return to the *status quo ante bellum.* This met the aspirations of the majority of teachers and of the urban population. If the first period saw the Minister in action at the head of the reformists, in the second he had to yield to the anti-reformists. The Great Social Net (defined in the first period by the authority of the State and in the second by the urban classes) determined each time the strategy to be followed by its most faithful interpreter — the Minister-become-President, who had to assume the responsibilities that were compatible with the times and his rôle.

In Panama the Educational Reform was, to begin with, in perfect harmony with the project of society. When this project changed, the Reform became as alien to its context as in Costa Rica or Peru. The decision-maker could avail himself of the movements which were disrupting the educational system to influence the negotiations for the Treaty which, had they failed, would probably have enabled the 'alternative' society, which relied on the educational reform, to take shape.

In this case we can see that making use twice running of a strategy of breakdown was not the way to bring about changes. There was no lasting effective of collective apprenticeship outside the period 1972-76, during which the 'militants' of the Reform and the Minister kept up the appearances of a national debate. The Reform could not have been implemented in a climate of breakdown, and the strategy of 'non-negotiation' that was followed to impose the counter-reform was the natural corollary of the temporary mobilization of provisional allies with whom a negotiation presented scarcely any interest, either tactical or strategic.

With hindsight, the Panama case would appear to confirm the extent to which any non-negotiated educational reform is an exercise doomed, in the short term, to failure. In the event, the strategy of breakdown used in the first period was partly responsible for provoking the reaction to which the decision-maker had to yield in the second period by cutting himself off in the same way from support earlier considered useful. It might almost be thought that the rejection in both periods of a strategy of negotiation was deliberate on the part of the decision-maker: in the first period, to make the traditional forces aware of the arrival of a régime resolved to have no deal-

ing with the counter-revolutionaries, and in the second, in order not to an-
tagonise these same traditional forces by dealing with a reduced number of
reformists without any real power to negotiate, from the moment that the
State had ceased to cover them.

2.2. *The nature of the negotiators*

In addressing ourselves to the second question asked earlier, it seems useful
to examine certain consequences arising from the foregoing remarks on the
possibility and expediency of negotiation. Indeed, it was necessary in three
cases (Costa Rica, Guatemala, Peru) to bear in mind what should be
understood by a 'given collectivity', and to note in a fourth case (Panama)
that such a group — the reformists — was not, from the decision-maker's
viewpoint, worth negotiating with.

We have already referred to the idea of a collectivity placed either 'upstream'
or 'downstream' of the decision-maker. The position of the collectivity in
relation to the decision-maker is certainly significant. At the same time, it
seems obvious that the collectivity's situation in relation to the *receivers* of
the negotiated decision should also be defined.

It is by picturing the relative position that we hope to be able to identify
the 'collectivity'.

In theory, the decision-maker should apply a strategy of negotiation in
his relations with the collectivity most representative of those who will be
most affected by the decision — a precondition of which would be the identifying of the object of the negotiation itself. This collectivity is nothing else
than the 'ideal' system of action. Moreover, it is unthinkable that the decision-
maker should act otherwise than in agreement and direct liaison with the
responsible political authority in the government, in the name of which he
is acting.

A relationship could be imagined — represented diagramatically, by a
lozenge — in which the decision-maker (D) would be placed midway between the authority of the State (A) and the system of action (S), who would
join with him in a common apprenticeship of the changes which are bound
to have an impact on the public (P) — or the target-population — concerned
(pupils, students). The arrows show the direction of the currents of influence
before the decision.

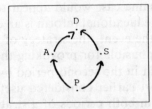

In the four cases in question, different forms of relationship can be
represented:

i) Costa Rica

The decision-maker is no longer supported by the authority, cuts himself off from the collectivity by a strategy of breakdown, and is mistaken regarding the project preferred by the public. On its side, the authority sticks to the system of action which obtains the support of the public. The following relation can be pictured:

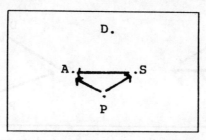

ii) Guatemala

The decision-maker has negotiated the support he receives from the authority but is ineffective in surrounding himself with a system of action to negotiate his position with it. The system, apart from the weak union forces, is not representative of the target-population. The dotted line suggests a possible line of communication:

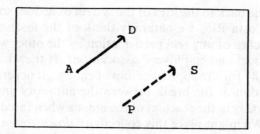

iii) Peru

The decision-maker has been ousted by the authority, which has re-established a relationship with the system of action, which in turn maintains communication with the target-population which is scarcely taken into account by the authority:

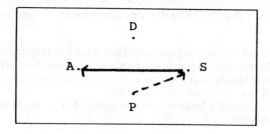

iv) Panama

The decision-maker remains attached to the authority which cuts itself off in a first period, from the population and, in a second period, from the system of action:

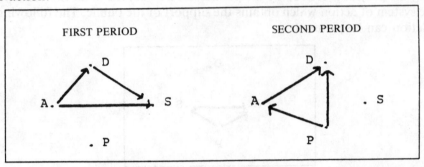

It would seem that none of the cases corresponds to the ideal picture. We must note that, naturally, in each case the idea of 'collectivity' or 'system of action' is implicitly different. But a closer look reveals that the authority remains the pole on which depends the final outcome of the project envisaged by the decision-maker. The authority can be joined by the decision-maker alone (Guatemala) or by the target-population and the system of action (Costa Rica).

Now let us come back to the idea of the system of action, sometimes called collectivity. In Costa Rica we naturally think of the teachers' unions and we recall the absence of any real participation by the other workers' unions and the professional and employers' associations. If the whole had formed an ideal collectivity for the apprenticeship of change, it nevertheless remains that the explanation of the break between the authority and the decision-maker lies principally in the reaction of the unions when faced by the strategy of breakdown. We might place this collectivity *downstream* from the decision, since the teachers considered themselves to be most affected by the *effect*[21] of the Reform (in their own view, they saw themselves as the objects of it, ignoring in the defence of their own interests those of the subjects of education: the pupils and students).

In Guatemala it is the collectivity which is missing, whether of the teachers/administrators or of the rural Indian populations. The organisms with which the decision-maker has negotiated — the Head of State, the Congress, and (through them) the real economic powers — are *upstream* of his position.[22]

21. Admittedly, in a democratic régime, the *effect* is felt downstream to begin with, and then — by the game of political representation — upstream, where the political authority cannot ignore, save at the risk of an electoral defeat, such feelings which, in turn, it will pass on to the decision-maker.

22. In this particular case the feedback effect mentioned in the footnote on the previous page does not appear.

We will conclude by noting that the decisions in Guatemala are the result of limited negotiation. The positioning of the collectivity upstream from the decision-maker reduces its meaning to either a formalism or a fiction. In may be said that if indeed there was change *and* negotiation in Guatemala, there was little collective apprenticeship.

In Costa Rica, in spite of the failures of the reform, there was in fact a national debate, a form of collective apprenticeship in which various local groups took part, called 'basic organizations' or 'living forces'. The wider communication circuit that developed formed a foundation for what could have led to a consensus, adapted to the real rhythm of the political changes (which had not developed as fast as the authors of the reform had wished).

We may ask whether the collectivity which was to act, in the end, as a brake on the reforming movement was not itself in the rearguard of the popular movement that it claimed to be part of. In the absence of any argument from other courses than the authors of the reforms, the claims of the collectivities could not easily be criticized.

For this more open country, it might be possible in this way to conceive a new scheme: the setting-up of a real association of the interested parties, not limited to the teachers alone. In grouping together (as the Costa Rican decision-maker had dreamed of doing, though without turning intention into action) *other* worker's unions, to which might be joined various associations and groups (consumers, chambers of commerce, of industry and of agriculture, parents' associations, students' organizations, cultural bodies, etc.), a more representative collectivity might have been established. It is and through such a collectivity that a real process of apprenticeship might have been started and developed. A system of action could then have been created, effectively carrying decisions arising from a collective apprenticeship.

Such an enlarged collectivity would present three considerable advantages:

i) It would oblige the unions to listen to viewpoints that differ from their own, while taking away from them at the same time their *de facto* monopoly over the educational phenomenon. An enlarged collectivity would probably be less attached to the existing scholastic institutions and customs.

ii) It would impose an attitude of compromise on the reformists, thus avoiding the rigorist and absolutist stance which is often the cause of the failure of reforms termed overall or integral. This collectivity would mediate the model of Educational Reform in relation to the realities of the general political development.

iii) It would allow the Minister to play the part of arbiter between the views and interests of the teachers on the one hand and the reformists on the other, and to cease being the prisoner of a system which made him both the judge and the advocate of his administrees — the teachers and the officials of the central administration. He would cease to react and would be able more fully to act in response to the needs of the really interested parties — the pupils, the students, and the citizens 'in a state of apprenticeship'. He would cease to be the Minister of Schools and Teachers, and could more fully defend the general interest.

Section 3. **Limits of change**

Earlier we considered the limits which change must respect and which are concerned with the structure of society, the passage of time, the nature of the strategy and the choice of opponents. For our final reflections we shall set as our objective a better definition of the intrinsic limit of change — that which is conditioned by time — and try to discover what kind of decision-maker best embodies this sense of time. Finally, we shall take our leave of Central America by assessing the significance of its educational reforms in relation to the temporal dimension they demand and the time and freedom of action available to the decision-maker responsible for them.

3.1. *Dynamic equilibrium and responsibility*
Rogers and Shoemaker define the long-term objective of an organised change as one that must produce 'a condition of dynamic equilibrium in the receiving system'.[23] The innovations must be introduced into the system at a moderate rate ('deliberate Speed'), carefully spaced out in relation to the system's capacity of adjusting itself to change.

This dynamic equilibrium admittedly only makes sense inside relatively stable structures whose volume scarcely varies. When profound structural modifications take place — a considerable increase in the public sector, for example — the rhythm of inputs of innovations and of outputs of the traditional system may be noticeably accelerated.

Whatever the intensity of the dynamic, it is understood that change does not consist in passing from a relatively unchanging state to another possessing other characteristics but provided with mechanisms forbidding further changes. It is not a matter of substituting one photo of a situation for another but rather of unwinding a film and watching a continuum in motion.

This applies particularly to education. It cannot be imagined that education — being simultaneously cause and effect of the social organization — can remain static if its aim is to be of service to man, whose nature is motion. Admittedly, if this motion is deliberately slowed down, or even prevented, education will have a slowing or stopping rôle, and the decision-maker will have to model himself on the existence of an excessively slow rhythm of life.

The decision-maker requires essentially this consciousness of time — a consciousness in which the lessons of his experience are inscribed — which fits into a continuum for his brief moment at the head of the Ministry of Education. He should not reject *a priori* what his predecessors have left for him,

23. Rogers and Shoemaker, op.cit., p.339.

nor should he refuse to leave for his own successors the fruits of his specific contribution to the construction of the national educational phenomenon. Lenin, a revolutionary if ever there was one was convinced of the necessity of respecting this sedimentation of experiences. In a speech to young communists in 1920 he referred to the reproaches and accusations levelled at Tsarist schooling, and while he recognized that it was 'a schooling of bookish study, of disciplining, of swotting', he urged his audience to 'distinguish what was bad in the old schooling and what was useful' so as to 'extract from it what is indispensable for communism', for, he added, 'you will commit a grave error if you attempt to deduce from them (the failings of former schooling) that it is possible to become a communist without having assimilated the riches accumulated by human knowledge'.[24]

Whether the passage of 'educational time' is relatively slow — or fast — as in a time of revolution, it is no exaggeration to say that every decision introducing a change must be conceived (before any other consideration) in function of this passage.

Rogers[25] distinguishes three forms of equilibrium in the introduction of changes:
— a stable equilibrium which corresponds to an almost total absence of change in the functions and structures of a system;
— a dynamic equilibrium which is reached when the rate of change in a social system is directly proportional to the system's capacity to cope with it;
— a disequilibrium which appears when the rate of change is too rapid to allow the social system to adjust to it.

The sensibility of the man who will estimate the nature of the equilibrium attained will also enable him to determine the nature of the other limits, and in particular those relating to the collectivity of apprenticeship. In other words, throughout the negotiation the decision-maker must act as a barometer, registering the highs and lows of pressure and making it possible to forecast a period of fair or else of unsettled weather, according to which he must slow down or accelerate the rhythm of collective apprenticeship. The sensibility and precision of this barometer will be a function of his experience, granted, but also of that of his associates — his sytem of action.

To revert to the Weberian classification already quoted, we may suppose that he who 'cannot put up with the ethical irrationality of the world'[26] would not be the decision-maker likely to introduce a sense of proportion in a process of collective apprenticeship and of negotiations. Once again, we conclude that in a design for change in the educational phenomenon, the description of the man who will be motivated by an *ethic of responsibility*

24. See Lenin, *Works*, Vol.31 (April-December 1920), speech to the Third Congress of the Russian Union of Communist Youth, 2 October 1920, Paris, Editions sociales, 1961.
25. Rogers, op.cit., p.339.
26. M. Weber, op.cit.

is a response, ideally, to the demands of a consciousness of time. And we have seen that it is time, more than any other influence, which conditions any change whatsoever in the realm of education.

It is around these two axes — the passage time enriched by collective experience, and the rôle of the decision-maker that we shall attempt in conclusion an impressionistic sketch of the conditions and prospects of educational reforms in Central America.

3.2. *Time and men in Central America*

Two cases have been studied — Guatemala and Costa Rica — another described — Panama, and we have cited examples or illustrations from the educational situations in Nicaragua, El Salvador and Honduras. But the six countries have hardly been given similar treatment, and, apart from the first two, any attempt at making comparisons would be out of the question. Nevertheless, we still have to 'place' education in these countries in relation to the passage of time and to the rôles of the men involved.

3.2.1. *Costa Rica and Panama*

Two countries, Costa Rica and Panama, appear very similar in their relation to the classic indicators: the average *per capita* income in each is higher than in any of the four neighbouring countries. In addition, the social pattern of an urban middle class is common to both. As regards education, we we have seen that the enrolment in primary education (nearly 90 per cent) and state expenditure on education (varying between 25 and 30 per cent of the national budget) are at comparable levels. Finally, we have seen that every attempt to introduce and overall Reform has been met by opposition from the urbanized classes and the teachers' unions.

The decision process has of course, been different, in the sense that the decision-makers reacted in radically different ways when faced with 'counter-reform'. One resisted, failed in his attempt, and disappeared from public life. The other was obliged to give way, failed, but survived politically. In the one case there was a hope of reforming the system; in the other there was a strategem which might have been useful but which was not used.

What really characterizes both Costa Rica and Panama is the nature of what we called earlier 'the social fabric', the meshes of which are too fine for education to be anything other than just one more element of a whole which is self-reproducing. Education has passed from the stage of being an instrument to being a symbol. For this reason, it is relatively untouchable.

In the perspective of time, it may be said that in both Panama and Costa Rica the rhythm of change, in a socio-political context which it would be an exaggeration to describe as liable to undergo profound changes in the short term, can only be slow. The decision-makers whom we have seen in action tended more towards conviction in Costa Rica than in Panama, and more to pragmatic realism in Panama than in Costa Rica. But in both countries the acquired gains of urbanization and the rise of a middle class are the guarantee of a stable education in which innovations will remain limited. In Rogers' terminology, this would be a *stable equilibrium.*

3.2.2. Guatemala, Honduras

If the rates of enrolment and of public expenditure on education are higher in Honduras than in Guatemala, the educational systems of the two countries can be described in the same way: they exist from day to day, and this cannot go on indefinitely. The children of the rural areas are practically excluded from any possibility of complete primary education, and secondary education still remains to a significant extent in private hands, while illiteracy rates among the adult population are still close to or above 50 per cent. All the same, there are men and institutions in these countries that could be mobilized to introduce the qualitative changes without which a wider coverage cannot be attained. In other words, to meet a latent and silent demand, which will become more and more audible with the passing of time, new teaching methods and curricula are needed (voluntary service, centres of interest, schooling and productive work, etc.) which will provide a form of education quickly and universally.

But the socio-political context, while noticeably different as regards the methods of imposing and maintaining public order, does not permit in either country, in 1981, any form of participative and popular education. The Guatemalan decision-maker whose methods we have studied, succeeded by patient work in introducing two minor changes in the system. These changes, given the Guatemalan microcosm, have a very limited effect, though they still show promise. But taking into account the relative slowness of his approach (for which we have tried to understand the reasons), we may ask whether it is realistic to imagine that his successors will be able to go on doing as much indefinitely, waiting for a critical mass of mini-decisions to be reached which will provoke a reaction from the authorities faced with the gradual transformation of their instrument of social reproduction for the service of other ends — and other clientèles.

Much the same is true in Honduras, with the creation and development of, first, a programme of out-of-school education for certain peasant populations and, second, an Institution for the training of higher-level educational personnel which has made use of self-learning techniques based on centres of interest (the needs, interests and problems of villagers).

This brings us back to the notion, already discussed, of the passage of time. Obviously, imperceptible and barely tolerated changes do not form part of a perspective of dynamic equilibrium. The decision-maker studied was able to adapt himself to the slow rhythm of the decisional movement. Will this be true of the marginalised groups who come into daily contact with relatives, friends or acquaintances who possess the instruments of knowledge and make use of the mass media? It is probable that in due course their needs will call for a response, independently of other demands.

Looked at from a different angle, it is possible that this educational frustration may itself bring about a demand for *educational responses* to deeply felt *educational needs*.

This being so, we may say that if Guatemala and Honduras possess men of responsibility, such men will not accept indefinitely that education in their countries remain static and out of date. Perhaps the equilibrium should be described as blocked rather than stable, in the sense that the beam of the balance is held in place, preventing the scale from falling either on the side of innovation or on that of tradition. Does not such as fixed equilibrium give warning of an inevitable disequilibrium in due course?

3.2.3. *El Salvador*

Between the two groups just described lies the exceptional case of El Salvador, where a 'Reform' was effectively carried out in the years 1967-1972. Less ambitious than those attempted in Costa Rica and in Panama, this Reform nevertheless saw an extension of schooling to nine years, changes in the curricula of the new 'basic' cycle, a very marked diversification of the second cycle of secondary education, the generalised use of television in the first-cycle class of secondary, the concentration of teacher training in a single Teacher-training City for the whole country, the creation of educational programmes for adults, and a network of 'houses of culture' — meeting-places for students and peasants.

The State gradually devoted greater and greater sums to education, almost reaching rates similar to those in Costa Rica and Panama. Enrolment increased considerably, and had not the events of 1980-81, which practically led to a state of civil war in certain parts of the country, greatly affected the data, it might have been said that the country was on the point of crossing a qualitative threshold and would in a few years be carried to levels approaching those of Costa Rica and Panama.

El Salvador was beginning to reap the benefits of a long effort, slow and gradual, commenced ten years earlier when the decision-maker of those days, a dynamic and energetic Minister, decided 'to attack all the principal problems at the same time'[27] to ensure that the efforts mobilised during his ministerial mandate would have an effect, he sought at the same time as launching his attack on all fronts, 'the means of perpetuating the changes and structural processes which had been set in motion'.[28] Re-appointed as Minister, he set up an office for planning and organisation (1972-1978). This

27. See the article by N. McGinn, E. Shiefelbein and D.P. Warwick, 'Educational planning as a political process: two case studies from Latin America', *Comparative education review,* Vol.23, No.2, June 1979, p.223.
28. Ibid. p.231.

was a period of consolidation of effort, reflecting a sort of solidarity in time between two successive ministers.

This investment in time was accompanied by the application the ethic of responsibility. The combination of the two factors gave El Salvador an educational system which has functioned in depth and has borne fruit. Even though the fruit is suffering in the storm now shaking the country, it is not perhaps entirely unconnected with an undeniable general awareness of socio-political conditions which are especially difficult for the rural population.

The case of education in El Salvador might be classified as at least a state of *dynamic equilibrium.*

3.2.4. *Nicaragua*

A brief description of the literacy crusade was given in Part One of this study.[29] This is only one aspect — even if the most spectacular — of the taking in hand of the entire phenomenon by the Government of National Reconstruction which put an end ot the more than forty years' régime of the Somoza family. The new government carried to power by the Sandinist People's Revolution put into practice its programme on its arrival in July 1979. With regard to education it declared:

'A thorough reform of the aims and content of national education will be carried out, so that it may become a key factor in the process of humanist transformation of Nicaraguan society and may be oriented in a critical and liberating direction. The said reform will be of an overall nature: from pre-school education right up to the level of higher education.'[30]

Clearly, the education desired by the new Government was to be new and, as its Minister of Education said, its 'aims and objectives must respond to the new values proclaimed by our Revolution. If our revolutionary process proposes to build a more just, more humane, more egalitarian and more fraternal society, the objectives and the philosophy of national education cannot be the same as in the past. They must reflect the new values so that education, in all its forms, can contribute effectively to form the New Man who must bring them to life.'

The new Government immediately embarked on an accelerated programme of activities, containing a set of fundamental changes conceived to 'place education at the service of the masses, separating itself clearly at the same time from the vertical, fragmentary and élitist education of the past.'[31] These changes affected both the methods and structures of education as well as those of the administration.

29. See above, Part I, Chapter 2, section 3.
30. *Programa de Gobierno de Reconstrucción Nacional,* Junta de Reconstrucción Nacional, Algún lugar de Nicaragua, 18 June 1979, Chap.3-5(a), p.14.
31. Carlos Tunnerman, *La educación en el primer ano de la revolución popular Sandinista,* Managua, Ministerio de Educación, July 1980. Introduction, pp.i-ii.

Education was declared free at all levels, and the literacy crusade was to be followed up by a permanent action of post-literacy and 'popular' education for adults.

This overall Reform accompanied a socio-political change and the instrument that was the educational system was no longer of use to reproduce a society that had been in great part eliminated. But this raises the essential question: though there had been an undeniable opening of the social structures and a movement towards mobility which had not happened previously, could this really be called a radical change?

If the new schooling was to serve a new Society, was it not necessary to avoid simply restoring the previous schooling — for the benefit of a greater number, it is true, but preserving its selective system and its memorising methods — in short, the methods of traditional learning?

But the existence of schools of the traditional type, both in the public and private sectors, rendered difficult and hardly realistic a policy — theoretically possible — of a clean sheet. Also, the eventual widening of the system to include sections of the population which had not hitherto had access to it could hardly be envisaged without a proportional increase in real resources (teachers, headmasters, organisers, not to mention constructional materials, transport, etc.).

The national literacy campaign showed the creative capacity of the new authorities, who were able to motivate an exceptional voluntary service for a long period and showed a rare capacity for oganisation and infrastructure. This capacity appears to have been placed at the disposal of the New Education, and it cannot be ruled out that with time, Nicaragua might orient itself essentially in this direction.

In the meantime, the decision-maker must find out how to insert himself in a continuum wherein he cannot ignore the past — even if he repudiates it — but the future of which will show whether he has succeeded in imposing on it a real change of direction.

It is clear that of all the Central-American countries, Nicaragua is the one whose Reform tends to follow really new directions because the society itself which it serves is no longer the same.

The months and the years to come will show whether this change is in line with the Project of society. It will be important to study the tendency — natural in all human undertakings — to crystallise (perhaps even fossilise) what has been gained. Then, the education extracted from the ore of a formalism preserved by intermediary bodies, such as the teachers, can become the instrument of a society no longer, but of a new administrative bureaucratic order.

Then we shall be able to say whether the healthy disequilibrium which still existed two years after the Revolution has led to a dynamic equilibrium or a stable one.

Also from
Trentham Books

GREAT EXPECTATIONS AND MIXED PERFORMANCE:
THE IMPLEMENTATION OF HIGHER EDUCATION REFORMS IN EUROPE
Ladislav Cerych and Paul Sabatier

This work analyses the original aims, results and the factors explaining the achievements of seven higher education reforms in different European countries. Its authors interpret the findings of a series of case studies and examine the British Open University, the Swedish 25/4 Admission Scheme, the Norwegian Regional Colleges and the German "Comprehensive" University. The book uses the technique of implementation analysis and provides an illuminating comparison, by Burton Clark, of contemporary higher education policy implementation in Europe and the USA.

"Cerych and Sabatier have given us the most useful analysis now available, and likely to be so for a long time, of important systems of higher education undergoing change and attempted change in a unique and crucial period of their existence."
Clark Kerr

1986
ISBN 0 948080 02 7
Price £13.95. 276 pages, A5

THE CRISIS OF REDISTRIBUTION IN EUROPEAN WELFARE STATES
J.P. Jallade

European welfare states are in crisis. Governments everywhere are trying to restore the financial balance of social budgets, either by cutting benefits or by increasing taxes and contributions, or both. Who, then, will bear the brunt of these adjustments? Can a flexible and equitable solution be achieved? This book examines the redistribution efficiency of European welfare states, above all the income redistribution arising for social benefits (such as family allowances, pension systems, health care and unemployment compensation) and the taxes or contributions which finance them. However, the present crisis is also political inasmuch as European societies, more aware of the price to be paid for more protection and social equality, are asking "how egalitarian a society do we want or can we afford?"

After a discussion of the basic issues involved, five empirical studies analyse the redistributive effects of social security in the United Kingdom, Sweden, Hungary, the Netherlands and France; and the final chapter assesses the outlook for redistributive efficiency in Europe.

"A brilliant analysis" *Journal of Public Policy*.

October 1987
ISBN 0 948080 13 2
Price £15. 261 pages, 165mm x 242mm

THE EEC AND EDUCATION
Guy Neave
Introduction by Lord Asa Briggs

No multi-national organisation has ever initiated and funded so great a range of educational activities as the European Economic Community. In this authoritative volume undertaken with official support, Guy Neave of the European Institute of Education and Social Policy and the University of London Institute of Education presents the first published account of the Commission's full range of activities.

"A definitive account . . . written with both clarity and persistence."
Education

"Education was a late starter in the EEC and still struggles under considerable handicaps. Despite this, obvious progress has been made. Guy Neave's new book is an excellent source of information with which to develop an evaluation."
Studies in Higher Education

1984, Reprinted 1988
ISBN 0 9507735 4 9
Price £10.50. 203 pages, A5

EMPLOYMENT AND UNEMPLOYMENT IN EUROPE
Edited by J.P. Jallade
Introduction by Shirley Williams

This volume presents the most thoroughgoing analysis of one of the major issues affecting Western European society. It includes contributions by most of the major European experts including the President of the European Commission Jacques Delors. The volume is introduced by Shirley Williams who has worked closely with the contributors both in her ministerial career and in her recent association with the Policy Studies Institute.
1981
ISBN 0 9507735 0 6
Price £7.95. 234 pages, A5

Trentham Books Ltd.,
151, Etruria Road,
Stoke-on-Trent, Staffordshire,
ST1 5NS, England
Telephone: 0782 274227
Telex: Telser G367257 I C LIGHT
FAX: 0782 411115